BEGINNING ITALIAN GRAMMAR

BEGINNING ITALIAN GRAMMAR

BY VINCENZO CIOFFARI
Modern Language Editor, D. C. Heath and Company

D. C. HEATH AND COMPANY, BOSTON

Map by
RICHARD C. BARTLETT, JR.

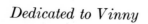

Dedicated to Vinny

PREFACE

The aim of this *Beginning Italian Grammar* is to present in a compact and complete form the basic elements of the Italian language. Since proper speech habits are essential for the knowledge of a foreign language, we have not only given an Introduction to Italian Pronunciation, but we have supplemented it with explanations and examples at the beginning of each lesson of Part I. By the time the student reaches Part II his habits should be firmly established.

The book is composed of twenty-six lessons divided into two parts of thirteen lessons each. Part I provides the basic sounds, the essential vocabulary, and the skeleton structure without which knowledge of the language would be impossible. Part II increases the vocabulary, expands the grammatical structure, and furnishes the exercises necessary to attain a firm grasp of the language. At the same time we have attempted to introduce enough elements of Italian culture and customs to arouse interest and provide topics for discussion.

In the section on Pronunciation we have presented all the significant sounds of Italian in the order of their importance for the English speaker. After the vowels we have stressed the sounds which have no counterpart in English, so that the student can learn to distinguish them and form them correctly. Even the student who is interested only in a reading knowledge will assign a mental pronunciation to the words he sees; it will be to his advantage to assign the correct one from the start.

In the section on Current Usage our aim has been to furnish the standard Italian used by all good speakers of the language regardless of the region from which they come. It is, of course, the language of Tuscany as modified by the language of Rome, without the regionalisms peculiar to either section. The vocabulary is carefully controlled, so that no more than about thirty new words are introduced in each lesson. Grammatical points are likewise controlled; no construction is introduced which is not presented in the lesson itself or in previous lessons.

In the section on Structure we have presented briefly and concisely all the fundamentals of construction. Current usage has been the determining factor in the order of presentation and in the choice of points to be treated. The emphasis has always been on general rules rather than on exceptions.

The Language Practice is a new experiment. Here the student is expected to learn to guess correctly from the subject matter. In Part I the English in parallel columns serves as a check. In Part II there is no English, but the more difficult words are given in footnotes, and the student is trained to answer questions according to sense rather than according to word-for-word equivalents. All words appearing in the Language Practice are included in the end vocabulary. In Part II the section on pronunciation is replaced by a study of useful expressions and idiomatic phrases.

The book can be used for a full year of college work by taking up a lesson a week, with ample time for supplementary readers. It can be used for a concentrated one semester course by taking up two lessons a week; as such it will form a solid basis for courses leading to the study of literature. It can be used for a two-year course in academic high schools by implementing it with readers, conversational materials, and individual projects. The book will then serve as the core from which the class can expand along the lines of greatest interest. It covers adequately all the requirements of regents and college board examinations.

The author is indebted to his many friends who have gone over the manuscript in mimeographed form and given him the benefit of their criticism and suggestions. The following professors in Italy have each gone over two or three lessons: Signorina Giuseppina Campanile (Pisa); Signorina Maria Pia Gallo (Messina); Dott. Antonio Mattu (Cagliari); Signora Laura Combatti (Trieste); Signora Barbara Bruno Asero (Catania); Dott. Dario Gazzoni-Pisani (Roma); Dott. Guido Bistolfi (Alessandria); Signorina Clara Enrico (Genova); Signorina Alma V. Tron (Genova); Signora Margherita Pottino (Roma); Signorina Alma Sabatini (Roma). The author owes a special debt of gratitude to those who have patiently gone over the whole of the manuscript: Dr. Carlo Vacca, of Wellesley High School; Mr. Gino Bigongiari, of Columbia and Long Island Universities; Prof. Camillo Merlino, of Boston University; and Prof. Rocco Montano, of the Istituto Universitario di Magistero "Suor Orsola Benincasa" di Napoli and of the Catholic University of America. As in all previous works, most of the credit goes to the patient and silent collaborator, Mrs. Angelina Grimaldi Cioffari. Whatever shortcomings the book may have are the author's own, since he has been the final judge of what was to be included.

VINCENZO CIOFFARI

TABLE OF CONTENTS

Preface   v

List of Photographs   xv

Introduction on Pronunciation   xvii
Alphabet. Vowels. Consonants. Combined Letters. Long
Consonant. Stress and Written Accent. Diphthongs and
Triphthongs. Syllabication. Capitalization. Apostrophe.
Punctuation.

PART ONE

1   *La famiglia Gentile*   1
Pronunciation: Consonants **b, d, f, l, m, n, p, t, v;**
  Vowels **a, e, ɛ, i, o, ɔ, u.**
Gender. Articles. Interrogative Form. Negative Form.
Language Practice: "Buɔn giorno."

2   *La casa*   7
Pronunciation: **gn, gli; r, rr.**
Plural of Nouns. Agreement of Adjectives. Special Mascu-
line Words. Summary of the Definite Article. Position
of Adjectives. Contractions with **a** and **in.**
Language Practice: "Dove abita Lɛi?"

3   *La strada*   14
Pronunciation: **t**-sound; **y**-sound; **w**-sound.
Subject Pronouns. Forms of Address. Present Indicative
of the First and Second Conjugations. Present Indicative
of **ɛssere** and **avere.**
Language Practice: "Dov'ɛ un ristorante?"

ix

4   *Un viaggio a Firenze*   21

Pronunciation: **s**-sound; open and close **e** and **o**.
Present Indicative of the Third Conjugation. Present
   Indicative of **volere, potere, andare.** Plural of Indefinite
   Articles and Partitive Construction. Uses of the Articles.
   Purpose. Days of the Week.
Language Practice: "Le presento . . ."

5   *La stazione di Roma*   29

Pronunciation: **z**-sound; **ch**-sound; **j**-sound.
Present Indicative of **venire, fare, dare.** Expressions of
   Time. Numerals from 1 to 20. Possessive Adjectives.
   Interrogatives.
Language Practice: "A che ora parte il treno?"

6   *Cercando alloggio*   37

Pronunciation: **k**-sound; **g**-sound; Long Consonant.
Past Participle. Present Perfect Tense. Present Perfect of
   Verbs Conjugated with **essere.** Irregular Past Participles.
   Direct Object Pronouns (**lo, la, li, le**). The Particle **ne.**
   Months and Seasons.
Language Practice: "La colazione."

7   *Venezia*   45

Pronunciation: **ch-** and **k**-sounds; **j-** and **g**-sounds; Missing
   Letters.
Present Indicative of **dovere, dire, sapere.** Future Tense.
   Direct Object Pronouns (Cont.). Weather.
Language Practice: "Lei che cosa fa?"

8   *La casa di Flora*   52

Pronunciation: Written Accent.
Agreement of Past Participles. Indirect Object Pronouns.
   Position of Object Pronouns with Infinitives. Adjective
   bello. Verbs Conjugated with **essere.** Irregular Past
   Participles.
Language Practice: "Dove posso comprare . . .?"

9 *Consigli e invito*   60
   Pronunciation: **sk**-sound; **sh**-sound.
   Imperative. First Person Plural Commands. Polite Com-
       mands. Complete Imperative. Position of Object Pro-
       nouns. Orthographical Changes. Relative Pronouns.
   Language Practice: "Che tempo fa oggi?"

10 *Napoli e il giro di Amalfi*   68
   Pronunciation: Review of Sounds.
   Reflexive Verbs. Reflexive for the Passive. Demonstratives.
       Numerals Above 20.
   Language Practice: "La passeggiata."

11 *Il secolo decimoquarto*   76
   Pronunciation: Writing from Sounds.
   Past Definite. Irregular Verbs in Past Definite. Com-
       parison of Adjectives. Irregular Comparatives. *In* After
       a Superlative. *Than* in Comparison. Ordinal Numerals.
   Language Practice: "Il genio italiano."

12 *I nostri pasti*   84
   Pronunciation: Intonation.
   Imperfect Tense. Verbs Irregular in the Imperfect. Imper-
       fect and Past Definite. Table of Contractions. Double
       Object Pronouns. Special Meaning of **da.**
   Language Practice: "Il fidanzamento."

13 *Mestiere o professione?*   92
   Pronunciation: Dictation.
   Conditional: Forms and Uses. Disjunctive Personal Pro-
       nouns: Uses. The Verb **piacere:** Forms and Use.
   Language Practice: "Gli sport."

                       PART TWO

14 *La moda*   103
   Demonstratives. Particles **ci, vi,** and **ne.**
   Language Practice: "La cinematografia."

15 *In un negozio*   109
Table of Pronouns. Position of Object Pronouns (Cont.).
Infinitive with **fare.** Possessive Pronouns.
Language Practice: "Milano."

16 *Le belle arti*   118
Present Subjunctive: Formation. Uses of the Subjunctive:
Noun Clauses; Adjective Clauses. Present Subjunctive
of Irregular Verbs.
Language Practice: "La serenata."

17 *In salotto*   126
Uses of the Subjunctive: Polite Commands; Impersonal
Expressions. Present Perfect Subjunctive. Infinitive with
Expressions of Emotion. Reflexive for First Person Plural.
Present Subjunctive of Irregular Verbs.
Language Practice: "L'università di Bologna."

18 *La geografia dell'Italia*   134
Comparison of Adjectives (Cont.).   Absolute Superlative.
Comparison of Equality. Comparison of Adverbs. Trans-
lation of *than* (Cont.).
Language Practice: "Due Italiani in America."

19 *L'arte e i musei*   142
Imperfect Subjunctive. Subjunctive in Adverbial Clauses.
Optative Subjunctive. Formation of Adverbs. Table of
Relative Pronouns.
Language Practice: "Torino."

20 *Lettera a una compagna di scuola*   151
Compound Tenses of the Indicative. Auxiliary with Reflexive
Verbs. Uses of the Compound Tenses of the Indicative.
Sapere and **conoscere.**
Language Practice: "Il Boccaccio."

21 *Una passeggiata*   159
Irregular Verbs in the Past Definite. Distinction between
Present Perfect, Past Definite, and Imperfect. Uses of the
Gerund.
Language Practice: "Galileo Galilei."

22   *Nella pensione*   167
Double Object Pronouns (Cont.). Definite Article with Possessives. Object pronouns with **fare** + Infinitive. Metric System.
Language Practice: "La famiglia."

23   *Una gita a Castel Gandolfo*   175
Sequence of Tenses. Compound Tenses of the Subjunctive. Subjunctive in Indirect Questions; with Indefinite Words. Summary of Plural of Nouns.
Language Practice: "La Città del Vaticano."

24   *Il pranzo — Cibi e bevande*   184
Compound Tenses of Verbs Followed by the Infinitive. Infinitive as a Substantive; with Prepositions; with Adjectives; with Nouns; Complementary.
Language Practice: "Leonardo da Vinci."

25   *A zonzo per la città*   193
Contrary-to-fact and *Should-would* Sentences. Past Participle. Object Pronouns with Participles.
Language Practice: "La Conca d'Oro."

26   *In ferrovia*   200
Suffixes. Augmentatives. Diminutives. Suffixes with Adjectives.
Language Practice: "Sonetto di Petrarca (LXI)"

Appendix of Verbs   209

Italian-English Vocabulary   217

English-Italian Vocabulary   236

Index   249

Map of Italy   136

PHOTOGRAPHS

Colosseum — Rome (*Ewing Galloway*)   3
Castel Sant'Angelo (*Ewing Galloway*)

Triton Fountain (*Jacobs from Three Lions*)   10

Open-air Restaurant (*Owen from Black Star*)   16
Playing Checkers (*Paula Horn from Monkmeyer*)

Florence — David and Perseus (*Gendreau*)   23
Florence — Street and Cathedral (*Gendreau*)

Railway Station in Rome (*Arts and Architecture*)   31
Esedra Fountain (*Foto Alinari*)

Chianti Vendor (*Roberts*)   39
Siena — Mangia Tower (*ENIT*)

St. Mark's Square (*ENIT*)   47
Gondola on Canal (*Roberts*)

Adoration of the Shepherds, by Giorgione (*National Gallery
    of Art — Kress Collection*)   54
Flora (*detail*), by Titian (*Uffizi Gallery — Florence*)

Lake Como (*ENIT*)   62

Amalfi (*ENIT*)   71

Dante Monument at Trento (*Foto Alinari*)   77

Trevi Fountain (*ENIT*)   86
Boy looking into fountain

Soccer Game (*Wide World*)   96
Rome's Grand Prix Race (*Wide World*)

Italian Fashions (*Town and Country*)   105

Milan Cathedral (*Gendreau*)   115
Milan — Piazza della Repubblica (*Locchi*)

La Scala (*Gendreau*)   119
Toscanini (*Wide World*)

Bologna (*Foto Alinari*)   131

The Annunciation, by Fra Filippo Lippi (*National Gallery of
    Art — Kress Collection*)   143
Portrait of a Youth, by Pintoricchio (*National Gallery of
    Art — Kress Collection*)

Pompeii (*Norman Gordon from Black Star*)   153

Pisa (*Roberts*)   164

Woman doing her washing (*Jacobs from Three Lions*)   169
Livorno (*Locchi*)

Castel Gandolfo (*ENIT*)   176
Swiss Guards at the Vatican (*ENIT*)

Man studying at home (*Paul Pietzsch from Black Star*)   187

Mt. Etna (*Silberstein from Monkmeyer*)   196
Taormina (*Silberstein from Monkmeyer*)

Cortina (*Black Star*)   202

INTRODUCTION ON PRONUNCIATION

In this brief introduction on Italian pronunciation we present only the general rules, avoiding exceptions and uncommon cases, whose pronunciation is indicated by special type in the text. These general rules are expanded with exercises at the beginning of each of the thirteen lessons of Part I.

Since Italian is practically a phonetic language, the same symbol represents the same sound under similar circumstances. All syllables are pronounced clearly and distinctly, without slurring the vowels. Italian is pronounced more forward in the mouth than English, with intonation that extends over whole phrases rather than individual words.

Alphabet. The Italian alphabet has twenty-one letters, namely all the letters of the English alphabet except j,[1] k, w, x, y.

Vowels. The five vowel letters actually represent seven vowel sounds, because **e** and **o** both have an open and a close sound. The vowel sounds correspond approximately to the following English sounds:

a	like the *a* in *father* (Midwestern)	madre, padre
e (close)	like the *a* in *day* (without *i*-glide)	perchè, tre
ε (open)	like the *e* in *met* or *let*	è, Ɛnzo
i	like the *i* in *machine* or *ee* in *feet*	Gina, Gentile
o (close)	like the *o* in *go* (without *u*-glide)	sono, molto
ɔ (open)	like the *o* in *for*	stɔria, cɔsa
u	like the *oo* in *boo* or *moon*	uno, studia

[1] The letter **j** is sometimes seen in older Italian, where it represents the i-sound before another vowel or is used in place of **ii**. The other letters sometimes occur in foreign words.

In this book we have used the symbols ɛ and ɔ to represent open **e** and open **o,** but in printed Italian these symbols do not exist. The ɛ and ɔ occur only in stressed syllables; when unstressed, **e** and **o** are always close.

Consonants. The following consonants are pronounced approximately as in English: **b, d, f, l, m, n, p, q, t,** and **v.** In pronouncing **d, l, n,** and **t** the tip of the tongue touches the back of the upper teeth and produces a more dental sound than the corresponding English. The sound **p** does not have the explosive puff of the English *p.* The **n**-sound has a slight nasal quality before a **k-** or hard **g**-sound.

The letters **c** and **g** have two sounds:
1. A hard sound before **a, o,** or **u** (like *k* in *keep* or *g* in *go*).
2. A soft sound before **e** or **i** (like *ch* in *church* or *j* in *James*).

To represent the soft sound before **a, o,** or **u** an **i** is inserted after the **c** or **g** (**cia, cio, ciu;** or **gia, gio, giu**).

To represent the hard sound before **e** or **i** an **h** is inserted after the **c** or **g** (**che, chi;** or **ghe, ghi**).

h   is always silent.

r   is a trill produced by the tip of the tongue flapping up and down against the gums behind the upper teeth. Double **rr** has a longer trill.

s { sometimes like the *s* in *soap, sit* (UNVOICED)   casa, basta
{ sometimes like the *s* in *rose* (VOICED)   prɔ*s*a, chiɛ*s*a

In this book the voiced *s* is printed in italics to distinguish it from the unvoiced **s.**

z { frequently like the *ts* in *cats* (UNVOICED)   zio, grazie
{ sometimes like the *ds* in *beds* (VOICED)   me*z*zo, pran*z*o

Combined Letters. There are two combinations of letters which produce sounds that have no exact parallel in English.

gn   like *ny* in *canyon,* but as a single sound   bagno, ogni
gli [1]   like the *lli* in *million,* but as a single sound   fam*i*glia, figli

---

[1] **Gli** retains its separate sounds in a few words like **negligente, anglicismo,** etc.

There are other combinations of letters which have sounds that do have an approximate parallel in English.

ch and **gh**	always a hard sound in Italian (**ch** = *k;* **gh** = *g* of *go*)	chi, laghi
chi	followed by **a, e, o,** or **u** is pronounced like *ky*	chiɛsa, vɛcchio
qu	always like *kw*	quanto, quattro
sc	always like *sh* when before **e** or **i**	scɛna, finisci
sc	always like *sk* when before **a, o,** or **u**	scala, scopa
sci	followed by **a, o,** or **u** has an *sh*-sound	lascia, lascio

Long Consonant (Double Consonant). The double consonant in Italian is longer and more emphatic than the single consonant.[1] It is not two consonants in rapid succession, but a holding of the vowel preceding the consonant and a slightly heavier explosion when the consonant does come out.

Anna	AN-na	fratello	fra-TƐL-lo
sorella	so-RƐL-la	ballo	BAL-lo

This long consonant is produced not only when you have two consonants, but also when a single consonant comes after certain one-syllable words like **a, e, ɛ̀, da, ciɔ̀,** etc.

a me = am-ME   ɛ̀ mio = ɛm-MI-yo   da casa = dak-KA-sa

Stress and Written Accent. In Italian the stress falls generally on the next to the last syllable in a word, but there are many exceptions. For example:

1. In the third person plural of verb forms the stress is regularly on the third syllable from the end in many tenses.

2. Words ending in –ɛsimo or –*i*ssimo are stressed on the third syllable from the end.

3. Verb forms which add a pronoun retain the stress on the syllable which had it before the pronoun was added.

In pronouncing Italian notice that words of more than one syllable which have a stress on the last syllable carry a written accent (`). In this book we use only the grave accent (`), but in books printed in Italy you will find also the acute accent (´),

---

[1] There is no distinction in pronunciation between the single **z** and double **zz**.

and sometimes even the circumflex (^). Since the type of accent
used does not indicate the quality of the vowel except by agreement, we find it more convenient to use only one type in our
textbooks.

The written accent is used on certain words of one syllable to
distinguish them from similar words which have a different
meaning.

chè, because	**che,** that
dà, gives	**da,** from, by
è [ɛ], is	**e,** and
là, lì, there	**la,** the; **li,** them
nè, neither, nor	**ne,** of it
sè, himself	**se,** if
sì, yes	**si,** himself

In this book the stress is indicated in one of three ways: (1) by
the written accent; (2) by the special characters ɛ and ɔ;
(3) by printing the stressed vowel in italics whenever that vowel
is in any position other than the second vowel from the end.

Diphthongs and Triphthongs. Two vowels pronounced
as one syllable form a diphthong. The vowels **a, e,** and **o** combine with the vowels **i** or **u** to form a diphthong (**st*u*dia, Lɛi,
fiore**). The vowels **i** and **u** combine with each other to form a
diphthong (**più, guida**). The vowels **a, e,** and **o** do not form
a diphthong when they are combined with each other (**aereo**).
In a diphthong the **a, e,** or **o** is the vowel which bears the stress
(**piano, colɛi, pɔi**). In the diphthongs formed only with **i**[1]
and **u** the second vowel is stressed (**piuma, Guido**).

A triphthong is a vowel cluster containing a diphthong plus a
third vowel. The triphthong is pronounced like a single syllable if
the middle vowel is **a, e,** or **o** (**vuɔi, miɛi**). It is pronounced like
two syllables if the middle vowel is **i** or **u** (**aiutare, p*a*io**).

Syllabication. Italian words are divided into syllables
according to the following rules:
1. Every vowel or diphthong forms the core of a syllable.

---

[1] When the **i** is in the sound **gli** or is used to soften **c** or **g**, it does not form
a diphthong (**f*i*glio, giorno, giardino**).

2. A single consonant between vowels goes with the syllable which follows.

3. Double consonants between vowels are separated.

4. Two dissimilar consonants or more than two consonants are separated so that the second syllable contains sounds which can begin words in Italian:

> **al-to**   because there is no word which can begin with **lt.**
> **la-dro**   because there are words which begin with **dr.**
> **la-scia** because there are words which begin with **scia.**

As a result you will find that **s** followed by another consonant goes with the syllable which follows. With combinations of **l** or **r** with another consonant, the two are separated if the **l** or **r** comes first, but they are not separated if the **l** or **r** comes second.

Capitalization. Capitals in Italian are used about the same as in English, with the following exceptions:

1. Months and days of the week are written with a small letter.

2. **Io** is written with a small letter, but **Lɛi** and **Loro** (when meaning *you*) and the corresponding object pronouns and possessives are generally written with a capital.

3. Names of languages or adjectives of nationality are written with a small letter.

4. When an adjective of nationality is used as a substantive denoting a person, it is written with a capital.

5. Titles of books or chapters are written with small letters, except, of course, for the first letter of the title or any word which has a capital in its own right.

The rules of capitalization are flexible in Italian and vary greatly from one printer or from one person to another.

Apostrophe. The apostrophe is used in Italian whenever certain short words ending in a vowel are followed by a word beginning with a vowel. This happens regularly with (*a*) most of the articles; (*b*) the object pronouns **mi, ti, si, ci, vi, lo,** and **la;** (*c*) demonstrative adjectives; (*d*) the preposition **di;** (*e*) the adjectives **bɛllo, buɔno, grande,** and **santo.**

Punctuation. Following are the names of the punctuation signs:

.	punto *or* punto fermo	—	lineetta
,	virgola	-	stanghetta
;	punto e virgola	. . .	punti sospensivi
:	due punti	« »	virgolette
?	punto interrogativo	( )	parentesi
!	punto esclamativo	[ ]	parentesi quadra

The punctuation signs are used about the same in Italian as in English. The only important distinction is that Italian uses a different type of quotation marks for direct quotations and the dash instead of quotation marks to denote a change of speaker in conversation.

PART ONE

PRONUNCIATION

In Italian, as in English, there are only a limited number of sounds which make up the language. Many sounds are similar in both languages, as for example, those represented by the consonants *b, d, f, l, m, n, p, t,* and *v.* Other sounds have no exact parallel in the two languages.

The vowels. The sounds represented by the letters *a, e, i, o, u* are quite different from English. Listen carefully as you hear them and you will notice that when the vowel is stressed it is pronounced as follows:

a is like the English *a* in father	padre
e $\begin{cases} \text{is sometimes like the } e \text{ in } met \text{ or } let \\ \text{and sometimes like the } a \text{ in } day \text{ (without the} \\ \quad y\text{-glide)} \end{cases}$	Ɛnzo perchè
i is like the *i* in *machine,* or the *ee* in *feet*	Gentile
o $\begin{cases} \text{is sometimes like the } o \text{ in } for \\ \text{and sometimes like the } o \text{ in } go \text{ (without the} \\ \quad u\text{-glide)} \end{cases}$	scuɔla Roma
u is like the *oo* in *boo*	studia

As an aid to pronunciation we have indicated the sound of *e* in *met* (called open *e*) by the symbol ɛ and the sound of *o* in *for* (called open *o*) by the symbol ɔ, to distinguish them from the other sounds of *e* and *o* (called close sounds). Remember, however, that printed Italian does not make any such distinctions.

CURRENT USAGE

La famiglia Gentile

In the following selection you will be able to recognize many words, even though you have never seen or heard them before. Read loudly, clearly, and without inhibitions.

La famiglia Gentile è italiana. Il padre è Carlo; la madre è Anna. Carlo è il marito; Anna è la moglie. Carlo e Anna sono marito e moglie.

Enzo Gentile è il figlio di Carlo e di Anna. Gina è la
5 figlia. Enzo è il fratello di Gina; Gina è la sorella di Enzo. Enzo e Gina sono fratello e sorella. Carlo ed Enzo sono padre e figlio. Anna e Gina sono madre e figlia. Ora basta con il padre, la madre, il figlio, la figlia, il fratello e la sorella.

10   La famiglia abita a Roma. Roma è la capitale d'Italia. È una città molto bella. Carlo Gentile è professore di storia. La moglie fa il lavoro di casa. Enzo studia medicina; Gina va a scuola di ballo.

La famiglia Gentile è felice. E perchè no? Il padre e la
15 madre lavorano a Roma. Il figlio e la figlia studiano a Roma. La città è molto bella. Sì, la famiglia è felice.

STRUCTURE

1. Gender. Nouns in Italian are either masculine or feminine; there are no neuter nouns. Those denoting a male are masculine (**padre, fratello**). Those denoting a female are feminine (**madre, sorella**). Nouns denoting anything else may be either masculine (**ballo**), or feminine (**capitale**).

In general, words ending in **–o** in the singular are masculine, words ending in **–a** are feminine, and words ending in **–e** may be either masculine or feminine (**padre, madre**).

2. Articles. The little word preceding a noun is called an article. When it indicates a definite person or thing it is called the definite article and corresponds to the English *the*. When it

The Colosseum and the Castel Sant'Angelo have marked the Roman landscape from time immemorial. Rome is truly the Eternal City.

indicates *any* person or thing, it is called indefinite and corresponds to the English *a* or *an*.

The definite article before a masculine noun which does not belong to a special class is **il.** Before a feminine noun the definite article is **la.** The indefinite article before a masculine noun which does not belong to a special class is **un.** Before a feminine noun the indefinite article is **una.** You will learn about the special class and the plural of these articles in the next lesson.

il padre, *the father*   **la** madre, *the mother*
un padre, *a father*   **una** madre, *a mother*

3. Interrogative Form. To ask a question in Italian the subject may be placed after the verb.

È Carlo il marito? *Is Charles the husband?*

The simplest way of asking a question is to keep the order of the positive statement and change the inflection of the voice.

La famiglia abita a Roma? *Does the family live in Rome?*

Remember that in a question the English word *do* or *does* is not expressed in Italian.

4. Negative Form. To make a sentence negative in Italian the word **non** is placed before the verb.

La famiglia non abita a Roma. *The family does not live in Rome.*

LANGUAGE PRACTICE

Piccolo dialogo

In the Language Practice you will have simple selections containing words and expressions which may or may not have been presented in the previous lessons. This exercise is intended for guessing and getting the gist of the subject matter. The ability to make a good guess is very important in learning a language. The words in these sections are not included in Word Lists of each lesson, nor are they used in the exercises until they have appeared in the active part of the lesson. The words are included in the end vocabulary, however.

Read aloud for recognition only and act out in class or with a fellow student.

— Buɔn giorno, signorina Sabatini.

Good morning, Miss Sabatini.

— Buɔn giorno, signor Crespi. Come sta?

Good morning, Mr. Crespi. How are you?

— Bɛne, grazie. E Lɛi?

Fine, thank you. And you?

— Anch'io stɔ bɛne, grazie. Bɛlla giornata!

I'm fine too, thank you. Beautiful day!

— Bɛlla davvero! Come sta Suo padre?

Really beautiful! How is your father?

— Molto bɛne. Come sta Sua madre?

Very well. How is your mother?

10

— Non c'ɛ̀ male. Stiamo tutti bɛne.

Fairly well. We are all well.

— Ne sono molto contɛnta. Dia i miɛi saluti.

I'm very happy over it. Give them my regards.

— Grazie; saluti anche ai Suɔi. Arrivederla!

Thanks; regards to your family 15 too. So long!

EXERCISES

I. Questions. Answer the following in complete sentences in Italian:

1. Ɛ̀ Carlo il padre? 2. Carlo e Anna sono marito e moglie? 3. Gina è la figlia di Carlo e di Anna? 4. Carlo ed Ɛnzo sono padre e figlio? 5. Ɛnzo e Gina sono fratɛllo e sorɛlla? 6. La famiglia abita a Roma? 7. Ɛ̀ una città molto bɛlla Roma? 8. Carlo Gentile è professore di stɔria? 9. Studia medicina Ɛnzo? 10. Ɛ̀ felice la famiglia?

II. Place the correct definite and indefinite article before each of the following words:

1. famiglia 2. padre 3. madre 4. marito 5. moglie 6. figlio 7. figlia 8. fratello 9. sorɛlla 10. capitale 11. città 12. professore 13. stɔria 14. casa 15. medicina 16. ballo

III. Make the following sentences negative:

1. La famiglia è felice. 2. Il figlio studia a Roma. 3. La madre fa il lavoro di casa. 4. La città è molto

bella. 5. Ɛnzo va a scuɔla di ballo. 6. Il padre è professore di stɔria. 7. La città è la capitale d'Italia. 8. Carlo ed Ɛnzo sono padre e figlio. 9. La famiglia abita a Roma. 10. Gina studia medicina.

IV. Pronounce carefully the following words:

1. famiglia, Anna, italiana, madre, figlia, città.
2. Gentile, è, perchè, Ɛnzo, e, bella.
3. il, figlio, marito, Gina, figlia, Gentile, sì.
4. sono, con, ora, molto, professore, scuɔla, stɔria, lavorano, nɔ, non.
5. una, studia, studiano.

V. Write the Italian for the following:

1. The family is Italian. 2. Charles and Anna are husband and wife. 3. Enzo is the son of Charles. 4. Gina is the daughter of Anna. 5. Anna and Gina are mother and daughter. 6. Does the family live in Rome? 7. Is Rome the capital of Italy? 8. Enzo is not a professor of history. 9. The husband does not do the housework. 10. Yes, the city is very beautiful.

WORD LIST

NOUNS

ballo *m.* dancing, dance
capitale *f.* capital
Carlo Charles
casa *f.* house, home
città *f.* city
famiglia *f.* family
figlia *f.* daughter
figlio *m.* son
fratɛllo *m.* brother
Italia *f.* Italy
lavoro *m.* work; **lavoro di casa** *m.* housework
madre *f.* mother
marito *m.* husband
medicina *f.* medicine
moglie *f.* wife
padre *m.* father

professore *m.* professor
Roma *f.* Rome
scuɔla *f.* school; **scuɔla di ballo** *f.* dancing school
sorɛlla *f.* sister
stɔria *f.* history

ADJECTIVES

bɛllo, –a beautiful
felice happy
italiano, –a Italian

VERBS

abita lives
basta (it is) enough
è is
fa does
lavorano (they) work

sono (they) are
studia studies
studiano (they) study
va goes

OTHER WORDS

a to, at; a Roma in Rome
alla (a + la) to the

con with
di of
e (ed) [1] and
molto very
ora now
perchè why; e perchè no?
and why not?
un, una a, an

PRONUNCIATION

The *gn-* and *gli-*sounds. There are some sounds in Italian which have no counterpart in English. Notice the pronunciation of **bagno.** The **gn** resembles the English *ny* in *canyon*, but it is a single sound. Notice the pronunciation of **famiglia.** The **gli-**sound resembles the English *lli* in *million*, but it is a single sound.

The *r-*sound. The **r** in Italian is a characteristic trill produced by the tip of the tongue flapping up and down against the gums behind the upper teeth. A single **r** (other than initial) is usually so short that it sounds like a single flap. A double **r** (or initial **r**) is a longer trill. Notice the pronunciation of the following:

single **r:** grande, quattro, primo, pranzo, mentre
double **r:** pianterreno, Roma

[1] Sometimes before a vowel, and especially before **e**, the form **ed** is used for *and*.

CURRENT USAGE

La casa

La famiglia Gentile ha una bella casa. La casa non è grande; è una casa comoda. Ha otto stanze, quattro al pianterreno e quattro al primo piano. La cucina, il salotto, la sala da pranzo, e lo studio sono al pianterreno. Al primo
5 piano ci sono tre camere da letto e la stanza da bagno.

La casa è in Via Toscana, vicino a Villa Borghese. Villa Borghese è un parco di Roma grande e bello. Vicino a Villa Borghese c'è la famosa Via Vittorio Veneto, dove ci sono grandi caffè. La vita a Roma è bella, anche per la famiglia
10 di un professore.

La casa ha un giardino con molti fiori. Il professore passa molto tempo nel giardino. Coltiva i fiori e studia libri di storia. Anche Enzo studia nel giardino. L'aria è fresca e i fiori sono belli. Gina, però, passa il tempo alla scuola di
15 ballo, dove balla per molte ore.

Dov'è la madre mentre tutti studiano? La povera madre è in cucina. Prepara il pranzo per la famiglia.

STRUCTURE

5. Plural of Nouns. In Italian nouns form the plural by changing the final vowel. Words ending in **–o** in the singular change the **–o** to **–i**. Words ending in **–a** change the **–a** to **–e**. Words ending in **–e** change the **–e** to **–i**. Words ending in an accented vowel do not change.

giardin**o** — giardin**i**   professor**e** — professor**i**
cas**a** — cas**e**   caffè — caffè

Nouns ending in **–io** in the singular simply drop the **–o** for the plural, unless the **i** is stressed, and then you have **–ii.**

stud**io** — stud**i**   **zio**, *uncle* — **zii**

6. Agreement of Adjectives. In Italian, adjectives agree in gender and number with the noun they modify. The masculine singular form is used with a masculine singular noun, the feminine singular form with a feminine singular noun, etc. Notice:

9

parco bɛllo	pɔvera madre
casa cɔmoda	grandi caffɛ̀
bɛlla casa	molti fiori

Adjectives like **cɔmodo**, which end in −o in the masculine singular, end in −a in the feminine singular, −i in the masculine plural, and −e in the feminine plural. We can call these four-form adjectives.

Adjectives like **grande**, which end in −e in the masculine singular, do not change for the feminine singular and end in −i in the plural for both genders. We can call these two-form adjectives.

7. Special Masculine Words. Masculine words beginning with a **z**, an **s** followed by a consonant, or a vowel, are treated as a special group. They take the definite article **lo** instead of **il** (**lo studio**, *the study*). The **lo** becomes **l'** before a vowel (**l'amico**, *the friend*). These special words take the indefinite article **uno** instead of **un** (**uno studio**, *a study*), but **un** is retained before a vowel (**un amico**, *a friend*).

8. Summary of the Definite Article. All the forms of the definite article are as follows:

	SINGULAR	PLURAL	
MASC.	**il**	**i**	before ordinary masculine words. il fratɛllo, i fratɛlli
	lo	**gli**	before masculine words beginning with **z** or **s** + consonant. lo zio, gli zii lo studio, gli studi
	l'	**gli**	before words beginning with a vowel. l'amico, gli amici
FEM.	**la**	**le**	before feminine words beginning with a consonant. la stanza, le stanze
	l'	**le**	before feminine words beginning with a vowel. l'aula, *the classroom*, le aule

*The fountains of Rome have long inspired poets,
musicians, and artists. The Fountain of the
Triton is one of the most powerful creations of
the sculptor Bernini.*

9. Position of Adjectives. In Italian the adjective normally comes after the noun instead of before it, as in English.

una casa comoda, *a comfortable house*

Some common adjectives and all numerals generally come before the noun.

la povera madre, *the poor mother*

When two adjectives modify the same noun they usually come after it and are joined by **e.**

un parco grande e bello, *a large and beautiful park*

10. Contractions. When some prepositions are followed by the definite article, usually the two contract into a single word. Notice:

a + il = al	in + il = nel
a + lo = allo	in + lo = nello
a + la = alla	in + la = nella
a + i = ai	in + i = nei
a + gli = agli	in + gli = negli
a + le = alle	in + le = nelle
a + l' = all'	in + l' = nell'

You will have more of these contractions later on.

LANGUAGE PRACTICE

Piccolo dialogo

For recognition only.   Act out in class or with a fellow student.

— Dove abita Lei?	Where do you live?
— Abito in Via Toscana.	I live on Toscana street.
— È grande la casa dove abita?	Is the house where you live large?
— Sì, è grande. Ha dieci stanze.	Yes, it is large. It has ten rooms.
— C'è un giardino?	Is there a garden?
— Sì, c'è un bel giardino.	Yes, there is a beautiful garden.
— Lei passa molto tempo nel giardino?	Do you spend a great deal of time in the garden?

5

— Sì, studio e coltivo i fiori.   Yes, I study and cultivate the flowers.

— Cɔsa studia Lɛi?   What are you studying?
— Studio medicina. E Lɛi?   I am studying medicine. And you?
5 — Anch'io studio medicina.   I am studying medicine, too.
— Caspita! E dove sono tanti malati?   Heavens! And where are so many sick people?
— Pazienza! Iddio provvede.   Be patient! The Lord will provide.

EXERCISES

I. Questions. 1. Ha una bɛlla casa la famiglia Gentile? 2. Ci sono ɔtto stanze al pianterreno? 3. Ci sono quattro stanze al primo piano? 4. Dov'è la casa? 5. Villa Borghese è un parco? 6. Dov'è la famosa Via Vittɔrio Vɛneto? 7. La casa ha un giardino? 8. Il professore coltiva i fiori? 9. Passa il tɛmpo nel giardino Gina? 10. Dov'è la madre?

II. Supply the correct definite and indefinite articles for the following words:

1. casa 2. piano 3. cucina 4. salɔtto 5. sala da pranzo 6. studio 7. camera da lɛtto 8. stanza da bagno 9. caffè 10. vita 11. giardino 12. fiore 13. tɛmpo 14. libro di stɔria 15. aria 16. ora 17. pranzo

III. Supply the definite article for the following words and then change the article and the noun to the plural:

1. pranzo 2. ora 3. aria 4. libro 5. tɛmpo 6. fiore 7. giardino 8. vita 9. caffè 10. stanza 11. camera 12. studio 13. sala 14. salɔtto 15. cucina 16. piano 17. 'casa

IV. Combine a noun from line A with an adjective from line B and supply the definite articles; then change the expressions to the plural. The same adjective may be used with more than one noun.

A. giardino, libro, fiore, pranzo, caffè, vita, camera, sala, cucina, stanza, casa, madre
B. pɔvero, bɛllo, cɔmodo, grande, felice, italiano

V. Write the Italian for the following:

1. Charles has a beautiful house. 2. The house has eight rooms, four on the first floor and four on the second floor. 3. The kitchen and the dining room are on the first floor. 4. The bathroom is on the second floor. 5. The house is near Villa Borghese. 6. There are many large cafés. 7. Does the house have many flowers? 8. Does the professor cultivate the flowers? 9. Where is Gina while Enzo studies? 10. The mother prepares the dinner for the family.

WORD LIST

NOUNS

aria *f.* air
caffè *m.* café
camera *f.* room; **camera da letto** *f.* bedroom
cucina *f.* kitchen
fiore *m.* flower
giardino *m.* garden
libro *m.* book
ora *f.* hour
parco *m.* park
piano *m.* story, floor; **al primo piano** on the second floor
pianterreno *m.* ground floor, first floor; **al pianterreno** on the ground floor, on the first floor
pranzo *m.* dinner
sala da pranzo *f.* dining room
salotto *m.* living room
stanza *f.* room; **stanza da bagno** *f.* bathroom
studio *m.* study
tempo *m.* time
via *f.* road, street
vita *f.* life

ADJECTIVES

comodo, –a comfortable
famoso, –a famous
fresco, –a cool
grande big, large
molto, –a much, a great deal of
molti, –e many
povero, –a poor
primo, –a first
vicino, –a near

VERBS

coltiva (he) cultivates
ha (it) has
passa (he) spends (*time*)
prepara (she) prepares

OTHER WORDS

anche also
ci there; **c'è** there is; **ci sono** there are
dove where
mentre while
otto eight
per for
però however
quattro four
tre three
tutti everyone, all

PRONUNCIATION

The *t*-sound. The t-sound in Italian is similar to the English, but it is more dental and is not accompanied by the released puff of air which is characteristic of the English *t*. Listen carefully as you hear:

strada, troviamo, appartamento, distante, soltanto, quattro

The *y*-sound. The y-sound in Italian is not represented by the letter *y*, but by the letter *i*, whenever the **i**-sound is followed by any other vowel sound. Listen carefully for the **y**-sound in the following:

graziose, piani, propria, negozio, chiesa; io, via [1]

Notice that the y-sound does not occur when the letter *i* forms part of the consonant sound, as in **giardino, famiglia, figlio.**

The *w*-sound. The w-sound is produced whenever *u* is followed by another vowel sound, although the letter *w* itself does not exist in the Italian alphabet. Listen carefully as you hear:

quattro, qualsiasi, quasi, vuole; sua, due [2]

CURRENT USAGE

La strada

La strada dove abita la famiglia è bella. Le case sono piccole e graziose. Non ci sono grandi edifici perchè la

---

[1] When the i-sound is stressed, the y-sound is in addition to the i-sound. You actually hear i-yo, vi-ya. [2] When the u-sound is stressed, the w-sound is in addition to the u-sound. You actually hear su-wa, du-we.

14

strada non è commerciale. Troviamo invece case a due
piani, semplici, con un bel [1] giardino e con alberi e fiori. Ogni
famiglia ha la propria casa.

Il mercato però non è distante; soltanto tre o quattro
isolati. Anche il mercato è piccolo e comodo. C'è un sarto, 5
un barbiere, una modista, e un calzolaio. C'è, per di più,
un negozio di abiti, un pizzicagnolo, e un caffè. La famiglia
Gentile compra quasi tutto lì vicino, perchè nei negozi vendono tutto.

La chiesa dove va la famiglia è proprio dirimpetto alla 10
casa. Ma poi a Roma non mancano chiese. Roma ha molte
chiese. La più grande chiesa del mondo è San Pietro. Però
quasi ogni strada ha la sua piccola chiesa. Roma, Città
Eterna, pensa bene alla vita eterna.

STRUCTURE

11. Subject Pronouns. The subject pronouns in Italian are
as follows:

SINGULAR	PLURAL
io, I	**noi,** we
tu, you (*fam.*)	**voi,** you (*fam.*)
Lei, you (*pol.*)	**Loro,** you (*pol.*)
egli, he	**essi,** they (*m.*)
essa, she	**esse,** they (*f.*)

12. Forms of Address. Italian has various ways of expressing
the word *you*. **Tu** is used when addressing a close friend or a
member of one's own family. **Voi** is used when addressing several
close friends, members of the family, or when addressing a large
group. **Lei** [2] is the common form for addressing the average person

---

[1] Notice that **bello** becomes **bel** before a masculine singular noun which
does not belong to the special class.   [2] The polite forms **Lei** and **Loro,** together with their corresponding object pronouns and possessives, are generally
written with a small letter at present in Italy. We follow the older usage in
this book because it is more convenient for both teachers and students.

Via Vittorio Veneto has the elegance of sophisticated society, but the common folk enjoy themselves just as much in some shaded nook of the streets of Rome.

you will meet; it is a more polite form than **tu.** **Loro** is the plural of **Lɛi** and is used when addressing more than one person.

In many sections of Italy, particularly south of Rome, **voi** is used as the polite form of address rather than **Lɛi.** It is used when addressing one person or more than one. Foreigners, however, will find no need for this form of address.

13. Present Indicative of the First and Second Conjugations. In Italian the ending of the verb varies in person and number according to the subject. Therefore each verb in each tense will have forms for the first, second, and third person singular and for the first, second, and third person plural.

Verbs are always designated by their general form, which is called the infinitive. Regular verbs fall into three main classifications, known as conjugations. Those whose infinitive ends in –**are** belong to the first conjugation. Those whose infinitive ends in –**ere** belong to the second conjugation. Those whose infinitive ends in –**ire** belong to the third conjugation.

In the first conjugation the endings of the present indicative are as follows:

comprare, *to buy*	
io compr–**o**	noi compr–**iamo**
tu compr–**i**	voi compr–**ate**
egli, essa, Lɛi compr–**a**	essi, esse, Loro compr–**ano**

In the second conjugation the endings of the present indicative are as follows:

vendere, *to sell*	
io vend–**o**	noi vend–**iamo**
tu vend–**i**	voi vend–**ete**
egli, essa, Lɛi vend–**e**	essi, esse, Loro vend–**ono**

14. Present Indicative of *ɛssere* and *avere*. The two most common irregular verbs are **ɛssere,** *to be,* and **avere,** *to have.* The present indicative forms of the two verbs are as follows:

	ɛssere	avere
io	sono	hɔ
tu	sɛi	hai
egli, essa, Lɛi	è	ha
noi	siamo	abbiamo
voi	siɛte	avete
essi, esse, Loro	sono	hanno

Notice that the **h** is not pronounced in Italian.

LANGUAGE PRACTICE

Piccolo dialogo

For recognition only. Act out in class or with a fellow student.

— Scusi, dov'è un ristorante?

Pardon me, where is there a restaurant?

— Un ristorante? Perchè? Vuɔl mangiare?

A restaurant? Why? Do you want to eat?

5 — Sì che vɔglio mangiare. Hɔ molto appetito.

Yes, I do want to eat. I am very hungry.

— Non ha fatto la prima colazione stamattina?

Didn't you have breakfast this morning?

— Sì hɔ fatto la prima colazione. 10 Ma adɛsso sono le dodici.

Yes, I did have breakfast. But it is now twelve o'clock.

— Non è pɔi tardi. Qui facciamo colazione alle due.

It isn't at all late. Here we have lunch at two o'clock.

— Fino alle due non pɔsso aspettare. Dov'è un ristorante?

I can't wait until two o'clock. Where is there a restaurant?

15 — Un ristorante di lusso o un ristorante modɛsto?

An expensive restaurant or a modest restaurant?

— Un ristorante dove pɔsso mangiare.

A restaurant where I can eat.

— Ma non vede che questo è un 20 ristorante? Io sono il proprietario.

But don't you see that this is a restaurant? I am the proprietor.

— E allora entriamo. Vɔglio mangiare piuttɔsto che conversare.

Let's go in then. I want to eat rather than talk.

EXERCISES

I. Questions. 1. Sono piccole le case nella strada dove abita la famiglia Gentile? 2. Ci sono grandi edifici? 3. Ci sono case a due piani? 4. È distante il mercato? 5. È grande il mercato? 6. C'è un sarto e una modista? 7. Vendono tutto nei negozi? 8. Dov'è la chiesa dove va la famiglia? 9. È grande la Chiesa di San Pietro? 10. Pensa alla vita eterna Roma?

II. To conjugate means to give all the forms of a given tense of a verb. Conjugate the following verbs in the present indicative:

abitare, vendere, essere, avere

III. Supply the appropriate subject pronouns for the following verb forms and translate:

coltivano	vende	siamo	avete
coltivi	vendono	sono	hanno
comprate	vendete	siete	abiti
compra	troviamo	è	abita
compro	abbiamo	hɔ	vendo

IV. Supply the correct forms of the verbs indicated for the following pronouns:

1. io (abitare)
2. Lei (vendere)
3. essa (avere)
4. Loro (essere)
5. voi (trovare)
6. noi (comprare)
7. tu (essere)
8. voi (coltivare)
9. Lei (avere)
10. egli (vendere)
11. Lei (abitare)
12. noi (vendere)
13. egli (essere)
14. essa (trovare)
15. Loro (essere)
16. noi (abitare)
17. io (essere)
18. io (avere)
19. egli (trovare)
20. essa (comprare)

V. Write the Italian for the following:

1. There are no large buildings in the street. 2. Instead there are two-story houses. 3. The houses are simple, with (a) garden, trees, and flowers. 4. Is the shopping district very far? 5. Only three or four

blocks.   6. The shopping district has a tailor, a hat shop, a barber, and a shoemaker.   7. Is there a dress shop besides?   8. Does the family buy almost everything near there?   9. Is the church right opposite the house?   10. Every street has its little church.

WORD LIST

NOUNS

albero m. tree
barbiεre m. barber
calzolaio m. shoemaker
chiεsa f. church
Città Etεrna f. Eternal City
edificio m. building
isolato m. block
mercato m. shopping district
modista f. hat shop
mondo m. world
negozio m. store, shop; **negozio di abiti** m. dress shop
pizzicagnolo m. grocer
San Piεtro Saint Peter's
sarto m. tailor
strada f. street

ADJECTIVES

commerciale commercial
distante distant, far
etεrno, –a eternal
grazioso, –a pretty
piccolo, –a small

proprio, –a one's own
semplice simple
il suo, la sua his, her, its

VERBS

comprare to buy
mancare to lack
pensare to think
trovare to find
vendere to sell

OTHER WORDS

bεne well, carefully
dirimpetto a opposite
invece instead
lì adv. there
ma but
ogni every
perchè because
per di più moreover, besides
poi then
proprio adv. directly
quasi almost
soltanto only
tutto everything

PRONUNCIATION

The s-sound. The s-sound is sometimes a pure hissing sound such as you hear in the English words *hissing* or *soap*. At other times it is closer to the **z** of the English words *dozen* or *doze*. The hissing type is called voiceless. The **z**-type is called voiced, because the vocal cords are called into play. The sound represented by double *s* in Italian is always voiceless. Listen to the pronunciation of the following:

voiceless **s**	*voiced* **s**
spesso	chiesa
sono	visita
sì	bisogno
nessuno	
casa	

We have indicated the voiced *s* throughout the book by printing it in italics.

Open and close *e* and *o*. Listen again carefully for the distinction between open ε and close **e**, and open ɔ and close **o**. The native speaker of Italian makes the distinction without realizing it.

e	**ε**	**o**	**ɔ**
spesso	Firεnze	sono	trɔvano
provvede	sεmpre	giorno	prɔprio
fresco	sorεlla	mondo	perɔ

CURRENT USAGE

Un viaggio a Firenze

I genitori di Carlo Gentile abitano a Firenze. Egli fa
spesso il viaggio da Roma a Firenze per vedere i genitori, i
fratelli e le sorelle. Parte da Roma il sabato mattina e
arriva a Firenze nel pomeriggio. Poi parte da Firenze la
5 domenica nel pomeriggio e arriva a Roma la sera. Così
può passare un giorno con i genitori.

Firenze è il centro della cultura italiana. Ogni casa e
ogni strada ha la sua importanza storica. Il Duomo, il
Battistero, e il Campanile di Giotto formano il gruppo cen-
10 trale. A poca distanza ci sono altri edifici di importanza
storica: Santa Croce, il Bargello, gli Uffizi, il Palazzo Pitti,
ecc. Firenze è famosa nella storia, nella letteratura, e
nell'arte.

Gli stranieri che vanno in Italia passano molto tempo a
15 Firenze. Visitano le chiese e i musei. Vedono le opere
d'arte di Michelangelo, Raffaello, Botticelli, Tiziano, Giotto,
Leonardo da Vinci, Andrea del Sarto, e tanti altri artisti.
La città di Firenze è un vero museo.

Le donne però, preferiscono Firenze perchè vi trovano
20 negozi di lusso, specialmente negozi di borsette, gioielli, ecc.
Vogliono sempre comprare. Quando un Americano arriva
a Firenze, consegna alla moglie tutto il suo denaro e va
all'albergo a riposare.

STRUCTURE

15. Present Indicative of the Third Conjugation. Verbs
ending in **–ire** are classified as third conjugation. Some of these
verbs follow the pattern of **finire** and others the pattern of **partire**.

Who could imagine that Perseus, the bronze masterpiece of Benvenuto Cellini, would be standing in the open air in Piazza della Signoria?

No matter from what street you approach, you get a glorious view of the Duomo of Florence, standing next to the Baptistry and the Campanile.

finire, *to finish*	partire, *to leave*
io fin–**isco**	io part–**o**
tu fin–**isci**	tu part–**i**
egli, essa, Lɛi fin–**isce**	egli, essa, Lɛi part–**e**
noi fin–**iamo**	noi part–**iamo**
voi fin–**ite**	voi part–**ite**
essi, esse, Loro fin–*iscono*	essi, esse, Loro part–**ono**

Verbs which follow the pattern of **finire** are marked **isco** in the end-vocabulary: **preferire** (**isco**). Other verbs of the third conjugation follow **partire.**

16. Present of *volere, potere, andare.* These are three of the most common verbs which are irregular in the present indicative. The forms are as follows:

	volere, *to wish*	**potere,** *to be able*	**andare,** *to go*
io	vɔglio	pɔsso	vado
tu	vuɔi	puɔi	vai
egli, essa, Lɛi	vuɔle (vuɔl) [1]	puɔ̀	va
noi	vogliamo	possiamo	andiamo
voi	volete	potete	andate
essi, esse, Loro	vɔgliono	pɔssono	vanno

17. Plural of Indefinite Articles. Strictly speaking, Italian has no plural of indefinite articles. The partitive is used instead. It is formed by **di** + definite article and is translated by *some.* The forms are as follows:

MASCULINE
- **dei**   plural of **un** (cannot be used before a vowel).
  dei musɛi, *some museums*
- **degli**   plural of **uno** (used also before a vowel).
  degli straniɛri, *some foreigners*
  degli amici, *some friends*

---

[1] Many short words, particularly verb forms ending in **–le** or **–re**, drop the final **–e** before words beginning with a consonant.

I thought one used just un + una. Why uno?

FEMININE   **delle**   plural of **una** and **un'**.

delle donne, *some ladies*

delle *a*ule, *some classrooms*

18. Partitive Construction.   When the preposition **di** is combined with the singular of the definite article, it indicates that only part of whatever is mentioned is taken into account.   It is translated by *some*.

del pane, *some bread*   della medicina, *some medicine*

19. Uses of the Articles.   The definite article is generally repeated before each noun and must agree in gender and number with the noun it modifies.

V*i*sitano le chiese e i mus*e*i.   *They visit the churches and museums.*

The definite article is used in Italian but not required in English in the following instances:

1. Before a noun about which you want to express a general characteristic.

L'arte è b*e*lla.   *Art is beautiful.*

2. Before the name of a language (except immediately after the verb **parlare** or after the prepositions **in** or **di**).

Carlo st*u*dia l'italiano.   *Charles studies Italian.*

BUT →   La classe d'italiano.   *The Italian class.*

The indefinite article is used about the same as in English except for the following instances:

1. The indefinite article is omitted with a predicate nominative denoting a profession or a trade, but not modified by an adjective.

Il padre è professore.   *The father is a professor.*

2. If the predicate nominative is modified, the indefinite article is used.

Il padre è un bu*o*n professore.   *The father is a good professor.*

20. Purpose. The purpose for which an action is done is expressed by **per** followed by the infinitive.

Va a Firenze per vedere i genitori. *He goes to Florence to see his parents.*

21. Days of the Week. The days of the week are as follows:

(la) **domenica,** Sunday
(il) **lunedì,** Monday
(il) **martedì,** Tuesday
(il) **mercoledì,** Wednesday
(il) **giovedì,** Thursday
(il) **venerdì,** Friday
(il) **sabato,** Saturday

Notice that the days of the week are written with a small letter in Italian.

LANGUAGE PRACTICE

Piccolo dialogo

For recognition only. Act out in class or with a fellow student.

— Le presento il signor Perry.
May I present Mr. Perry?

— Lieto di far la Sua conoscenza, signor Perrini.
Pleased to make your acquaintance, Mr. Perrini.

— Il piacere è mio, ma non mi chiamo Perrini. Mi chiamo Perry.
The pleasure is mine, but my name is not Perrini. My name is Perry.

— Come, non è italiano Lei?
Why, aren't you Italian?

— No, signore, non sono italiano. Sono americano.
No, sir, I am not Italian. I am an American.

— Di che parte degli Stati Uniti, per favore?
From what part of the United States, please?

— Sono della Virginia.
I am from Virginia.

— Della Virginia? E la Virginia non è regione italiana?
From Virginia? And isn't Virginia an Italian region?

— No, non è regione italiana.
No, it is not an Italian region.

— Sì, ma ha il nome italiano. E poi, Lei parla bene l'italiano.
Yes, but it has an Italian name. And besides, you speak Italian well.

— Tante grazie. Lei è molto gentile. Scusi, come si chiama?
Thank you very much. You are very kind. Pardon me, what is your name?

— Mi chiamo Lorenzo Perrini, e sono fiorentino.	My name is Lorenzo Perrini, and I am a Florentine.
— Sono molto lieto di far la Sua conoscenza. Adoro Firenze.	I am very happy to make your acquaintance. I adore Florence.
— Allora resti a Firenze e prenda il nome di Perrini.	Then stay in Florence and take the 5 name of Perrini.

EXERCISES

I. Questions. 1. Dove abitano i genitori di Carlo Gentile? 2. Perchè Carlo fa spesso il viaggio da Roma a Firenze? 3. Quando parte da Roma e poi quando parte da Firenze? 4. Ha importanza storica Firenze? 5. Dove sono il Duomo, il Battistero, e il Campanile di Giotto? 6. Dove sono Santa Croce, il Bargello, gli Uffizi, e il Palazzo Pitti? 7. Passano molto tempo a Firenze gli stranieri? 8. È un vero museo la città di Firenze? 9. Perchè le donne preferiscono Firenze? 10. Le donne vogliono sempre comprare?

II. Supply the proper subject pronoun for the following verb forms and translate:

preferiamo	può	parto
preferisce	vai	partite
preferiscono	vado	vuoi
possono	andate	vuole
potete	parte	vogliamo

III. Supply the proper form of the present indicative:

1. noi (potere). 2. voi (andare). 3. egli (volere). 4. Lei (volere). 5. essi (finire). 6. Loro (partire). 7. io (preferire). 8. tu (preferire). 9. voi (potere). 10. io (andare). 11. essi (volere). 12. esse (potere). 13. noi (preferire). 14. Loro (finire). 15. Lei (partire).

IV. Translate the following: *dei*   *degli*

1. some ladies 2. some palaces 3. some foreigners *degli* 4. some jewels 5. some museums 6. some hotels 7. not far away 8. Sunday morning 9. they visit 10. expensive shops *essi visitano negozi di lusso*

V. Write the Italian for the following:

1. He wants to see the parents, brothers, and sisters.
2. He does not leave Rome (on) [1] Saturday afternoon.
3. Does he arrive in Rome (in) the evening? 4. Every street has its importance. 5. The Cathedral and the Bell Tower form the central group. 6. The other buildings are also beautiful. 7. The city is famous in [the] [2] history, [the] literature, and [the] art. 8. The foreigners who go to Italy are happy. 9. They visit the museums and churches. 10. They always want to buy many things.

WORD LIST

NOUNS

albergo *m.* hotel
Americano *m.* American
arte *f.* art
artista *m. or f.* artist
Bargello *m. a museum in Florence*
battistero *m.* baptistry
borsetta *f.* handbag
Campanile di Giotto *famous bell tower in Florence*
centro *m.* center
cultura *f.* culture
denaro *m.* money
distanza *f.* distance
donna *f.* lady
duomo *m.* cathedral
edificio *m.* building
Firenze *f.* Florence
genitori *m. pl.* parents
gioiello *m.* jewel
giorno *m.* day
gruppo *m.* group
importanza *f.* importance

letteratura *f.* literature
lusso *m.* luxury; **di lusso** luxurious, expensive
mattina *f.* morning
museo *m.* museum
opera *f.* work; **opera d'arte** *f.* masterpiece
Palazzo Pitti *m.* Pitti Palace, *art gallery in Florence*
pomeriggio *m.* afternoon
Santa Croce *a famous church in Florence*
sera *f.* evening
straniero *m.* foreigner
Uffizi *m. pl. art gallery in Florence*
viaggio *m.* trip; **fa il viaggio** takes the trip

ADJECTIVES

altro, –a other
centrale central
poco, –a little; **a poca distanza** not far away
storico, –a historic, historical

[1] Do not translate English words in parentheses.   [2] Translate into Italian English words in brackets.

tanto, −a so much; *pl.* so
  many
vero, −a true, real

vedere to see
visitare to visit
volere to want

VERBS

andare to go
arrivare to arrive
consegnare to turn over
formare to form
partire to depart
preferire (isco) to prefer
potere to be able
riposare to rest

OTHER WORDS

che who
così thus, in this way
da from
ecc. etc.
quando when
sɛmpre always
specialmente especially
spesso often

PRONUNCIATION

The *z*-sound. The z-sound is sometimes like the English ts-sound in *cats*, as for example in the words **zio** or **negɔzio.** It is formed in the front part of the mouth, with the tongue right behind the upper teeth. Listen for it in words like: **stazione, grazie, Tiziano, Uffizi, Palazzo.**

At other times the sound represented by the letter **z** is voiced, that is the vocal cords accompany the sound, which is now made with less explosion, allowing the air to pass between the tongue and the teeth. The closest to it is the sound in the English word *beds*. Listen for it in words like **pranzo, mɛzzo.** In this book you will find this type printed with an italic *z*.

The *ch*-sound. The **ch**-sound is about the same as the English, but in this case the spelling is troublesome. The **ch**-sound is represented by **c** before **e** or **i** (**ce, ci**) and by **ci** before **a, o,**

or **u** (**cia, cio, ciu**). The **i** is not pronounced as a separate
vowel in **cia, cio, ciu**; it simply indicates that the **c** has a **ch**-
sound. Listen for it in the following words: **edificio, commercio,
Cioffari, città, centro.**

The *j*-sound. The **j**-sound is also about the same as in the
English words *James* or *gentle*. In Italian this sound is represented by **g** before **e** or **i** (**ge, gi**) and by **gi** before **a, o,** or **u**
(**gia, gio, giu**). The **i** in these three groups is not pronounced
separately; it simply indicates that the **g** has a **j**-sound. Listen
for it in the following words: **pomeriggio, giardino, Giuseppe.**

CURRENT USAGE
La stazione di Roma

Oggi arriva a Roma un amico di Enzo. È uno studente
inglese che viene a passare l'estate in Italia. Si chiama
Riccardo Webster. Enzo va alla stazione perchè l'amico
non conosce Roma.

5   La stazione principale si chiama Roma Termini. Lì arrivano e di lì partono treni per tutte le parti d'Europa. La
stazione è grande e bella. Ci sono belle sale d'aspetto:
una per la prima e una per la seconda classe. Ogni sala
d'aspetto ha il proprio ristorante. (Lo sapete che i treni
10 italiani hanno due classi?)

C'è un ufficio informazioni dove si possono chiedere informazioni su qualsiasi treno. Gl'impiegati sono cortesi e
rispondono subito a tutte le domande. Enzo va all'ufficio
informazioni e domanda:

15   — A che ora arriva il treno di Londra?

L'impiegato gli dice che il treno arriva alle sedici e due,
sul binario numero dodici. Sono già le sedici meno dieci,
perciò Enzo va subito a ricevere il suo amico.

The main hall of the Termini Station is resplendent with
glass walls and marble floors. Within sight, in Piazza
dell'Esedra, is one of the most graceful fountains of Rome.

STRUCTURE

22. Present Indicative of *venire, fare, dare*

	venire, *to come*	**fare,** *to do*	**dare,** *to give*
io	vɛngo	faccio	dɔ
tu	viɛni	fai	dai
egli, essa, Lɛi	viɛne	fa	dà
noi	veniamo	facciamo	diamo
voi	venite	fate	date
essi, esse, Loro	vɛngono	fanno	danno

23. Expressions of Time.   Italian has two expressions for asking for the time.

Che ora ɛ?   } *What time is it?*
Che ore sono?

Both are equally good, but **Che ora ɛ?** is the more common.

Ɛ l'una. *It's one o'clock.*
Ɛ mezzogiorno. *It's noon.*
Ɛ mezzanɔtte. *It's midnight.*
Sono le sɛtte. *It's seven o'clock.*
Sono le tre e mɛzzo (*or* mɛzza). *It's half-past three.*
Sono le nɔve meno un quarto. *It's a quarter to nine.*
Il trɛno parte alle sedici. *The train leaves at four* PM.

Before a singular word the hour is expressed by ɛ; before a plural word it is expressed by **sono.** The hour itself is in the feminine (**l'una, le sɛtte**). Minutes or parts of the hour are expressed by **e** after the hour and by **meno** before the hour.

Train schedules and official events employ the twenty-four hour system, starting at midnight. This makes noon twelve o'clock, one o'clock in the afternoon thirteen o'clock, etc.

24. Numerals.   The cardinal numerals from 1 to 20 are as follows:

1 uno	6 sɛi	11 undici	16 sedici
2 due	7 sɛtte	12 dodici	17 diciassette
3 tre	8 ɔtto	13 tredici	18 diciotto
4 quattro	9 nɔve	14 quattordici	19 diciannɔve
5 cinque	10 diɛci	15 quindici	20 venti

25. Possessive Adjectives. Possessive adjectives are those which indicate possession. In Italian the possessive adjective agrees in gender and number with the object possessed (and not with the possessor, as in English). The forms are as follows:

MASCULINE		FEMININE		MEANING
Sing.	*Pl.*	*Sing.*	*Pl.*	
il mio	i miei	la mia	le mie	my
il tuo	i tuoi	la tua	le tue	your (*fam. sing.*)
il suo	i suoi	la sua	le sue	his, her, its
il Suo	i Suoi	la Sua	le Sue	your (*pol. sing.*)
il nostro	i nostri	la nostra	le nostre	our
il vostro	i vostri	la vostra	le vostre	your (*fam. pl.*)
il loro	i loro	la loro	le loro	their
il Loro	i Loro	la Loro	le Loro	your (*pol. pl.*)

Notice that the definite article is used as part of the possessive adjective. However, the article is not used with certain words denoting a member of the family and unmodified (**padre, madre, fratello, sorella, cugino, zio,** etc.).

mio padre e mia madre, *my father and mother*

But if the noun is modified, the article is used.

la mia cara madre, *my dear mother*

26. Interrogatives. The most common interrogative pronouns in Italian are:

chi? *who? whom?*
che? *what?*
che cosa? *what?*
cosa? *what?*

Notice that **chi?** is used both as the subject and the object of a verb.

Chi arriva? *Who is arriving?*
Chi vuole? *Whom do you want?*

The most common interrogative adjectives are **che?** (*what?*), **quale?** (**qual?**), *pl.* **quali?** (*which?*), **quanto, –a?** (*how much?*), and **quanti, –e?** (*how many?*).

> Che libro vuole?   *What book does he want?*
> Quale treno, per favore?   *Which train, please?*
> Quante classi ci sono?   *How many classes are there?*

LANGUAGE PRACTICE

Piccolo dialogo

—Scusi, signore, a che ora parte il treno?

—Quale treno, per favore?

—Il treno per Napoli. Vado a
5   visitare mio cugino.

—Ah, sì! Via Formia?

—Non so. Vado a Napoli.

—Che biglietto ha?

—Non ho biglietto. Posso fare il
10   biglietto in treno?

—In treno costa di più. A che ora vuol partire?

—Voglio partire presto.

—Presto, va bene. C'è un treno
15   fra dieci minuti.

—Dove posso fare il biglietto?

—Allo sportello numero sette, qui a sinistra. Faccia presto.

—Ecco, vado subito. Tante
20   grazie.

—Prego. Buon viaggio, e saluti al cugino.

Excuse me, sir, at what time does the train leave?

Which train, please?

The train for Naples. I am going to visit my cousin.

Oh, yes. Via Formia?

I don't know. I am going to Naples.

What ticket do you have?

I don't have a ticket. Can I get the ticket on the train?

It costs more on the train. At what time do you want to leave?

I want to leave right away.

All right, immediately. There is a train in ten minutes.

Where can I get the ticket?

At window number seven, here to the left. Be quick.

Here I go, quickly. Thank you so much.

You are welcome. Have a nice trip, and regards to your cousin.

EXERCISES

I. Questions. 1. Chi arriva oggi a Roma? 2. Chi va alla stazione a ricevere l'amico? 3. È italiano Riccardo Webster? 4. A quale stazione arrivano i treni di Londra? 5. Ci sono buone sale d'aspetto nella stazione? 6. Che c'è in ogni sala d'aspetto? 7. Dove si possono chiedere informazioni? 8. Sono cortesi gl'impiegati? 9. A che ora arriva il treno di Londra? 10. Che ora è già quando Enzo va a ricevere il suo amico?

II. Give the following hours in Italian:

7:20	12:00 m	8:30	1:12
10:19	3:20	11:15	5:25
4:05	9:17	6:08	9:10

(On the twenty-four hour system)

1:15 PM	5:05 PM	10:00 AM
3:10 PM	7:30 PM	9:10 PM

III. Translate orally:

my friend	her class	their waiting room
his station	your (*fam.*) office	their restaurant
our hotel	your (*pol.*) restaurant	our train
their students	our question	your (*pol.*) father
your (*pol.*) train	my number	my uncle

IV. Supply the correct form of the verb indicated and translate:

1. tu (venire)	6. essi (dare)
2. voi (venire)	7. essi (venire)
3. io (fare)	8. Lei (fare)
4. egli (fare)	9. tu (dare)
5. noi (dare)	10. noi (fare)

V. Translate the English words in parentheses:

1. (Who) arriva oggi? 2. (Who) viene alla stazione? 3. (Whom) vuole vedere Enzo? 4. (What) è una sala d'aspetto? 5. (What) c'è in ogni sala d'aspetto? 6. (What) treno arriva alle sedici? 7. (Which) è il binario numero dodici? 8. (Which) treni hanno due classi? 9. (What) chiede Lei nel ristorante? 10. A (what) ora arriva il treno?

VI. Write the Italian for the following:

1. I am going to meet my friend because he does not know Rome. 2. His name is Richard, not Joseph. 3. The trains arrive there and depart from there. 4. They go to all parts of Europe. 5. There are beauti-

ful waiting rooms in the station. 6. This waiting room is for the second class. 7. Do you know that the trains are comfortable? 8. I go to the information desk and I ask. 9. Does the train arrive at four PM? 10. It is already ten minutes to ten.

WORD LIST

NOUNS

amico *m.* friend
binario *m.* track
classe *f.* class
domanda *f.* question
estate *f.* summer
Europa *f.* Europe
impiegato *m.* clerk, employee
informazioni *f. pl.* information
Londra *f.* London
numero *m.* number
ora *f.* hour, time; **a che ora?** at what time?
parte *f.* part
Riccardo Richard
ristorante *m.* restaurant
Roma Termini *main station in Rome*
sala d'aspetto *f.* waiting room
stazione *f.* station
studente *m.* student
treno *m.* train
ufficio informazioni *m.* information desk

ADJECTIVES

cortese courteous
inglese *adj.* English

principale principal
secondo, –a second
sedici sixteen; **alle sedici** at 4:00 PM

VERBS

chiamarsi to be called; **si chiama** his name is
chiedere to ask for
conoscere to know
dire to say; **dice** says
ricevere to receive, meet
rispondere to answer
sapere to know
venire to come

OTHER WORDS

di lì from there
già already
gli to him
lo him, it
meno minus
oggi today
perciò therefore
qualsiasi any
su on
subito quickly

PRONUNCIATION

The *k*-sound. The **k**-sound in Italian is similar to the English *c* in *cat*. In spelling it is represented by **c** before **a, o,** or **u** (**ca, co, cu**) and by **ch** before **e** or **i** (**che, chi**). Therefore the spelling of the **k**-sound before the five vowels is **ca, che, chi, co, cu.** Listen for it in the following words:

amico, Riccardo, scusi, che, chi

The *g*-sound. The **g**-sound in Italian is similar to the English *g* in *go*. It is represented by **g** before **a, o,** or **u** (**ga, go, gu**) and by **gh** before **e** or **i** (**ghe, ghi**). The spelling of the **g**-sound before the five vowels is: **ga, ghe, ghi, go, gu.** Listen for it in the following words:

impiegato, alberghi, negozio, botteghe, gusto

The long consonant. In Italian the double consonant in writing is really a long consonant in pronunciation. It is not two consonants in rapid succession, but a holding of the position of the vocal organs forming the consonant with a slightly heavier explosion of that consonant when it does come out. This long consonant occurs not only when there are two consonants in the middle of a word, but also at the beginning of a word when there is a single consonant following words like **a, e, da.** Listen to the following:

otto, faccio, alle, bella, Riccardo
e due, a che ora, da lì partono

37

CURRENT USAGE

Cercando alloggio

Stamattina Ɛnzo e Riccardo hanno fatto colazione e sono usciti presto. Hanno preso l'autobus e sono andati vicino all'università. Lì hanno cercato una stanza per Riccardo, perchè è venuto a Roma per studiare. Volete sentire come
5 hanno fatto?

— Buɔn [1] giorno, signora. Il mio amico Riccardo cerca una stanza.

— Bɛne, signori. Sono studɛnti?

— Sì, signora, siamo studɛnti.

10 — E vɔgliono due stanze?

— Nɔ, signora. Io sono di quí.

— Anche i Romani prɛndono stanze.

— Lo sɔ,[2] ma io abito coi miɛi genitori, in Via Toscana.

— Hɔ capito. E Lɛi, signore, di dov'è?

15 — Sono inglese. Sono venuto per studiare l'italiano.

— Bravo, quí ci sono molti studɛnti. Vuɔle una stanza grande?

— Una stanza cɔmoda.

— Ɛcco una bɛlla stanza, a mille lire il giorno.

20 — Lɛi forse non ha capito. Non sono un ricco Americano, sono un pɔvero Inglese.

— Hɔ capito. Ɛcco una stanza cɔmoda, a seicɛnto lire il giorno.

— Che ne dici, Ɛnzo? La prɛndo?

25 — Sì, mi sembra buɔna. Ci sono ristoranti quí vicino?

— Sì, ci sono ristoranti. Ma abbiamo pensione quí in albɛrgo, se vuɔle.

— La pensione quanto cɔsta?

— La stessa stanza, con pensione, viɛne a mille e duecɛnto
30 lire il giorno.

— Allora prɛndo la stanza con pensione, Ɛnzo?

---

[1] **Buɔno** becomes **buɔn** when it is used before a masculine singular noun which does not begin with a **z** or an **s** + consonant. [2] **Lo sɔ**, I know.

This unusual view of Siena is a favorite with all those who have visited the city of the famous Palio. The donkey is not a participant in the horse race, but is a familiar sight in many Italian cities.

— Sì, sì, meglio con pensione, Riccardo.

E così Riccardo ha trovato la stanza, ed i due amici sono
tornati a casa. (E voi avete imparato il passato prossimo.)

STRUCTURE

27. Past Participle. The past participle of regular verbs is
formed by taking the stem and adding –**ato** for the first conjugation, –**uto** for the second, and –**ito** for the third. Notice the
following models:

I	II	III
parlare, *to speak*	vendere, *to sell*	finire, *to finish*
parlato, *spoken*	**venduto,** *sold*	**finito,** *finished*

28. Present Perfect Tense (*Passato Prossimo*). The present perfect tense expresses an action which has taken place in the
recent past, or rather in a period of time not yet completed. It is
mentally connected with the present by the speaker. In English
it usually corresponds to *I have spoken* or *I spoke, he has finished*
or *he finished*, etc. The present perfect is formed by the present
of the verb **avere** (or in some cases **essere**), followed by the past
participle of the verb to be conjugated. Study these models:

I	II	III
parlare	**vendere**	**finire**
io ho parlato	ho venduto	ho finito
tu hai parlato	hai venduto	hai finito
egli, essa, Lei ha parlato	ha venduto	ha finito
noi abbiamo parlato	abbiamo venduto	abbiamo finito
voi avete parlato	avete venduto	avete finito
essi, esse, Loro hanno parlato	hanno venduto	hanno finito

29. Present Perfect of Verbs Conjugated with *essere*.
Many verbs are conjugated with **essere** instead of **avere**. You
will learn these verbs as you go along because they will always
be so indicated when they are first given. Notice that when a

verb is conjugated with εssere the past participle is treated as an adjective and agrees with the subject in gender and number.

Following are models of verbs conjugated with εssere:

	I **andare,** *to go*	II **cadere,** *to fall*	III **partire,** *to leave*
io	sono andato, –a	sono caduto, –a	sono partito, –a
tu	sεi andato, –a	sεi caduto, –a	sεi partito, –a
egli	è andato	è caduto	è partito
essa	è andata	è caduta	è partita
Lεi	è andato, –a	è caduto, –a	è partito, –a
noi	siamo andati, –e	siamo caduti, –e	siamo partiti, –e
voi	siεte andati, –e	siεte caduti, –e	siεte partiti, –e
essi	sono andati	sono caduti	sono partiti
esse	sono andate	sono cadute	sono partite
Loro	sono andati, –e	sono caduti, –e	sono partiti, –e

30. Irregular Past Participles. Some common verbs have irregular past participles. Keep these in mind in forming the present perfect.

fare — **fatto**   εssere — **stato** (takes εssere)
prεndere — **preso**   venire — **venuto** (takes εssere)

31. Direct Object Pronouns (*lo, la, li, le*). The direct object pronouns for the third person are as follows:

lo, him *or* it referring to a masculine singular person or thing.
la, her *or* it referring to a feminine singular person or thing.
li, them referring to masculine plural persons or things.
le, them referring to feminine plural persons or things.

La prεndo? *Do I take it?*
Li vediamo spesso. *We see them often.*

These object pronouns generally come directly before the verb in Italian. There are many more pronouns and many more rules about them, but at present learn only these forms.

32. The Particle *ne*. The particle **ne** is a direct object pronoun which refers to something that has been mentioned before. It is a combination of the preposition **di** + a pronoun, and has a great variety of meanings: *of it, of them, some, some of it, some of them,* etc.

Che ne dici?   What do you think of it?

33. Months and Seasons

gennaio, January	**luglio,** July
febbraio, February	**agosto,** August
marzo, March	**settembre,** September
aprile, April	**ottobre,** October
maggio, May	**novembre,** November
giugno, June	**dicembre,** December

All the names of the months are masculine and are generally written with a small letter in Italian.

primavera *f.* spring	**autunno** *m.* autumn, fall
estate *f.* summer	**inverno** *m.* winter

LANGUAGE PRACTICE

La colazione

La colazione è il primo pasto del giorno. Come il sole entra per la finestra e porta luce, così la colazione entra per la bocca e porta nutrimento.

In Italia ci sono due colazioni: la prima quando uno si alza, e la seconda a mezzogiorno. La prima si chiama caffè, perchè infatti non è altro che caffè con latte, e un panino con burro. La seconda colazione si chiama più generalmente pranzo, e allora finalmente si può mangiare.

L'Americano che va in Italia si trova in difficoltà nei primi giorni.

Breakfast

Breakfast is the first meal of the day. Just as the sun enters through the window and brings light, so breakfast enters through the mouth and brings nourishment.

In Italy there are two breakfasts: the first when one gets up, and the second at noon. The first breakfast is called coffee, because in fact it is nothing more than coffee with milk, with a roll and butter. The second is called more generally lunch, and then at last one can eat.

The American who goes to Italy finds himself in trouble in the

Invece di cominciare il giorno con spremuta d'arancia, due uova con salsiccia, ecc. ecc., lo deve cominciare con un caffè ed un panino. Pazienza! Paese che vai, usanza che trovi.

first few days. Instead of starting the day with orange juice, two eggs with sausages, etc., etc., he has to begin it with coffee and a roll. Patience! When in Rome do as 5 the Romans do.

EXERCISES

I. Questions. 1. Hanno fatto colazione presto Enzo e Riccardo? 2. Che cosa hanno cercato vicino all'università? 3. Che cosa ha domandato la signora? 4. Perchè Enzo non vuole una stanza? 5. Vuole una stanza grande Riccardo? 6. È ricco Riccardo? 7. Ci sono ristoranti vicino all'albergo? 8. Quanto costa la pensione? 9. Riccardo ha trovato la stanza? 10. Dove sono tornati i due amici?

II. Conjugate the following verbs in the present perfect:

A. 1. studiare 2. abitare 3. capire
B. 1. uscire 2. cadere 3. tornare
C. 1. fare 2. prendere 3. venire 4. essere

III. Supply the correct form of the present perfect of the verbs indicated:

A. (*Conjugated with* **avere**) 1. Egli (trovare). 2. Noi (abitare). 3. Voi (capire). 4. Essi (studiare). 5. Lei (volere). 6. Loro (prendere). 7. Esse (fare). 8. Io (sentire). 9. Lei (capire). 10. Egli (imparare).

B. (*Conjugated with* **essere**) 1. Io (venire). 2. Lei (andare). 3. Loro (uscire). 4. Noi (partire). 5. Voi (cadere). 6. Esse (tornare). 7. Io (andare). 8. Lei (tornare). 9. Noi (fare). 10. Essa (prendere).

IV. Translate the following:

1. I take it (*m.*). 2. He sees them (*m.*). 3. We see them (*f.*). 4. I know it (*m.*). 5. They study it (*f.*). 6. He understands her. 7. They take it (*f.*). 8. They study them (*m.*). 9. We have them (*m.*). 10. She takes them (*f.*).

V. Write the Italian for the following:

1. Where did they take the bus and where did they go? 2. He wants a room because he came to Rome to study. 3. Are you Americans or are you Englishmen? 4. She lives with her parents in their house. 5. Here is a beautiful room, at six hundred lire a day. 6. There are no restaurants, but we have a good "pensione." 7. Did you take the room with board (**pensione**)? 8. Why do you want two rooms? 9. And so the two friends found a comfortable room. 10. Have you learned the present perfect?

WORD LIST

NOUNS

alloggio *m.* lodging
autobus *m.* bus
colazione *f.* breakfast, lunch
Inglese *m.* Englishman
lira *f.* lira (*Italian unit of currency, worth about* ⅙ *of a cent*)
passato prossimo *m.* present perfect
pensione *f.* boardinghouse, board (*lodging with meals*)
signora *f.* madam, lady
signore *m.* gentleman
Toscana *f.* Tuscany (*a region in Central Italy*)
università *f.* university

ADJECTIVES

bravo, –a good, fine
buono, –a good
duecento two hundred
mille a thousand
quanto, –a how much
ricco, –a rich
romano, –a Roman, from Rome
seicento six hundred
stesso, –a same

VERBS

capire (isco) to understand
cercare to look for, search
fare to make, do; **far colazione** to have breakfast
imparare to learn
prendere to take
sembrare to seem (*takes* **essere**)
sentire to hear
studiare to study
tornare to return (*takes* **essere**)
uscire to go out (*takes* **essere**)

OTHER WORDS

allora then
come how, what
Lei di dov'è? where are you from?
ecco here is, here are
forse perhaps
meglio *adv.* better
mi me, to me
presto early
quanto *adv.* how much
qui here; **di qui** from here
stamattina this morning

PRONUNCIATION

The *ch-* and *k*-sounds. These two sounds are more trouble-some in spelling than in pronunciation because the same basic letter **c** is used for both of them. Starting from the written letter, we can say that **c** is pronounced like a **k** before **a, o,** or **u** (**ca, co, cu**). It is pronounced like **ch** before **e** or **i** (**ce, ci**). In order to give **c** the soft (**ch**) sound before **a, o,** or **u,** you write an **i** after the **c** (**cia, cio, ciu**). In order to give **c** the hard (**k**) sound before **e** or **i,** you write an **h** after the **c** (**che, chi**).

The *j-* and *g*-sounds. These two sounds cause the same difficulty as the two previous ones in spelling because they are both represented by the same basic letter **g**. Again, starting from the written letter, we can say that **g** is pronounced hard (*g* as in *go*) before **a, o,** or **u**. It is pronounced soft (*j* as in *jump*) before **e** or **i**. In order to give **g** the soft (**j**) sound before **a, o,** or **u,** you write an **i** after the **g** (**gia, gio, giu**). In order to give **g** the hard (**g**) sound before **e** or **i,** you write an **h** after the **g** (**ghe, ghi**).

Missing Letters. The Italian alphabet has five letters less than the English alphabet: Italian has no **j, k, w, x, y.** Of course any of these may be found in foreign words. In the older spelling **j** was used as the consonantal **i**, but in modern spelling it is seldom used. The sounds which the five letters represent are written by corresponding Italian letters, as you have seen in the pronunciation exercises.

45

CURRENT USAGE
Venezia

Gina ha una compagna che ha la famiglia a Venezia. Si chiama Flora. La compagna ha invitato Gina a passare una settimana con la sua famiglia. Gina ha accettato con piacere. Farà il viaggio la settimana prossima.

5   Il viaggio da Roma a Venezia è lungo. Ci sono cinque ore di treno da Roma a Firenze e quattro ore da Firenze a Venezia. Gina prenderà il treno delle dieci, che arriverà a Firenze alle tre del pomeriggio, e a Venezia alle diciannove, cioè alle sette di sera.

10   Quando Gina arriverà a Venezia non potrà prendere un tassì. Dovrà prendere il vaporetto o la gondola, perchè a Venezia non ci sono tassì; infatti non ci sono automobili. Venezia è forse l'unica grande città del mondo dove non ci sono automobili. È un piacere passeggiare per le sue strade.

15   Venezia è una città meravigliosa. Le case formano una sinfonia di colori nell'acqua dei canali. La Piazza San Marco, con la Basilica e il Campanile, formano una veduta stupenda. La Riva degli Schiavoni e il Palazzo dei Dogi sono incantevoli. Il Lido di Venezia, poi, è rinomato in tutto 20 il mondo.

     Gina, che non ha mai visto Venezia, passerà una settimana meravigliosa con la sua compagna. Beato chi può passare una settimana a Venezia!

STRUCTURE

34. Present Indicative of *dovere, dire, sapere*

	dovere, *to owe, must*	**dire,** *to say*	**sapere,** *to know*
io	devo (debbo)	dico	so
tu	devi	dici	sai
egli, essa, Lei	deve	dice	sa
noi	dobbiamo	diciamo	sappiamo
voi	dovete	dite	sapete
essi, esse, Loro	devono (debbono)	dicono	sanno

Saint Mark's Square and the Rialto Bridge symbolize the beauty of Venice, the Queen of the Adriatic.

35. Future Tense. The future tense of regular verbs is formed as follows:

For the first and second conjugations, take the stem of the verb and add the endings: **–erɔ, –erai, –erà, –eremo, –erete, –eranno.** For the third conjugation take the stem and add the endings: **–irɔ, –irai, –irà, –iremo, –irete, –iranno.**

Notice the following model verbs:

	I	II	III
io	parlerɔ	venderɔ	finirɔ
tu	parlerai	venderai	finirai
egli, essa, Lɛi	parlerà	venderà	finirà
noi	parleremo	venderemo	finiremo
voi	parlerete	venderete	finirete
essi, esse, Loro	parleranno	venderanno	finiranno

As for the verbs which are irregular in the future, once you know the first person singular the rest of the forms follow the pattern of regular verbs.

andare, *to go*   1st person singular **andrɔ**
  FUTURE: andrɔ, andrai, andrà, andremo, andrete, andranno

avere, *to have*   avrɔ, avrai, avrà, avremo, avrete, avranno
dovere, *to have to*   dovrɔ, dovrai, dovrà, dovremo, dovrete, dovranno
ɛssere, *to be*   sarɔ, sarai, sarà, saremo, sarete, saranno
fare, *to do*   farɔ, farai, farà, faremo, farete, faranno
potere, *to be able*   potrɔ, potrai, potrà, potremo, potrete, potranno
vedere, *to see*   vedrɔ, vedrai, vedrà, vedremo, vedrete, vedranno
venire, *to come*   verrɔ, verrai, verrà, verremo, verrete, verranno

36. Direct Object Pronouns (Cont.). Personal pronouns of all three persons naturally have a direct object form. Following

is a table of the subject personal pronouns and the corresponding direct object pronouns:

	SINGULAR		PLURAL	
Subject	*Direct Object*		*Subject*	*Direct Object*
io	**mi,** *me*		noi	**ci,** *us*
tu	**ti,** *you*		voi	**vi,** *you*
egli	**lo,** *him, it*		essi	**li,** *them*
essa	**la,** *her, it*		esse	**le,** *them*
Lei	**La,** *you*		Loro	**Li, Le,** *you*

Generally the direct object personal pronoun comes immediately before the verb in Italian. Later you will learn the conditions under which it comes after the verb.

37. Expressions about the Weather. Following are some
of the common expressions about the weather:

> Che tempo fa? *How is the weather?*
> Fa caldo. *It's warm.*
> Fa freddo. *It's cold.*
> Fa fresco. *It's chilly.*
> Fa molto caldo. *It's hot.*
> Fa bel tempo. *The weather is fine.*
> Fa cattivo tempo. *The weather is bad.*

With expressions about the weather Italian uses **fa** (from **fare**).

LANGUAGE PRACTICE

Piccolo dialogo

For recognition only. Act out in class or with a fellow student.

— Lei che cosa fa in Italia, signorina Campanile?

What do you do in Italy, Miss Campanile?

— Sono professoressa d'inglese.

I am a teacher of English.

— In che città insegna?

In what city do you teach?

— Insegno a Pisa, città del famoso
Campanile.

I teach in Pisa, the city of the 5
famous bell tower.

— Ci sono molti studenti d'inglese in Italia?

Are there many students of English in Italy?

— Sì, ce ne sono molti. L'inglese è la lìngua più popolare.

Yes, there are many (of them). English is the most popular language.

— Perchè si studia tanto l'inglese?

Why do people study English so much?

5

— Si studia tanto perchè ha importanza commerciale e polìtica. Quando uno sa l'inglese, può sempre migliorare la sua posizione.

It is studied so much because it has commercial and political importance. When one knows English, he can always improve his position.

10

— Si usa molto l'inglese nel commercio in Italia?

Is English used a great deal in business in Italy?

— Sì, tutte le grandi case commerciali hanno relazioni con paesi di lìngua inglese.

Yes, all the big commercial houses have relations with English-speaking countries.

15

— Preferisce l'inglese d'Inghilterra o l'inglese degli Stati Uniti?

Do you prefer the English of England or the English of the United States?

— Io ho studiato l'inglese in Inghilterra, come molti dei miei amici. Adesso però, vogliamo imparare la pronunzia americana, perchè è più importante per noi.

I studied English in England, like many of my friends. Now, however, we want to learn the American pronunciation, because it is more important for us.

20

25 — Spero che troverà interessante il suo soggiorno qui in America.

I hope you will find your stay here in America interesting.

EXERCISES

I. Questions. 1. Come si chiama la compagna di Gina? 2. Quando farà il viaggio Gina? 3. Ci sono molte ore di treno da Roma a Venezia? 4. A che ora arriva a Venezia il treno? 5. Gina potrà prendere un tassì? 6. Che cosa dovrà prendere invece? 7. Ci sono molte automòbili a Venezia? 8. È bella la città di Venezia? 9. Che cosa formano la Piazza San Marco con la Basìlica e il Campanile? 10. È rinomato il Lido di Venezia?

II. Conjugate the following verbs:

  A. (*Future*) 1. formare 2. accettare 3. andare
 4. potere 5. fare 6. dovere 7. prendere.
  B. (*Present perfect*) 1. invitare 2. arrivare (*takes*

ɛssere) 3. prɛndere 4. fare 5. vedere 6. venire
(*takes* ɛssere) 7. andare (*takes* ɛssere).

III. Supply the correct form of the verb indicated in (*a*) the present, (*b*) the present perfect, and (*c*) the future:

1. Lɛi (dovere). 2. Noi (potere). 3. Egli (arrivare).
4. Essa (fare). 5. Loro (prɛndere). 6. Lɛi (capire).
7. Tu (imparare). 8. Voi (cercare).

IV. Use a direct object pronoun instead of the words in italics:

1. Passerà *la settimana* a Firɛnze. 2. Prenderemo *il treno* alle diɛci. 3. Faranno *il viaggio* la settimana prɔssima. 4. Vediamo *le case*. 5. Inviteremo *i compagni*. 6. Comprerete *l'automɔbile*. 7. Prenderemo *la gondola*. 8. Prɛndi *la stanza?* 9. Vediamo *le ragazze* spɛsso. 10. Lɛi dove passa *l'estate?*

V. Write the Italian for the following:

1. How is the weather? It's chilly. 2. The weather is fine this morning. 3. There are no taxis because the streets are canals. 4. It is a pleasure to walk where there are no cars. 5. The basilica and the square form a stupendous view. 6. When will you take the train from Florence to Venice? 7. I shall have to take a small steamer or a gondola. 8. Are there many enchanting things in the city? 9. He who has not seen Venice has not seen the world. 10. We shall take the trip next week and we shall spend three days in the city.

WORD LIST

NOUNS

acqua *f.* water
automɔbile *f.* automobile, car
basilica *f.* basilica
canale *m.* canal
colore *m.* color
compagna *f.* companion, friend
Flɔra *proper name*

Lido *m. famous beach on a reef near Venice*
Palazzo dei Dɔgi *m.* Doges' Palace
piacere *m.* pleasure
Piazza San Marco Saint Mark's Square (*in Venice*)
Riva degli Schiavoni *f. promenade near Saint Mark's Square*
settimana *f.* week

sinfonia *f.* symphony
tassì *m.* taxi
vaporetto *m.* small steamer
Venɛzia *f.* Venice
veduta *f.* sight, view

ADJECTIVES

beato, –a lucky
incantevole enchanting
lungo, –a long
meraviglioso, –a marvelous
prɔssimo, –a next
rinomato, –a famous
stupɛndo, –a stupendous
unico, –a only

VERBS

accettare to accept
dovere to have to, owe

invitare to invite
passeggiare to walk, stroll
visto *p.p.* of **vedere** seen

OTHER WORDS

chi he who, the one who
cioɛ̀ that is
infatti in fact

EXPRESSIONS

alle tre del pomeriggio at
three in the afternoon
cinque ore di trɛno five
hours on the train

PRONUNCIATION

Written Accent. In Italian you will find in some books three
types of written accents, the grave (`` ` ``), the acute (´), and the
circumflex (ˆ). The circumflex has practically disappeared now.
The acute accent is used by many Italian writers over the final
vowel of words which require an accent. However, the most
common practice in our textbooks is to use only the grave accent
whenever an accent is needed. Such is the practice followed in
this book.

Although in Italian most words are stressed on the next to the
last syllable, there are so many exceptions that it is hardly worth-
while to mention this as a rule. For that reason the stress is
indicated throughout this book either by the accent, by the special

characters ε and ɔ, or by printing the stressed vowel in italics whenever the stress does not fall on the next to the last vowel in the word.

Many of the standard Italian dictionaries use accents to indicate the quality of the vowels **e** and **o**. When accents are used for this purpose, the acute (´) accent indicates the close vowel and the grave (`) indicates the open vowel.

CURRENT USAGE

La casa di Flɔra

Gina è arrivata a Venεzia alle diciannɔve, alla stazione Santa Lucia. Flɔra è venuta a incontrarla con suo padre, il signor Bettini. Sono andati a casa in gondola. Com'è bεlla Venεzia vista dalla gondola! I motoscafi ed i vaporetti sono più veloci, ma perchè andare in fretta per i canali 5 di Venεzia?

La casa di Flɔra è vicino al Ponte di Rialto, dirimpεtto alla Casa del Petrarca. Non molto distante si trɔva il Teatro Goldoni, e un pɔco più lontano il Teatro Rossini. In casa del signor Bettini ci sono quadri di artisti veneziani 10 come Tiziano, il Tintoretto, Giovanni Bellini, e molti altri. Ci sono bεi vetri di Murano, la famosa *i*sola vicino a Venεzia, nell'Adri*a*tico. Tutto a Venεzia fa pensare alla poesia, alla m*u*sica e all'arte.

Gina è rimasta molto contεnta perchè la signora Bettini 15 l'ha ricevuta con grande cordialità. Le ha dato una camera accanto a quella di Flɔra, così le due compagne pɔssono passare la giornata insiεme. Perɔ ha detto loro di riposare prima del pranzo, perchè il vi*a*ggio è stato lungo. Gina non ha potuto riposare. Ha scritto una lεttera al babbo e gli 20 ha raccontato la sua prima impressione di Venεzia.

STRUCTURE

38. Agreement of Past Participles. When a verb is conjugated with **εssere** the past participle agrees in gender and number with the subject.

The Adoration of the Shepherds, by Giorgione, is one of the treasures of our own National Gallery in Washington.

The Flora (detail), by Titian, is one of the countless masterpieces in the Uffizi Gallery in Florence.

Gina è arrivat**a** a Venezia. *Gina arrived in Venice.*
Essi sono andat**i** in gondola. *They went in a gondola.*

When a verb is conjugated with **avere** the past participle remains unchanged unless there is a direct object preceding the verb. If the direct object comes before the verb, the past participle agrees with it in gender and number.

Gina ha scritto una lettera. *Gina has written a letter.*
Gina l'ha scritt**a**. *Gina has written it.*

39. Indirect Object Pronouns. The indirect object refers to the person *to whom* or *for whom* an action is done. The forms of the indirect object personal pronouns are as follows:

SINGULAR		PLURAL	
mi	to *or* for me	**ci**	to *or* for us
ti	to *or* for you (*fam.*)	**vi**	to *or* for you (*fam.*)
gli	to *or* for him ⎫	**loro**	to *or* for them
le	to *or* for her ⎭		
Le	to *or* for you (*pol.*)	**Loro**	to *or* for you (*pol.*)

The indirect object pronouns generally precede the verb, the same as direct object pronouns. However, the pronoun **loro** always comes after the verb.

Le ha dato una camera. *She gave her a room.*
Ha detto loro di riposare. *She told them to rest.*

Notice that when the object which comes before the verb is indirect, the past participle does not agree with it.

40. Position of Object Pronouns with Infinitives. When an object pronoun (other than **loro**) depends on an infinitive, it is attached to it after dropping the final **e**.

Flora è venuta a incontrar**la**. *Flora came to meet her.*

41. The Adjective *bello*. The adjective **bello** generally comes before the noun. In that position it has six forms, like the definite article.

SINGULAR	PLURAL	
bɛl	bɛi	before ordinary masculine nouns.
		il bɛl quadro — i bɛi quadri
bɛllo	bɛgli	before special masculine nouns.
		il bɛllo studio — i bɛgli studi
bɛlla	bɛlle	before feminine nouns.
		la bɛlla casa — le bɛlle case

Notice moreover that **bɛllo** and **bɛlla** drop the last vowel and take the apostrophe (**bɛll'**) before a word beginning with a vowel. When the adjective **bɛllo** comes after the noun, it has four forms, the same as any other similar adjective.

i quadri grandi e bɛlli, *the large beautiful pictures*

42. Verbs Conjugated with ɛssere. The following common verbs which you have learned so far are conjugated with **ɛssere** instead of **avere.**

andare, *to go*   rimanere, *to remain*
arrivare, *to arrive*   tornare, *to return*
cadere, *to fall*   venire, *to come*
ɛssere, *to be*

43. More Irregular Past Participles. Here are some additional common verbs whose past participle is irregular:

dire, *to say* — **detto**
ɛssere, *to be* — **stato**
rimanere, *to remain* — **rimasto**
scrivere, *to write* — **scritto**
vedere, *to see* — **visto** (*or* **veduto**)

LANGUAGE PRACTICE

Piccolo dialogo

For recognition only. Act out in class or with a fellow student.

— Mi dica, per favore, dove posso   Tell me, please, where can I buy
   comprare del formaggio?   some cheese?
— C'è una salumeria nella strada   There is a delicatessen in the street
   a dɛstra.   to the right.

— Posso comprare anche prosciutto cotto lì?

Can I buy boiled ham there, too?

— Sì, signore, si vende prosciutto cotto e prosciutto crudo.

Yes, sir, they sell boiled ham and smoked ham.

— Io sono americano e preferisco il prosciutto cotto. Lo adoperiamo molto in America, nei panini imbottiti.

I am an American and I prefer 5 boiled ham. We use it a great deal in sandwiches in America.

— Il panino imbottito è usanza americana. Noi in Italia preferiamo un pranzo completo.

The sandwich is an American custom. We in Italy prefer a full 10 meal.

— Quando viaggio, spesso mi preparo io stesso qualche cosa da mangiare a mezzogiorno. La sera preferisco pranzare in un buon ristorante.

When I travel I often prepare something for myself at noon. In the evening I prefer to eat in a good restaurant. 15

— Ebbene, nella salumeria troverà molti cibi. Ci sono formaggi, salami, mortadelle, scatole di tonno, scatole di acciughe, ecc.

Well, in the delicatessen you will find many foods. There are cheeses, salami, bologna, cans of tuna fish, cans of anchovies, etc. 20

— Grazie, signore. È molto gentile.

Thank you, sir. You are very kind.

— Prego, signore. Buon appetito!

Not at all, sir. Enjoy your dinner.

EXERCISES

I. Questions. 1. Quando è arrivata a Venezia Gina? 2. Chi è venuta a incontrarla? 3. Come sono andati a casa? 4. Sono veloci i motoscafi ed i vaporetti? 5. Quali artisti veneziani conosce Lei? 6. Quali teatri sono vicino al Ponte di Rialto? 7. Perchè è famosa l'isola di Murano? 8. Perchè è rimasta contenta Gina? 9. Possono passare bene la giornata insieme le due compagne? 10. Che cosa ha fatto Gina prima del pranzo?

II. Translate orally:

A. 1. They have arrived. 2. She has come. 3. We have gone. 4. You have been. 5. I have remained. 6. She has returned. 7. You (*pol. pl.*) have fallen. 8. Has she arrived? 9. Has Gina remained? 10. Have they been?

B. 1. He has said. 2. I have given. 3. She has seen. 4. We have received. 5. You have done. 6. You (*fam. sing.*) have written. 7. You (*fam. pl.*) have not been able. 8. He has not wanted. 9. You (*pol. pl.*) have said. 10. I have taken.

III. Supply the proper form of the verb in the person and number indicated:

A. (*Future*) 1. Io (arrivare). 2. Lɛi (avere). 3. Noi (ɛssere). 4. Gina (andare). 5. Le compagne (venire). 6. Tu (pensare). 7. Loro (vedere). 8. Voi (riposare). 9. La signora (ricevere). 10. Il babbo (capire).

B. (*Present Perfect*). 1. Flɔra (venire). 2. Il signore (arrivare). 3. Essi (rimanere) contɛnti. 4. Essa le (dare) una camera. 5. Il babbo (raccontare) la sua impressione. 6. Gli artisti (fare) i quadri. 7. Egli (venire) al teatro. 8. Essi (andare) in fretta. 9. Lɛi (passare) la giornata. 10. Noi (dire) loro di riposare.

IV. Substitute an indirect object pronoun for the words in italics:

1. Ha dato una camera *a Gina*. 2. Abbiamo detto *alle ragazze* di riposare. 3. Hɔ scritto una lɛttera *to you*. 4. Ha raccontato la stɔria *to us*. 5. Diremo *ai ragazzi* di prɛndere il motoscafo. 6. Ha dato l'automɔbile *to me*. 7. Scriviamo le lɛttere *ai genitori*. 8. Danno tutto *to you* (*fam. pl.*). 9. Parlerɔ *a mio padre* domani. 10. Direte *a Flɔra* la vɔstra impressione.

V. Write the Italian for the following:

1. When did she arrive in the city? 2. Her friend came to meet her at the station. 3. There is a beautiful little steamer in the canal. 4. The beautiful glass (*use plural*) of Murano is very famous. 5. Why did they rush through the streets of Venice? 6. Have you seen the paintings of artists like Tiziano, il Tintoretto, or Giovanni Bellini? 7. Everything in the city makes one

think of music and art.   8. Is my room next to the
one of my friend?   9. I told him to rest before dinner.
10. Why don't you tell her your first impression of
Venice?   *Perchè non dici*

WORD LIST

NOUNS

Adriatico *m.* Adriatic Sea
babbo *m.* daddy
Bellini (Giovanni) *Italian painter* (1426–1516)
cordialità *f.* cordiality
fretta *f.* hurry; **andare in fretta** to be in a hurry, rush
giornata *f.* day
Goldoni *most famous Italian playwright (1707–1793)*
gondola *f.* gondola
impressione *f.* impression
isola *f.* island
lettera *f.* letter
motoscafo *m.* motorboat
Murano *island near Venice, famous for its glass industry*
musica *f.* music
Petrarca Petrarch; *famous Italian poet (1304–1374)*
poesia *f.* poetry
ponte *m.* bridge; **ponte di Rialto** Rialto Bridge
quadro *m.* painting, picture

Rossini *famous Italian composer (1792–1868)*
teatro *m.* theater
Tintoretto *famous Italian painter (1518–1594)*
Tiziano *famous Italian painter (1477–1576)*
vetro *m.* glass

ADJECTIVES

veloce fast
veneziano, –a Venetian

VERBS

raccontare to tell
scrivere (*p.p.* **scritto**) to write

OTHER WORDS

accanto (a) next to
insieme (a) together (with)
lontano far
più more
prima di before
quella the one

PRONUNCIATION

The *sk*-sound. The **sk**-sound as in the English word *sky* is represented in Italian as follows: before **a, o,** or **u** it is **sc** (**sca, sco, scu**). Before **e** or **i** it is **sch** (**sche, schi**).

The *sh*-sound. The **sh**-sound as in the English word *shoe* is represented in Italian as follows: before **a, o,** or **u** it is **sci** (**scia, scio, sciu**). Before **e** or **i** it is **sc** (**sce, sci**).

Notice that the **ch** in Italian is never pronounced like **ch** in English. It is always like the English **k**-sound, even in syllables like **schia, schio,** or **schiu**.

CURRENT USAGE

Consigli di un padre a un figlio

Parla poco e con giudizio.
Impara bene e non dimenticare.
Parla solo quando ti fanno una domanda.
Finisci tutto quel che hai cominciato.
5   Scrivi spesso, ma non per chiedere denaro.

Consigli di un maestro agli studenti

State bene attenti in classe.
Non sprecate il tempo.
Imparate bene le lezioni.
Fate i compiti ogni giorno.
10   Studiate, studiate, e studiate.

60

Invito a un amico lontano

Vɛnga a stare con noi per qualche giorno. Faccia un viaggio da queste parti e pɔrti la Sua famiglia. Lasci tutto quel lavoro che sta facɛndo e si prɛnda un pɔ' di ripɔso. Il ripɔso è necessario per la salute e per lo spirito. Non dimentichi la frase « dolce far niɛnte »; è la medicina segreta dei dottori. Prɛndano il prɔssimo trɛno, Lɛi e Sua moglie, e pɔrtino anche i bambini. Li vedremo tutti con piacere. Saranno contɛnti del Loro viaggio. 5

STRUCTURE

44. The Imperative. The imperative is the form of the verb which indicates a command or a request. Strictly speaking, it has only the second person singular and the second person plural. The negative imperative for the second person singular has the same form as the infinitive. The negative for the second person plural has the same form as the affirmative.

IMPERATIVE

I	II
Affirmative — Negative	*Affirmative — Negative*
parla — non parlare	vendi — non vendere
parlate — non parlate	vendete — non vendete

III

Affirmative — Negative

finisci — non finire
parti — non partire
finite — non finite

45. First Person Plural Commands. When a command is given to a group which includes the speaker, it goes in the first person plural. In English it is translated by *let's*. The form is the same as the first person plural of the present indicative, both for the affirmative and the negative.

I	II	III
ascoltiamo, *let's listen*	vendiamo, *let's sell*	finiamo, *let's finish*

Lake Como, in northern Italy, offers many fascinating views such as the one above. The shores of the lake are dotted with villages whose colorful houses are mirrored in its waters.

46. Polite Commands. When a command is given to a person whom you are addressing in the **Lεi**-form, or to more than one person, whom you address as **Loro,** the verb goes in the present subjunctive, which you will learn completely in Lesson 16. At present notice the polite command forms of regular verbs. The negative form is the same as the affirmative.

I	II	III
parli (Lεi)	venda (Lεi)	finisca (Lεi)
parlino (Loro)	vendano (Loro)	finiscano (Loro)
		(parta — partano)

In these polite command forms the plural is always formed from the singular by adding **–no,** regardless of whether the verbs are regular or irregular. Notice some polite command forms:

cominciare:	**cominci — comincino**
dimenticare:	**dimentichi — dimentichino**
fare:	**faccia — facciano**
lasciare:	**lasci — lascino**
venire:	**vεnga — vεngano**

47. Complete Imperative. If all the various types of command forms are grouped together, you get the following forms:

	I	II	III
(io)	———	———	———
(tu)	parla (non parlare)	vendi (non vendere)	finisci (non finire)[1]
(Lεi)	parli	venda	finisca
(noi)	parliamo	vendiamo	finiamo
(voi)	parlate	vendete	finite
(Loro)	parlino	vendano	finiscano

48. Position of Object Pronouns. With the strictly imperative forms (**tu** and **voi**) and with the first person plural command (**noi**) all object pronouns except **loro** come after the verb and

[1] The forms of **partire** are: (tu) **parti,** (Lei) **parta,** (Loro) **partano.**

are attached to it. **Loro** always comes after the verb, but it is not attached.

> Finiscilo domani. *Finish it tomorrow.*
> Portalo a Maria. *Take it to Mary.*
> Diciamo loro di venire. *Let's tell them to come.*

When the imperative forms are in the negative, or when the commands are in the polite form, the object pronouns come before the verb, as they do regularly.

> Non lo portare a Maria. *Do not take it to Mary.*
> Lo finisca domani. *Finish it tomorrow.*
> Lo porti a Maria. *Take it to Mary.*

49. Orthographical Changes. Verbs ending in –**care** or –**gare** (like **dimenticare** and **pagare** [*to pay*]) add an **h** to the stem whenever the ending begins with **e** or **i**. This is done in order to preserve the **k**- or **g**-sound of the stem. Notice the present indicative, imperative, and future of the verb **dimenticare.**

PRESENT: dimentico, **dimentichi,** dimentica, **dimentichiamo,** dimenticate, dimenticano

IMPERATIVE: ——, dimentica, **dimentichi, dimentichiamo,** dimenticate, **dimentichino**

FUTURE: **dimenticherò,** etc.

Verbs ending in –**ciare** (like **cominciare** or **lasciare**) drop the **i** of the stem when the ending begins with an **i** or an **e**. Notice the future of **lasciare:**

> lascerò, lascerai, lascerà, lasceremo, lascerete, lasceranno

50. Relative Pronouns. The most common relative pronoun in Italian is **che,** corresponding to *who, whom, which,* or *that.* The relative pronoun is never omitted in Italian. **Che** may be used as the subject or as the object of a verb, but it cannot be used after a preposition. The common relative pronoun after a preposition is **cui,** corresponding to *whom* or *which.*

> Quel lavoro che sta facendo. *That work which you are doing.*
> L'amico a cui ho scritto. *The friend to whom I have written.*

There are other relative pronouns, which you will learn later on.

LANGUAGE PRACTICE

Piccolo dialogo

For recognition only.   Act out in class or with a fellow student.

— Guardi dalla finestra.   Che tempo fa oggi?

Look out of the window.   How is the weather today?

— Piove e tira vento.

It is raining and windy.

— Piove forte?   Fa freddo?

Is it raining hard?   Is it cold?

— Non piove forte, ma fa freddo.

It is not raining hard, but it is cold. 5

— Meglio così.   Quando fa caldo tuona spesso e lampeggia.

Better this way.   When it is warm, there is often thunder and lightning.

— Quando lampeggia ho paura. Mi nascondo nell'armadio.

When it is lightning, I am afraid. I hide in the closet. 10

— Il fulmine può arrivare anche nell'armadio.

Lightning can reach in the closet, too.

— Se arriva non mi trova, perchè mi nascondo bene.

If it reaches there it won't find me, because I hide well.

— Bravo, sei molto coraggioso. Preferisci l'inverno?

Fine, you are very brave.   Do you 15 prefer winter?

— Sì, preferisco l'inverno, quando nevica e fa freddo.

Yes, I prefer winter, when it snows and it is cold.

— La neve non mi piace, perchè con la neve è difficile guidare.

I don't like snow, because it is hard to drive with the snow. 20

— D'inverno io prendo sempre il treno.

In winter I always take the train.

— Sì, va bene, ma per me l'automobile è necessaria.

Yes, all right, but I need the car.

— Allora l'estate va bene per Lei e l'inverno va bene per me.

Then summer is all right for you 25 and winter is all right for me.

EXERCISES

I. Questions. 1. Lei parla sempre con giudizio?   2. Parla quando non Le fanno una domanda?   3. Scrive spesso a Suo padre per chiedere denaro?   4. Finisce sempre tutto quel che ha cominciato?   5. Sprecano il tempo gli studenti?   6. Chi fa i suoi compiti ogni giorno?   7. Chi impara bene le lezioni?   8. Il riposo è necessario per la salute?   9. Qual è la medicina segreta dei dottori?   10. Lei andrà a visitare un amico qualche giorno?

II. A. Give the complete imperative forms, both affirmative and negative, of the following verbs:

    1. imparare   2. dimenticare   3. finire   4. scrivere
    5. prendere   6. portare

B. Give only the polite command forms, both affirmative and negative, of the following verbs:

    1. venire   2. fare   3. lasciare   4. sprecare
    5. vedere   6. cominciare

III. Translate the following:

A. 1. Let's tell him everything. 2. Let's take it (*m.*) to Gina. 3. Do not finish (*pol.*) it today. 4. Do not speak (*pol.*) to her now. 5. Sell (*fam. pl.*) all that you have. 6. Finish (*pol. pl.*) them (*f.*) tomorrow. 7. Forget (*pol.*) it. 8. Let's take them (*m.*). 9. Write (*pol.*) to him, please. 10. Let's take it (*m.*) to Richard.

B. 1. The homework which I do. 2. The friend with whom I travel. 3. The question which they ask. 4. The teacher to whom we speak. 5. The rest which is necessary. 6. The train which you will take. 7. The friends we'll see. 8. The child to whom he writes. 9. We have spoken of it. 10. You will be glad of it.

IV. Translate the words in parentheses and read aloud:

1. (Leave) il lavoro che Lɛi fa. 2. (Work) molto se Lɛi vuɔle imparare. 3. Non (waste) tanto tɛmpo. 4. (Let's write) ogni giorno. 5. (Let's take) un viaggio in Eurɔpa. 6. (Come) a stare con noi quando pɔssono (Loro-*form*). 7. (Of them) abbiamo studiate due. 8. (Of it) parlano spesso. 9. (Of them) hanno comprati sɛi. 10. Il denaro (which) hɔ ricevuto. 11. Il lavoro (which) ha cominciato. 12. (To him) abbiamo dato un consiglio. 13. (To her) scriverɔ domani. 14. (To you, *pol.*) porteremo la medicina. 15. (To us) risponderanno quando potranno.

V. Write the Italian for the following:

1. He writes to him often because he wants money.
2. Learn the lessons if you want to learn the language.

3. Let's take the next train for Venice, where we shall see the family. 4. Will he take a little rest for his health? 5. Rest is also necessary for the morale. 6. They have an invitation from a friend far away. 7. The saying goes: "Happy life of ease." 8. He wastes his time, but he is very happy. 9. What is the secret medicine of the doctors? 10. Take the next train and bring your wife, too.

WORD LIST

NOUNS

bambino *m.* child
compiti *m. pl.* homework
consiglio *m.* advice
dottore *m.* doctor
frase *f.* phrase, saying
giudizio *m.* judgment; **con giudizio** with good sense
invito *m.* invitation
lezione *f.* lesson
maestro *m.* teacher
parte *f.* part; **da queste parti** to these parts
riposo *m.* rest
salute *f.* health
spirito *m.* morale

ADJECTIVES

attento, –a attentive; **stare attento** to pay attention
dolce sweet; **dolce far niente** happy life of ease
necessario, –a necessary
qualche some

quel, quella that; **quel che** what, that which
questo, –a this
segreto, –a secret

VERBS

cominciare to begin
dimenticare to forget
lasciare to leave
parlare to speak
portare to bring
sprecare to waste
stare (takes **essere**) to be, stay

OTHER WORDS

che that; who, whom
niente nothing
un po' a bit
solo *adv.* only

EXPRESSIONS

fare una domanda to ask a question
fare un viaggio to take a trip

PRONUNCIATION

Practice the following words, with particular attention to the sounds indicated.

ɛ	e	ɔ	o
niɛnte	spesso	pɔco	solo
provɛrbio	segreto	scuɔla	dolce
insiɛme	quello	cɔmodo	lezione
trɛno	vetro	ɔggi	dottore
albɛrgo	invece	automɔbile	famoso

gli	gn	r	rr
famiglia	bagno	arte	arrivare
consiglio	compagna	teatro	verrò
meraviglia	pizzicagnolo	quadro	pianterreno
mɛglio	ogni	incontro	a Roma

s	s	z	ʒ
impressione	musica	veneziano	pranzo
famoso	poesia	stanza	mezzogiorno
così	isola	accogliɛnza	azzurro
distante	chiɛsa	stazione	

ch	k	j	g
duecɛnto	che	dɔge	impiegato
diɛci	ricco	viaggio	Borghese
cucina	ɛcco	passeggiare	grandioso
invece	Carlo	già	golfo

68

CURRENT USAGE

Napoli e il giro di Amalfi

Ogni estate la famiglia Gentile va in villeggiatura per il mese di luglio. Quest'anno sono andati ad Amalfi, dove c'è una bella spiaggia. Si sono riposati e si sono divertiti.

Al principio della villeggiatura si sono fermati a Napoli 5 per un paio di giorni. La città ha una grande importanza storica. I disastri causati dal Vesuvio fanno dei dintorni di Napoli il centro [1] degli studi archeologici. Gli scavi di Pompei e di Ercolano hanno messo in luce la grandiosa civiltà romana di venti secoli fa. Enzo e Gina si sono 10 meravigliati dell'importanza storica di questa bella città.

Alla fine della villeggiatura la famiglia ha fatto il giro della riviera di Amalfi. Questa è una delle più belle gite d'Italia. L'autobus è partito da Napoli alle nove. Prima si è fermato a Pompei, dove tutti hanno visitato gli scavi. 15 Quegli scavi dimostrano che la città era una delle più belle dei tempi romani.

Dopo Pompei l'autobus ha fatto il lungo giro della riviera. Ci sono seicento curve lungo il giro, ed ogni curva apre una veduta incantevole. Il cielo limpido, il mare azzurro, le mon- 20 tagne, gli alberi, e le case formano una vera sinfonia di colori. Enzo e Gina non dimenticheranno mai questa gita.

STRUCTURE

51. Reflexive Verbs. A reflexive verb is one in which the action reverts back to the subject, as in the English sentence: "He sees himself in the mirror." Reflexive verbs are characterized by the fact that the infinitive has the reflexive pronoun **si** attached to it. Following are the forms of the present indicative of **lavarsi,** *to wash* (*oneself*).

---

[1] Make the surroundings of Naples into a center.

io mi lavo	noi ci laviamo
tu ti lavi	voi vi lavate
egli si lava	essi si lavano
essa si lava	esse si lavano
Lɛi si lava	Loro si lavano

The only feature which makes a verb reflexive is the reflexive pronoun; otherwise the verb retains its conjugation, whether it be regular or irregular. Reflexive verbs are conjugated with **ɛssere,** and the past participle agrees with the subject in gender and number. Notice the conjugation of **riposarsi,** *to take a rest,* in the present perfect.

io mi sono riposato, –a	noi ci siamo riposati, –e
tu ti sɛi riposato, –a	voi vi siɛte riposati, –e
egli si è riposato	essi si sono riposati
essa si è riposata	esse si sono riposate
Lɛi si è riposato, –a	Loro si sono riposati, –e

52. Reflexive for the Passive. The reflexive of the verb in the third person can express the idea of the passive when there is no particular one performing the action. When you say, for example, that *the excavations are found in Pompeii,* the passive is used in a general sense, meaning *one finds,* or *you find.* In Italian the idea is expressed by the reflexive form of the verb: **gli scavi si trɔvano a Pompɛi.** Likewise *Italian is spoken* is rendered by **si parla italiano.** In this passive construction the subject generally comes after the verb.

53. Demonstratives. The demonstrative is the word which points out or indicates a person or a thing. In English you can indicate something near the speaker (*this, these*) or something far from the speaker (*that, those*). In Italian there is also a demonstrative expressing a mid-position, that is, something near the person spoken to. For the present, however, we shall study only the first two types, which are more common.

*If you could only see this view of Amalfi in
its natural setting you would no longer
wonder why people rave so much about the
Amalfi drive.*

| questo, questa | this | refer to that which is near the |
| questi, queste | these | speaker. |

| quel, quello, quella | that | refer to that which is far away from the speaker and the person |
| quei, quegli, quelle | those | spoken to. |

The demonstrative adjective always comes before the noun it modifies and agrees with it in gender and number. In deciding which form of **quel** to use, keep in mind the following table:

SINGULAR	PLURAL	
quel	**quei**	before ordinary masculine nouns. quel giorno — quei giorni
quello	**quegli**	before special masculine nouns. quello zio — quegli zii
quella	**quelle**	before feminine nouns. quella famiglia — quelle famiglie
quell'	(**quegli** **quelle**)	before masculine or feminine singular nouns beginning with a vowel. quell'albero quell'aula quegli alberi quelle aule

54. Numerals. Numerals from 20 to 100 by tens.

20 venti	70 settanta
30 trenta	80 ottanta
40 quaranta	90 novanta
50 cinquanta	100 cento
60 sessanta	

To form the numerals from one multiple of ten to the next one notice the following rules:

For the 1 and the 8, drop the last vowel of the multiple and add **uno** or **ɔtto**: **ventuno, trentuno, ventɔtto, trentɔtto,** etc.

For the 3, add the word **tre** to the multiple and add an accent: **ventitrè, trentatrè,** etc.

For all the other numbers, simply add the smaller to the multiple: **ventisɛi, trentasɛtte,** etc.

In the multiples of 100 the smaller number comes before the larger one.

200	duecento	600	seicento
300	trecento	700	settecento
400	quattrocento	800	ottocento
500	cinquecento	900	novecento

The word for 1000 is **mille**. The plural of **mille** is **mila** and the multiples are formed by placing the smaller number before the larger one: **duemila, tremila,** etc.

From one million on the numbers are: **un milione, due milioni, tre milioni,** etc.

LANGUAGE PRACTICE

La passeggiata   The Stroll

For recognition only. Read aloud or have some other student read it to you.

La passeggiata è una delle più belle usanze italiane. Parecchie persone camminano insieme e conversano. I veri amici fanno la stessa passeggiata alla stessa ora ogni giorno. Se arriva l'ora della passeggiata e uno degli amici non si presenta, vuol dire che è malato.

La passeggiata non ha nè destinazione nè scopo. L'unica ragione è il piacere della compagnia. Quando uno passeggia gode non soltanto la compagnia dell'amico, ma l'amicizia delle persone che si incontrano lungo il cammino. L'usanza è così comune che all'ora del passeggio si incontrano almeno venti o trenta amici. La passeggiata è più piacevole del teatro o del cinematografo — e molto più economica. Un paio di scarpe dura parecchi anni. Con la passeggiata uno si riposa, mantiene l'amicizia, scambia idee, e si mantiene in salute.

The stroll is one of the most beautiful Italian customs. Several people walk together and talk. True friends take the same stroll at the same time every day. If the time for the stroll comes and one of the friends does not show up, it means that he is ill.

The stroll has neither a destination nor a purpose. The only reason is the pleasure of the company. When one strolls, he enjoys not only the company of his friend, but the friendship of the people he meets along the way. The custom is so common that during the strolling hour one meets at least twenty or thirty friends. The stroll is more pleasant than the theater or the movies — and much more economical. A pair of shoes lasts several years. With a stroll one rests, keeps up friendships, exchanges ideas, and keeps in good health.

EXERCISES

I. Questions. 1. Va spesso in villeggiatura la famiglia Gentile? 2. Che cosa ha fatto la famiglia ad Amalfi? 3. Quanti giorni si sono fermati a Napoli? 4. Che cosa hanno messo in luce gli scavi di Pompei e di Ercolano? 5. Di che cosa si sono meravigliati Enzo e Gina? 6. Qual è una delle più belle gite? 7. L'autobus dove si è fermato prima? 8. Che cosa dimostrano gli scavi di Pompei? 9. Ci sono molte curve lungo la riviera di Amalfi? 10. Sono belli i colori che si vedono lungo la riviera?

II. Conjugate the following verbs in the (*a*) present, (*b*) present perfect, and (*c*) future.

> 1. riposarsi   2. divertirsi   3. fermarsi   4. meravigliarsi

III. A. Supply the proper form of (*a*) **questo,** (*b*) **quello,** and translate:

> 1. estate   2. anno   3. spiaggia   4. giorno   5. disastro   6. centro   7. studi   8. secoli   9. gite   10. autobus   11. scavi   12. tempi   13. curva   14. mare   15. alberi

B. Write out and say the following numerals in Italian:

19	55	81	122	597
38	63	92	250	1010
43	77	110	411	3500

IV. Supply the proper form of the verb indicated and use each expression in a complete sentence in Italian.

> **A.** (*Future*) 1. Essi (fermarsi). 2. Egli (divertirsi). 3. Lei (riposarsi). 4. Noi (fermarsi). 5. Io (meravigliarsi).

> **B.** (*Present perfect*) 1. Tu (andare). 2. Essi (mettere). 3. Voi (fare). 4. Loro (visitare). 5. Questo (dimostrare).

> **C.** (*Present*) 1. I disastri (fare). 2. L'autobus (partire). 3. Le case (formare). 4. Essa (riposarsi). 5. Gina (meravigliarsi).

V. Translate into Italian:

1. This year we went to Amalfi because there is a beautiful beach. 2. Did they rest and did they enjoy themselves on (their) vacation? 3. Every city has its historical importance. 4. The archeological studies make the surroundings of Naples famous. 5. The Roman civilization of twenty centuries ago was grandiose. 6. Those mountains, those houses, and those trees are very beautiful. 7. Everyone visited the excavations when we stopped in Pompeii. 8. Every curve opens (on) an enchanting view on this drive. 9. We shall never forget this trip. 10. They go on a vacation every year, but they have never gone to Naples.

WORD LIST

NOUNS

Amalfi *a city near Naples*
anno *m.* year
cielo *m.* sky
civiltà *f.* civilization
curva *f.* curve
dintorni *m.pl.* surroundings
disastro *m.* disaster
Ercolano Herculaneum, *a city covered by lava when Vesuvius erupted in 79 A.D.*
fine *f.* end
giro *m.* tour, drive
gita *f.* trip
mare *m.* sea
mese *m.* month
montagna *f.* mountain
Napoli Naples, *the largest city in southern Italy*
paio *m.* pair, few; **un paio di giorni** a few days
Pompei Pompeii, *a city near Naples, buried by the ashes when Vesuvius erupted in 79 A.D.*
principio *m.* beginning; **al principio** in the beginning

riviera *f.* coast
scavo *m.* excavation
secolo *m.* century
spiaggia *f.* beach
Vesuvio *m.* Vesuvius, *a volcano near Naples*
villeggiatura *f.* country holiday; **in villeggiatura** on a vacation

ADJECTIVES

archeologico, –a archeological
azzurro, –a blue
grandioso, –a grandiose
limpido, –a clear

VERBS

aprire (*pp.* **aperto**) to open
causare to cause
dimostrare to show
divertirsi to have a good time, enjoy oneself
fermarsi to stop
meravigliarsi to be astonished
mettere to put; **mettere in luce** bring to light

OTHER WORDS	EXPRESSIONS
dopo after	**la più bɛlla gita** the most
fa ago	beautiful trip
lungo *prep.* along	**alle nɔve** at nine o'clock
mai never	
prima *adv.* first	

PRONUNCIATION

Writing from Sounds. A. Listen to the following words and write them from dictation:

ala — alla	vene — venne	sono — sonno	risa — rissa
cola — colla	pene — penne	rɔse — rosse	dici — dicci
cane — canne	casa — cassa	pɔso — pɔsso	visi — vissi
pani — panni	base — basse	ɛco — ɛcco	lino — l'inno

B. Now write the following from dictation:

pɔco — pɔchi	luɔgo — luɔghi	vacca — vacche	larga — larghe
ɛco — ɛchi	lungo — lunghi	amica — amiche	lunga — lunghe
ciɛco — ciɛchi	largo — larghi	ɔca — ɔche	voga — voghe
fuɔco — fuɔchi	prɛgo — prɛghi	parca — parche	paga — paghe

CURRENT USAGE

Il sɛcolo decimoquarto

Il sɛcolo decimoquarto fu il più importante della letteratura italiana. In quel sɛcolo vissero i tre maggiori scrittori

*The Dante Monument in Trento is the best known
of the countless monuments to the great Poet.*

italiani: Dante Alighieri, Francesco Petrarca, e Giovanni
Boccaccio.   Dante fu il maggior poeta italiano ed è considerato da molti il maggior poeta del mondo.   Il [1] Petrarca
fu uno dei migliori poeti e il più importante umanista dei
5 suoi tempi.   Il Boccaccio fu il migliore scrittore di prose e
uno dei migliori novellieri del mondo.

Dante passò la gioventù a Firenze ed i suoi anni maturi
in varie città dell'Italia.   Morì a Ravenna nel 1321 (mille
trecento ventuno).   Il Petrarca passò i primi anni in Toscana
10 e gli anni maturi in Francia, vicino alla città di Avignone.
Viaggiò per molte città della Francia e dell'Italia.   Il Boccaccio passò la prima parte della sua vita a Napoli, poi visse
quasi sempre in Toscana.

Dante aveva trentanove anni quando nacque il Petrarca.
15 Questi aveva nove anni quando nacque il Boccaccio.   Il
Boccaccio aveva soltanto otto anni quando morì Dante, ma
fu uno dei suoi più grandi ammiratori.   Studiò la vita e gli
scritti del famoso poeta e commentò parte della Divina
Commedia.   Dante, il Petrarca, e il Boccaccio servirono di
20 modello ai migliori scrittori di tutte le nazioni d'Europa;
ebbero un grande influsso sulla letteratura europea.

STRUCTURE

55. Past Definite.   The past definite (**passato remoto**) is
another of the past tenses in Italian.   It indicates an event which
took place at a definite time in the past and is not mentally connected with the present by the speaker.   The past definite is used
in relating historical events or in talking about personal events
which took place some time ago.

Dante fu il maggior poeta italiano.   *Dante was the greatest Italian
poet.*
Ebbero un grande influsso.   *They had a great influence.*

[1] The article is used before the surname of many famous people, but not
always nor with every famous person.

Notice the endings of regular verbs in the past definite.

		I	II	III
		parlare	**vendere**	**finire**
io		parl-**ai**	vend-**ei** (-**ɛtti**)	fin-**ii**
tu		parl-**asti**	vend-**esti**	fin-**isti**
egli, essa, Lɛi		parl-**ɔ**	vend-**è** (-**ɛtte**)	fin-**ì**
noi		parl-**ammo**	vend-**emmo**	fin-**immo**
voi		parl-**aste**	vend-**este**	fin-**iste**
essi, esse, Loro		parl-**arono**	vend-**erono** (-**ɛttero**)	fin-**irono**

56. Irregular Verbs in the Past Definite. Many verbs are irregular in the past definite. Notice the irregular forms of the verbs used in this lesson:

ɛssere	**vivere,** *to live*	**nascere,** *to be born*	**avere**
fui	**vissi**	**nacqui**	**ɛbbi**
fosti	**vivesti**	**nascesti**	**avesti**
fu	**visse**	**nacque**	**ɛbbe**
fummo	**vivemmo**	**nascemmo**	**avemmo**
foste	**viveste**	**nasceste**	**aveste**
furono	**vissero**	**nacquero**	**ɛbbero**

57. Comparison of Adjectives. The comparative form of an adjective expresses a greater degree of the quality of the adjective, as for example *green — greener; small — smaller; important — more important.* In Italian this comparative is generally formed by placing the word **più** before the adjective:

verde — più verde; p*i*ccolo — più p*i*ccolo; importante — più importante

The superlative of an adjective expresses the greatest degree of the quality of the adjective: *green — greenest; small — smallest; important — most important.* In Italian this superlative is formed by placing not only the word **più,** but also the appropriate definite article before **più.**

verde — il più verde; piccolo — il più piccolo; importante —
il più importante

There is another form of the superlative, which you will learn
later on.

58. Irregular Comparatives. In Italian as well as in English
there are some adjectives which change their form in the comparative and superlative, as for example: *good, better, best; bad, worse,
worst.* Notice the comparative of some of the common adjectives
which you have learned:

grande,[1] maggiore, il maggiore; buono, migliore, il migliore

59. "In" after a Superlative. The word *in* after a superlative is generally translated by **di.**

il maggior poeta del mondo, *the greatest poet in the world*

60. "Than" in Comparisons. The word *than* in comparisons
is usually translated by **di** before nouns, pronouns, and numerals.

Questa scuola è migliore di quella.   *This school is better than
that one.*
Abbiamo più di venti alunni.   *We have more than twenty students.*

Later you will learn more about the word *than.*

61. Ordinal Numerals. The ordinal numerals from the first
to the tenth are as follows:

1st	primo, –a	6th	sesto, –a
2nd	secondo, –a	7th	settimo, –a
3rd	terzo, –a	8th	ottavo, –a
4th	quarto, –a	9th	nono, –a
5th	quinto, –a	10th	decimo, –a

[1] The adjective **grande** has a regular as well as an irregular comparison.
When the regular comparison is used, the word refers to size; when the
irregular comparison is used, the word refers to age (*older*) or importance
(*greater*).

> la più grande casa, *the largest house*
> il maggior poeta, *the greatest poet*

LANGUAGE PRACTICE

For recognition only. Read it aloud or have some other student read it to you.

Il genio italiano

Dovunque leggiamo in un libro italiano, non troviamo altro che superlativi: il maggior poeta, il migliore scultore, il miglior pittore, il sommo scienziato, il miglior compositore — e sempre « del mondo ». È difficile credere che una piccola nazione abbia avuto tanti geni. Fatto sta che è una malattia contagiosa, e molti Italiani si credono di essere geni soltanto perchè sono Italiani.

Ma insomma, che ci possiamo fare! Se la natura ha voluto regalare a questa piccola nazione un Dante, un Michelangelo, un Raffaello, un Galileo, un Verdi, e tanti altri — perchè negarlo? E poi se la natura ha voluto mettere tutto insieme in un Leonardo da Vinci, si deve dire che non è vero? Alcune nazioni hanno petrolio, altre carbone, altre diamanti, ed altre . . . genio.

The Italian Genius

No matter where we read in an Italian book, we find nothing but superlatives: the greatest poet, the best sculptor, the best painter, the greatest scientist, the best com- 5 poser — and always "in the world." It is hard to believe that a small nation has had so many geniuses. The point is that this is a conta- gious disease and many Italians 10 think they are geniuses just because they are Italians.

After all, what can we do about it! If nature has decided to grant this small nation a Dante, a Mi- 15 chelangelo, a Raphael, a Galileo, a Verdi, and so many others — why deny it? And then if nature has decided to put everything to- gether in a Leonardo da Vinci, 20 must we say that it is not true? Some nations have oil, others coal, others diamonds, and others . . . genius.

EXERCISES

I. Questions. 1. Quale fu il più importante secolo della letteratura italiana? 2. Chi visse in quel secolo? 3. Chi è considerato il maggior poeta del mondo? 4. Perchè fu importante il Petrarca? 5. Fu gran novelliere il Boccaccio? 6. Dove passò la gioventù Dante Alighieri? 7. Viaggiò molto il Petrarca? 8. Quanti anni aveva Dante quando nacque il Boccaccio? 9. Fu grande ammiratore di Dante il Boccaccio? 10. Ebbero un grande influsso sulla letteratura europea questi tre grandi scrittori?

II. Conjugate the following verbs in the past definite (**passato remoto**):

    A. considerare, studiare, passare, viaggiare
    B. credere, morire, partire, vendere
    C. εssere, vívere, avere, nascere

III. Supply the correct form of the past definite of the verb indicated and then make complete, original sentences in Italian.

    1. Il Boccaccio (εssere). 2. Essi (vívere). 3. Noi (studiare). 4. Dante (nascere). 5. Lεi (viaggiare). 6. Egli (avere). 7. Essa (passare). 8. Io (studiare). 9. Voi (viaggiare). 10. Tu (finire).

IV. A. Make up original sentences using the noun and the comparative form of the adjective.

MODEL: casa — píccola. Questa casa è più píccola di quella.

    1. casa — grande. 2. città — píccola. 3. scuɔla — buɔna. 4. parte — grande. 5. trεno — lungo. 6. poεta — importante. 7. scrittore — interessante. 8. automɔbile — nuɔva. 9. campagna — bεlla. 10. fratεllo — grande.

B. Make up sentences using the noun and the superlative form of the adjective.

MODEL: ragazza — bεlla. Rɔsa è la più bεlla ragazza della classe.

    1. letteratura — interessante. 2. sεcolo — importante. 3. novelliεre — grande. 4. tεmpo — lungo. 5. vita — famosa. 6. casa — bεlla. 7. ammiratore — grande. 8. nazione — buɔna. 9. ɔpera — famosa. 10. umanista — importante.

V. Write the Italian for the following:

    1. That century was the most important one in our history. 2. The three greatest Italian writers lived in the same century. 3. He is the best prose writer and the best short-story writer in the world. 4. Where did Dante spend his youth and his mature years? 5. Who

died in Ravenna in 1321? 6. Who spent the first part
of his life in Naples? 7. Did you travel through many
cities when you went to Italy? 8. These three famous
writers served as models (*use singular*) for the best
writers in Europe. 9. The most important humanist
of his times was a great poet. 10. They all had a great
deal of influence on European literature.

WORD LIST

NOUNS

Alighieri: Dante Alighieri
*greatest Italian poet (1265–
1321)*
ammiratore *m.* admirer
Avignone *city in southern
France*
Giovanni Boccaccio *greatest Italian prose writer
(1313–1375)*
Divina Commedia *f.* Divine
Comedy
Francia *f.* France
gioventù *f.* youth
influsso *m.* influence
modello *m.* model
nazione *f.* nation
novelliere *m.* short-story
writer
poeta *m.* poet
prosa *f.* prose; **scrittore di
prose** prose writer
Ravenna *city in Romagna,
in north central Italy*
scritti *m. pl.* writings
scrittore *m.* writer

secolo decimoquarto 14th
century
umanista *m.* humanist

ADJECTIVES

europeo, –a European
importante important
maggiore *adj.* major; **il
maggiore** the greatest
maturo, –a mature
migliore *adj.* better; **il migliore** the best
vari, varie various

VERBS

commentare to write a commentary
considerare to consider
morire to die (takes **essere**)
nascere (*p.p.* **nato**) to be
born (*takes* **essere**)
servire to serve; **servire di
modello** serve as a model
viaggiare to travel
vivere (*p.p.* **vissuto**) to live
(generally takes **essere**)

PRONUNCIATION

Intonation. Intonation refers to the variations in the pitch of the voice which are characteristic of a phrase or a sentence in a language. The pronunciation of individual sounds may be similar in two people and yet the sentence may sound quite different. The intonation, for example, is one of the characteristic differences between the English of our northern states and that of our southern states.

In Italian intonation varies considerably from one region of Italy to the other, and all those intonations are different from English. Notice the approximate intonation of the following sentences:

Lɛi è italiano, signore?

Dove andiamo questo pomeri*g*gio?

Observe carefully and imitate clearly the intonation patterns you hear in the following sentences:

Dal pizzic*a*gnolo compravamo form*a*ggio, prosciutto, e cɔse s*i*mili.
Non possiamo mangiare bɛne senza spɛndere molto denaro.
Come si comportava il piccino di sɛtte anni?
Quanto era bɛlla la Fontana di Trɛvi!
« Paɛse che vai, usanza che trɔvi », dice il provɛrbio.

84

CURRENT USAGE

I nostri pasti

Quando eravamo a Roma abitavamo vicino alla Fontana di Trevi. Facevamo la prima colazione nella camera dell'albergo, perchè così era l'usanza. Non appena eravamo in piedi, suonavamo il campanello, e subito ce la portavano.

Per la seconda colazione preparavamo qualche cosa da 5 mangiare noi stessi lì in camera, quando avevamo appetito. Andavamo nei negozi e compravamo tutto il necessario. Dal pizzicagnolo compravamo formaggio, mortadella, salsiccia, prosciutto, e cose simili. Compravamo anche olive secche, acciughe, tonno in scatola, ecc. Poi dal fruttivendolo 10 compravamo arance, mele, pere, banane, pesche, uva, o altra frutta che si può mangiare facilmente in camera. Andavamo dal vinaio a comprare una bottiglia di vino. Poi, finalmente, dal fornaio compravamo pane e biscotti o paste. E così facevamo una bella colazione senza spendere 15 troppo.

La sera poi andavamo a pranzo in un vecchio ristorante vicino alla Fontana di Trevi. Si mangiava bene, e i camerieri erano molto cortesi. Avevano una grande pazienza con noi e col nostro piccino di sette anni, che non sempre si com- 20 portava bene. Eravamo sempre i primi ad arrivare, perchè noi siamo abituati a pranzare alle sei, e lì si pranzava alle otto. Ma « paese che vai, usanza che trovi », se lo stomaco lo permette.

STRUCTURE

62. The Imperfect Tense. The imperfect is another of the common past tenses in Italian. The imperfect expresses a continued, customary, or repeated action or a state of being in the past. For example, if we say *We were in Rome last year*, the sentence expresses a continued action, or one might say a state of being in the past. It goes in the imperfect in Italian: **Eravamo a**

The Trevi Fountain needs no introduction to moviegoers.

Wouldn't you like to be that little boy looking for coins?

Roma l'anno scorso. When we say *We used to buy oranges*, the sentence expresses a repeated or a customary action and goes in the imperfect: **Compravamo arance.**

The imperfect tense is generally regular in Italian, even for most verbs which are otherwise irregular. It is formed by taking the infinitive, dropping the last three letters, and adding the following endings for each conjugation:

I	II	III
comprare	vendere	finire
compr–**avo**	vend–**evo**	fin–**ivo**
compr–**avi**	vend–**evi**	fin–**ivi**
compr–**ava**	vend–**eva**	fin–**iva**
compr–**avamo**	vend–**evamo**	fin–**ivamo**
compr–**avate**	vend–**evate**	fin–**ivate**
compr–*avano*	vend–**evano**	fin–*ivano*

63. Verbs Irregular in the Imperfect. The imperfect of the verb **essere** is as follows:

ero, eri, era, eravamo, eravate, erano

For other irregular verbs, learn the first person singular of the imperfect and the rest of the forms always follow the same pattern. Notice two of the common irregular verbs:

fare, *to do*   facevo, facevi, faceva, facevamo, facevate, facevano
dire, *to say*   dicevo, dicevi, diceva, dicevamo, dicevate, dicevano

64. Imperfect and Past Definite. Notice that the imperfect expresses a continued, customary, or repeated action in the past, whereas the past definite expresses a single act or a historical event in the past. The tense which you use expresses the idea which you wish to convey. If you say **Fui a Roma l'anno scorso,** you mean that you were there at that time and later you stopped being there. If you say **Ero a Roma l'anno scorso,** you intimate simply that you were there, without intimating anything about not being there later.

65. Table of Contractions. So far you have had some of the contractions which are formed by the combination of a preposition and an article. Let's list them all now.

	il	lo	la	i	gli	le	l'
a, to, at	al	allo	alla	ai	agli	alle	all'
con, with	col	con lo	con la	coi	con gli	con le	con l'
		(collo)	(colla)		(cogli)	(colle)	(coll')
da, from	dal	dallo	dalla	dai	dagli	dalle	dall'
di, of	del	dello	della	dei	degli	delle	dell'
in, in	nel	nello	nella	nei	negli	nelle	nell'
per, through	pel	per lo	per la	pei	per gli	per le	per l'
su, on	sul	sullo	sulla	sui	sugli	sulle	sull'

66. Double Object Pronouns. When a direct and an indirect object pronoun both depend on the same verb, the indirect comes before the direct (except **loro**), and the last letter of the indirect object pronoun becomes −**e**.

Ce la portavano. *They brought it to us.*

If the indirect object pronoun is **gli** or **le,** it becomes **glie** and is attached to the direct object pronoun. The forms of the double object pronouns therefore are:

me lo	te lo	glielo	ce lo	ve lo
me la	te la	gliela	ce la	ve la
me li	te li	glieli	ce li	ve li
me le	te le	gliele	ce le	ve le

The double object pronouns will be taken up more completely in Lesson 22. At this point they are given for recognition only.

67. Special Meaning of *da*. The preposition **da** + a word denoting a person means *at the place* where the person is to be found ordinarily. It may be translated *at the house of, at the place of,* etc.

Andavamo dal vinaio. *We went to the wine-seller's.*

LANGUAGE PRACTICE

For recognition only.   Read aloud or have some other student read it to you.

Il fidanzamento

Una bell'idea questo fidanzamento all'uso antico, se uno ha la pazienza di aspettare. L'usanza italiana ha le sue ragioni. In molte piccole città è ancora questa. Una madre con una figlia disponibile cerca un buon partito fra gli amici. Quando le pare di aver trovato un giovane adatto, ne parla al marito, e questi a sua volta ne parla al padre del giovane. Se le due famiglie sono d'accordo, allora si cerca la maniera di far incontrare i due giovani, in una festa familiare o in qualche visita. Se i giovani trovano simpatia l'uno per l'altra, si permette al giovane di far visita alla ragazza. Indi ne segue il fidanzamento, che può durare tre o quattro mesi, o otto o dieci anni. I giovani che non si annoiano durante il fidanzamento finiscono per sposarsi, con la speranza che poi non si annoieranno quando sarà troppo tardi.

The Engagement

This idea of an old-fashioned engagement is fine, if one has the patience to wait. The Italian custom has its reasons. In many small cities it is still as follows. A 5 mother who has an eligible daughter looks for a good prospect among her friends. When she thinks she has found a suitable young man, she tells her husband about it, and 10 he, in turn, talks with the young man's father. If the two families agree, then some way is found to get the two young people together, at a party or through a social call. 15 If the young people like each other, permission is given for the young man to call on the girl. From this comes the engagement, which may last three or four months, or eight 20 or ten years. The young people who do not get bored with each other during the period of engagement end up by getting married, with the hope that they will not 25 get bored when it is too late.

EXERCISES

I. Questions. 1. Dove si fa la prima colazione quando si è all'albergo? 2. Che cosa facevamo noi non appena eravamo in piedi? 3. Dove facevamo la seconda colazione? 4. Che cosa compravamo nei negozi? 5. Che cosa si vendeva dal pizzicagnolo? 6. Che cosa si vendeva dal fruttivendolo? 7. Dove andavamo per comprare il vino? 8. Chi vendeva pane, biscotti, e paste? 9. Dove andavamo a pranzo la sera? 10. Erano cortesi i camerieri? 11. A che ora si pranzava? 12. Che proverbio ha imparato Lei?

II. Supply the proper form of the imperfect of the verb indicated:

1. Io (essere) abituato a pranzare alle sei, ma lì (pranzare) alle otto. 2. Egli (comportarsi) bene perchè i camerieri (essere) cortesi. 3. Essa non (avere) pazienza e non (volere) aspettare. 4. (Mangiare) bene voi quando (essere) in Italia? 5. Si (spendere) troppo denaro e non si (fare) buona colazione. 6. Le mele, pere, e pesche (essere) buone, ma l'uva non (essere) buona. 7. Il vinaio (vendere) vino e noi lo (comprare). 8. Essi (comprare) tonno in scatola e (preparare) la colazione. 9. La mortadella (essere) migliore della salsiccia, che (essere) troppo secca. 10. Ogni mattina io (andare) alla sua porta e (suonare) il campanello.

III. Make up original sentences in Italian containing the following expressions:

1. vicino a. 2. essere in piedi. 3. la prima colazione. 4. la seconda colazione. 5. tutto il necessario. 6. dal pizzicagnolo. 7. dal fruttivendolo. 8. una bottiglia di vino. 9. far colazione. 10. andare a pranzo. 11. comportarsi bene. 12. il primo ad arrivare. 13. alle sei. 14. senza spendere. 15. essere abituato a.

IV. Use the correct form of the imperfect or the past definite, according to the sense:

1. Tu mi (dire) sempre che la Fontana di Trevi (essere) la più bella fontana di Roma. 2. Quando il treno (partire) egli (comprare) ancora il biglietto. 3. Noi non (trovare) molto dal pizzicagnolo e (tornare) a casa senza comprare niente. 4. Io (mangiare) le pesche e le banane perchè (avere) appetito. 5. Un giorno il vinaio ci (vendere) una bottiglia di vino. 6. (Mangiare) frutta perchè si (potere) mangiare facilmente in camera. 7. Il prosciutto (essere) migliore della mortadella, che non mi (piacere). 8. Quando (nascere) il Boccaccio, Dante (avere) quarantotto anni.

9. Quando (arrivare) il treno, noi (essere) alla stazione.
10. Il tonno in scatola mi (piacere) molto, ma le acciughe non (costare) tanto.

V. Translate into Italian:

1. He used to live near the Trevi Fountain because
there was a good hotel there. 2. Did you always ring the
bell as soon as you woke up? 3. Who brought you
your breakfast when you were hungry? 4. Where can
we buy canned tuna fish, dry olives, and such things?
5. We bought everything we needed at the grocer's
and at the fruit vendor's. 6. You have forgotten the
wine. Didn't you buy it at the wine dealer's? 7. Without spending money she cannot have a good breakfast.
8. In the evening I want to go to a restaurant.
9. When the waiters were courteous, the dinner seemed
better. 10. "When in Rome, do as the Romans do,"
says the proverb.

WORD LIST

NOUNS

acciuga *f.* anchovy
appetito *m.* appetite; **avere
appetito** to be hungry
arancia *f.* orange
banana *f.* banana
biscotto *m.* cookie, biscuit
bottiglia *f.* bottle
cameriere *m.* waiter
campanello *m.* bell
Fontana di Trevi *f.* Trevi
Fountain
formaggio *m.* cheese
fornaio *m.* baker
frutta *f.* fruit
fruttivendolo *m.* fruit vendor
mela *f.* apple
mortadella *f.* bologna
oliva *f.* olive
paese *m.* country

pane *m.* bread
pasta *f.* pastry
pazienza *f.* patience; **avere
una grande pazienza** to
have a great deal of pa-
tience
pera *f.* pear
pesca *f.* peach
piccino *m.* little fellow
piede *m.* foot; **essere in
piedi** to be up and around
prosciutto *m.* ham
salsiccia *f.* sausage
scatola *f.* can
stomaco *m.* stomach
tonno *m.* tuna fish
usanza *f.* custom
uva *f.* grapes
vinaio *m.* wine-seller, wine
dealer
vino *m.* wine

ADJECTIVES

abituato, –a accustomed
secco, –a dry
simile similar
vεcchio, –a old

VERBS

abitare to live, dwell
comportarsi to behave
mangiare to eat; **qualche
  cɔsa da mangiare** something to eat

permettere to permit
pranzare to dine
spεndere to spend
suonare to ring

OTHER WORDS

appena hardly; **non appena** as soon as
facilmente easily
finalmente finally
qualche some
senza without
troppo *adv.* too much

PRONUNCIATION

Si scriva sotto dettatura (*Write from dictation*):

Anεddoto su Rossini

Rossini, durante una fredda giornata dell'invεrno del mille ottocεnto tredici, εra rimasto a lεtto a comporre.   Mentre scriveva un duetto, un fɔglio gli cadde a tεrra.   Piuttɔsto che muɔversi e prεnder freddo, si mise a comporre un nuɔvo duetto.   Composto il secondo duetto, venne un suo amico che gli raccolse il fɔglio caduto.   Allora Rossini cantɔ tutti e due i duetti, e l'amico scelse il migliore.

CURRENT USAGE

Mestiɛre o professione?
(Meditazioni di un giovane)

Che mestiɛre potrɛi fare? Mio fratɛllo Giorgio è falegname e guadagna bɛne, ma a me non piace fare il falegname. Potrɛi fare il barbiɛre, come il cugino Antɔnio.
Comprerɛi una bottega e lavorerɛi per conto mio. Ma l'orario è lungo e non si guadagna molto. Che mestiɛre allora? 5
sarto? calzolɑio? muratore? elettricista? Ah, ɛcco un bɛl
mestiɛre! Tutte le case hanno apparecchi elɛttrici e tutti
gli apparecchi hanno bisogno di riparazioni. Come elettricista avrɛi la mia automɔbile, non ci sarɛbbe orɑrio fisso,
e mi farɛi ricco in pɔco tɛmpo. Che altro di mɛglio si po- 10
trɛbbe desiderare?

Ma vediamo un pɔ'. Perchè non pensare a qualche professione? Cɛrto bisognerɛbbe andare all'università, ma la
vita di studɛnte non sarɛbbe tanto brutta. L'avvocato
esɛrcita una buɔna professione; se è bravo può farsi una 15
bɛlla clientɛla. Preferirɛi però la professione del mɛdico,
come lo zio Tommaso, ma per lui non c'è mai ripɔso; dɛve
lavorare giorno e nɔtte. Ci sarɛbbe anche la professione
dell'ingegnɛre, ma non m'interɛssa affatto; prɔprio non è
per me. 20

Cɛrto si potrɛbbe fare anche il professore, ma lì ci vuɔle
intelligɛnza e paziɛnza. Il professore dɛve studiare sɛmpre,
insegnare per lunghe ore, e rassegnarsi a fare una vita
modɛsta. È una vita che non interɛssa molto a noi giɔvani.

Quindi cɔsa fare? Non sɔ; ci penserɔ domani. 25

STRUCTURE

68. Conditional. In Italian the present conditional is formed
by taking the first person singular of the future of any verb,
regular or irregular, dropping the –ɔ, and adding the following
endings: **–ɛi, –esti, –ɛbbe, –emmo, –este, –ɛbbero.**

Notice the present conditional of regular verbs:

I	II	III
comprerɛi	venderɛi	finirɛi
compreresti	venderesti	finiresti
comprerɛbbe	venderɛbbe	finirɛbbe
compreremmo	venderemmo	finiremmo
comprereste	vendereste	finireste
comprerɛbbero	venderɛbbero	finirɛbbero

Here is the present conditional of some common irregular verbs:

andare andrɛi, andresti, andrɛbbe, andremmo, andreste, andrɛbbero

avere avrɛi, avresti, avrɛbbe, avremmo, avreste, avrɛbbero

dovere dovrɛi, dovresti, dovrɛbbe, dovremmo, dovreste, dovrɛbbero

ɛssere sarɛi, saresti, sarɛbbe, saremmo, sareste, sarɛbbero

potere potrɛi, potresti, potrɛbbe, potremmo, potreste, potrɛbbero

vedere vedrɛi, vedresti, vedrɛbbe, vedremmo, vedreste, vedrɛbbero

venire verrɛi, verresti, verrɛbbe, verremmo, verreste, verrɛbbero

volere vorrɛi, vorresti, vorrɛbbe, vorremmo, vorreste, vorrɛbbero

69. Uses of the Conditional. The conditional expresses what would happen under certain conditions, which may be expressed or implied. The present conditional corresponds to the English *should* or *would*, as for example *we would speak, he would come, I should be pleased*, etc.

Avrɛi la mia automobile. *I would have my own car.*
Non sarɛbbe tanto brutta. *It would not be so bad.*

70. Disjunctive Personal Pronouns. The disjunctive personal pronouns are those which are used independently of a verb.

The forms are as follows:

SINGULAR	PLURAL
me, me	**noi,** us
te, you (*fam.*)	**voi,** you (*fam.*)
lui, him (**esso,** it)	**loro** (**essi**), them (*m.*)
lɛi, her (**essa,** her, it)	**loro** (**esse**), them (*f.*)
Lɛi, you (*pol.*)	**Loro,** you (*pol.*)

sè (reflexive third person) himself, herself, themselves, etc.

71. Uses of Disjunctive Pronouns. The disjunctive pronouns are used:

1. After prepositions.

Per lui non c'è ripɔso. *For him there is no rest.*

2. In exclamations.

Beato lui! *Lucky he!*

3. For emphasis or contrast, in which case the pronoun always follows the verb.

Vɔglio te, non lɛi. *I want you, not her.*

4. **Lui, lɛi,** and **loro** are used after the verb **ɛssere** as predicate nominative.

È lui; sono loro. *It is he; it is they.*

5. **Lui, lɛi,** and **loro** are used in a compound subject or object.

Io, lui, e lɛi siamo rimasti. *He, she, and I remained.*

72. The Verb *piacere*. **Piacere** is the only verb in Italian which can be used to translate the English verb *to like*. When used in this sense,[1] **piacere** has only the third person singular and the third person plural in each tense. It is conjugated with **ɛssere**.

PRESENT INDICATIVE	piace, piacciono
FUTURE	piacerà, piaceranno
PRESENT PERFECT	è piaciuto (–a), sono piaciuti (–e)
PAST DEFINITE	piacque, piacquero
IMPERFECT	piaceva, piacevano

[1] With the meaning *to please*, **piacere** has all forms. Present Indicative: **piaccio, piaci, piace, piacciamo, piacete, piacciono.**

Soccer is a popular sport in Italy.

*The Grand Prix de Rome is given not just
in art, but in a popular automobile race.*

Since Italian has no verb meaning *to like*, English sentences containing this verb must first be reworded, using the verb *to please*.

We like the profession. = The profession pleases us.

The sentence then translates directly into Italian by using the correct form of **piacere** and placing the subject of the verb *to please* after the verb. If this subject is singular, the verb is in the third person singular. If this subject is plural, the verb is in the third person plural. If the subject is an action, the verb is in the singular.

We like the profession. = The profession pleases us. = Ci piace la professione.

He likes the girls. = The girls please him. = Gli piacciono le ragazze.

She likes to work. = To work pleases her. = Le piace lavorare.

Notice that the subject in English (*we, he, she*) becomes the indirect object in Italian (**ci, gli, le**). The indirect object **loro** generally comes after the verb.

Piace loro lavorare giorno e notte. *They like to work day and night.*

If the subject of the verb *to like* is a noun, that word must be introduced by **a** in Italian.

Mary likes the gloves. = The gloves are pleasing to Mary. = A Maria piacciono i guanti.

LANGUAGE PRACTICE

Gli Sport

Gli sport favoriti in Italia sono parecchi. Fra le donne c'è lo sport di ciarlare e criticare le amiche. Fra gli uomini c'è lo sport di guardare le giovani che passano e commentare. Ma, parlando sul serio, fra gli sport favoriti troviamo il calcio, il ciclismo, il baseball,

Sports

There are several favorite sports in Italy. Among women there is the sport of gossiping and criticizing one's friends. Among men there is the sport of looking at the young women passing by and commenting on them. But, seriously speaking, among the favorite sports we find

98   BEGINNING ITALIAN GRAMMAR

il tennis, il nuoto, lo sci, le corse di automobili, le corse di cavalli, il polo, e tanti altri giochi conosciuti in America. Infatti, molti degli sport sono simili nelle due nazioni. Mentre in America si gioca molto il foot-ball, in Italia il calcio è più popolare. Mentre in America la bicicletta è piuttosto rara, in Italia è molto comune, e si usa per trasporto, per esercizio, e per corse. In Italia poi c'è uno sport che è poco conosciuto in America, cioè l'alpinismo. In America l'alpinismo si fa principalmente con gli ascensori, nei grattacieli delle grandi città. Due generazioni fa gli sport erano poco sviluppati in Italia, ma adesso sono così sviluppati come negli Stati Uniti.

soccer, bicycle riding, baseball, tennis, swimming, skiing, auto races, horse races, polo, and so many other games known in America. In fact, many of the sports are alike in both nations. While in America they play a great deal of football, in Italy soccer is more popular. While in America the bicycle is rather rare, in Italy it is very common, and is used for transportation, exercise, and races. In Italy, however, there is a sport which is scarcely known in America, namely mountain climbing. In America mountain climbing is done mostly with elevators, in the skyscrapers of large cities. Two generations ago sports were little developed in Italy, but today they are as developed as in the United States.

EXERCISES

I. Supply the correct form of the conditional and read aloud:

1. Egli (potere) fare il falegname, ma non gli (piacere). 2. Voi (dovere) fare il barbiere, perchè (essere) un bel mestiere. 3. (Volere) fare il sarto Lei? Le (piacere) fare il sarto? 4. Come muratore io (guadagnare) bene e (avere) la propria automobile. 5. Non ci (essere) orario fisso e ci (essere) molte vacanze. 6. Lei (andare) all'università e (fare) la vita di studente. 7. Noi (preferire) la professione del medico e non ci (piacere) la professione d'ingegnere. 8. L'avvocato (avere) una bella clientela e (essere) ricco. 9. Per lui non ci (essere) riposo e per me non ci (essere) denaro. 10. Essa (studiare) sempre e (imparare) molto.

II. Translate the English pronoun in parentheses and complete the sentence in Italian:

1. Per (me) preferirei... 2. Vanno da (them) per... 3. Il cugino Antonio abita con (us)...

4. Non hanno bisogno di (her) . . .   5. A (him) non
interessa . . .   6. Deve lavorare con (you, *fam.*) . . .
7. Per (you, *pol.*) non c'è riposo . . .   8. Verrò con
(you, *fam. pl.*) . . .   9. Con (them) mi farei ricco . . .
10. Non pensare a (her) . . .

III. Translate into Italian:

1. He likes the profession.   2. I like to work.   3. We
like the movies.   4. They like to study.   5. She likes
the university.   6. Do you like the houses?   7. Does
he like the trades?   8. She likes the barber.   9. I like
to rest.   10. We like to teach.   11. They like this life.
12. You (*fam.*) like these books.   13. You (*pol.*) like
Rome.   14. We like Florence and Venice.   15. I like
to sleep.

IV. Form complete sentences in Italian using the following
expressions:

1. guadagnare bene.   2. fare il barbiere.   3. per
conto mio.   4. apparecchi elettrici.   5. orario fisso.
6. in poco tempo.   7. la vita di studente.   8. non è
tanto brutta.   9. giorno e notte.   10. non interessa
affatto.   11. ci vuole.   12. cosa fare?

V. Translate into Italian:

1. I should like to learn a trade, but I don't like to
work hard (**molto**).   2. The hours are too long for us;
we prefer more rest.   3. Did you say that he would
like to be a tailor, a shoemaker, or a barber?   What an
ambition!   4. They would get rich in a short time,
but they would not be happy.   5. Would you come
with us in our new automobile, or would you go with
them?   6. All [the] electrical appliances need repairs if
we use them a great deal.   7. The doctor has a good
profession, but there is never any rest.   8. That profession does not interest him at all; it's not for him.
9. One could be a professor, but who wants to be a
professor?   It is not for us.   10. One would need too
much intelligence and too much patience.

WORD LIST

NOUNS

Antɔnio Anthony
apparecchio *m.* appliance
avvocato *m.* lawyer
bisogno *m.* need; **aver bi-sogno di** to need
bottega *f.* shop
clientɛla *f.* clientele
conto *m.* account; **per conto mio** for myself
cugino *m.* cousin
elettricista *m.* electrician
falegname *m.* carpenter; **fare il falegname** to be a carpenter
Giorgio George
giovane *m.* young man; *f.* young lady; *adj.* young
ingegnɛre *m.* engineer
intelligɛnza *f.* intelligence
mɛdico *m.* doctor
meditazione *f.* meditation
mestiɛre *m.* trade
muratore *m.* mason
nɔtte *f.* night
orario *m.* hours, schedule
professione *f.* profession
riparazione *f.* repair
Tommaso Thomas

ADJECTIVES

brutto, –a bad, disagreeable
elɛttrico, –a electrical

fisso, –a fixed; **orario fisso** *m.* fixed hours
modɛsto, –a modest, simple

VERBS

bisognare to need to, have to
desiderare to desire, want
esercitare to practice (*a profession*)
farsi to become; **farsi ricco** to become rich
guadagnare to earn
insegnare to teach
interessare to interest
lavorare to work
rassegnarsi to resign oneself

OTHER WORDS

affatto at all
cɛrto certainly
domani tomorrow
male *adv.* bad
pɔco little; **un pɔ'** a little
quindi therefore

EXPRESSIONS

che altro di mɛglio? what could be better? what more?

PART TWO

CURRENT USAGE

La mɔda

Questa mɔda è una bɛlla cɔsa. La natura si rinnɔva una vɔlta l'anno, nella primavɛra, ma la mɔda si rinnɔva quattro vɔlte l'anno. C'è la mɔda d'inverno, che nei negɔzi comɪncia in lᴜglio. C'è la mɔda di primavɛra, che si mette in mostra a Natale. C'è la mɔda d'estate, che fa pensare a giornate 5 sulla spiᴀggia. E c'è la mɔda d'autunno, che fa pensare a fɛste e balli.

Andiamo a passeggio e vediamo la mɔda. Vede quella signorina con quell'ᴀbito corto? La pɔvera signorina sɛnte freddo, ma la mɔda è sevɛra e non le permette di portare 10 un ᴀbito più lungo. Vede quel cappɛllo su quella signora alta? Non è un parasole; è un cappɛllo. Quando tira vɛnto la pɔvera signora dɛve tenɛrsi il cappɛllo con tutte e due le mani. Ma che si può fare se la mɔda è così?

Vede quei giᴏvani senza cappɛllo e quegli altri in mᴀniche 15 di camɪcia? Fa freddo e pɔssono prɛndere un raffreddore, ma preferɪscono il raffreddore pur di seguɪr la mɔda.

Guardi un pɔ' anche il Suo vestito. A che sɛrve cotesta cravatta? Le riscalda forse il pɛtto? E cotesti bottoni alle mᴀniche della giᴀcca? E cotesto fazzoletto nel taschino? 20 Tutto fa parte della mɔda. Nella natura ci sono bɛi ciɛli, bɛgli ᴀlberi, bɛlle fɔglie, e bɛi colori. Nella mɔda ci sono bɛi cappɛlli, bɛgli ᴀbiti, e bɛlle giᴏvani. Come ammiriamo la natura così possiamo ammirare anche la mɔda.

103

Useful Expressions

una vɔlta l'anno once a year
si mette in mostra is displayed
fa pensare a makes one think of
andiamo a passeggio let's go for a walk
tira vɛnto the wind is blowing
tutte e due le mani both hands
in maniche di camicia in shirt sleeves
prɛndere un raffreddore to catch a cold
pur di seguir la mɔda as long as they are in style
a che sɛrve? of what use is?
fa parte della mɔda forms a part of fashion

Questions. 1. Quando si rinnɔva la natura? 2. Quando comincia la mɔda di primavɛra? 3. A che fa pensare la mɔda d'autunno? 4. Quando possiamo vedere la mɔda? 5. Sɛnte freddo la signorina con l'abito corto? 6. Va bɛne il cappɛllo grande quando tira vɛnto? 7. Che preferiscono quei giovani senza cappɛllo e quegli altri in maniche di camicia? 8. Si prɛnde facilmente un raffreddore? 9. A che sɛrve la cravatta? 10. Ci sono bɛlle cɔse nella natura?

STRUCTURE

73. Demonstratives. In Lesson 10 you learned the forms of the demonstrative adjectives **questo** and **quello.** When a demonstrative is not followed by the noun it modifies it is used as a pronoun. Following are all the forms of the demonstratives that may be used either as adjectives or as pronouns.

ADJECTIVES OR PRONOUNS

	Sing.	*Pl.*		
MASC.	questo	questi	} this, these	Refers to that which is near the speaker.
FEM.	questa	queste		
MASC.	cotesto	cotesti	} that, those *(near you)*	Refers to that which is near the person spoken to.
FEM.	cotesta	coteste		
	(also spelled codesto)			

Italian fashions lead the day.
—Just ask any girl.

Notice that in Italian there is the intermediate demonstrative **cotesto** (**codesto**) indicating an object near the person addressed. English has no such distinction. However, **cotesto** and all its forms are seldom used in ordinary conversation.

The following forms may be used as adjectives only or as pronouns only:

	ADJECTIVES ONLY		PRONOUNS ONLY		
	Sing.	*Pl.*	*Sing.*	*Pl.*	
MASC.	quel *(that)*	quei *(those)*	quello *(that)*	quelli *(those)*	Refers to that which is away from both the speaker and the person spoken to.
	quello (quell')	quegli			
FEM.	quella (quell')	quelle	quella	quelle	

Questa mɔda è una bɛlla cɔsa.   *This style is something beautiful.*
A che sɛrve cotesta cravatta?   *What is that tie for?*
Vede quei giovani?   *Do you see those young men?*

74. The Particles *ci*, *vi*, and *ne*. **Ci** is used to indicate any vague place or a place which has been previously mentioned; it may be translated by *here*, *there*, *to this place*, or *to that place*. In literary Italian **vi** is often used instead of **ci**.

Ci andiamo spesso.   *We go there often.*
Ci sono bɛi colori.   *There are beautiful colors.*
Vi ritornerɔ.   *I shall go back there.*

Ci and **vi** cannot be used when there is any emphasis on the place mentioned (**lì** or **là** is used instead). Their position with respect to the verb is the same as that of conjunctive object pronouns.

The particle **ne,** in addition to meaning *some of it, some of them,* etc., may refer to a place previously mentioned. In that case it carries the meaning of *from there, from that place.*

Se ne tornɔ subito.   *He came back from there immediately.*

LANGUAGE PRACTICE

Si legga senza tradurre:

La cinematografia [1]

La cinematografia è adesso una delle grandi industrie in Italia. Prima della guerra [2] pochi artisti italiani apparivano [3] sullo schermo. [4] Ora quasi ogni pellicola [5] rinomata [6] ha qualche artista italiano, e le donne sono più note [7] degli uomini in questo campo. [8] Anche quelli che non conoscono l'Italia conoscono i nomi di Anna Magnani, Gina Lollobrigida, Silvana 5 Mangano, Sophia Loren, Marisa Pavan, Vittorio de Sica, Aldo Fabrizi, e di tanti altri. Il cinema italiano è molto apprezzato [9] perchè è semplice e naturale; ha portato sullo schermo una sincerità che rende le pellicole vere opere d'arte.

Si risponda alle seguenti domande senza tradurre:

1. Apparivano molti artisti italiani sullo schermo prima della guerra?
2. Sono note le artiste italiane dello schermo? 3. Lei conosce i nomi di Magnani, Lollobrigida, e Mangano? 4. È semplice e naturale l'arte italiana? 5. Che ha portato sullo schermo l'arte italiana?

ESERCIZI

I. Furnish the proper demonstrative adjective or pronoun in the following sentences:

1. (This) primavera sarà più bella di (that one).
2. (These) negozi hanno più abiti di (those). 3. (That) signorina porta sempre (that) abito lungo. 4. (That) cappello sarebbe buono per (that) avvocato. 5. (Those) giovani che vanno a (that) università sono sempre senza cappello. 6. (That, *near you*) giacca e (that, *near you*) cravatta sono molto eleganti. 7. (That, *near you*) bottone non va con (that) altro bottone. 8. (This) parasole è più grande di (that) cappello. 9. (Those) abiti sono più eleganti di (these). 10. (That) inverno faceva più freddo di (that) autunno.

---

[1] movie industry.   [2] war.   [3] appeared.   [4] screen.   [5] film.   [6] famous.
[7] noted.   [8] field.   [9] appreciated.

II. Si traducano le parole inglesi tra parentesi (Translate the English words in parentheses):

1. (Beautiful) alberi e (beautiful) foglie fanno (beautiful) la primavera.   2. Le (beautiful) giovani portano dei (beautiful) cappelli.   3. (It is) freddo e possiamo (catch) un raffreddore.   4. Quella (beautiful) cravatta va bene con (that) abito.   5. La moda (makes one think of the) giornate sulla spiaggia.   6. Sono andati (for a walk) mentre (the wind was not blowing).   7. (Both) le signorine sono uscite con (both) i giovani.   8. Non sentono freddo (as long as they are in style).   9. (Of what use is) la moda se non c'è denaro?   10. (Three times a year) compriamo abiti nuovi.

III. Form complete sentences using the following words:

1. maniche, camicia, giovane.   2. bottone, giacca, servire.   3. Natale, festa, inverno.   4. cotesto, fazzoletto, taschino.   5. signora, tenersi, cappello.   6. cappello, grande, parasole.   7. ammirare, giovani, belle.   8. riscaldare, abito, petto.   9. permettere, portare, cappello.   10. preferire, raffreddore, moda.

IV. Si traduca in italiano (Translate into Italian):

1. We like those stores and we go there often.   2. If they come back from there soon, they can be here for Christmas.   3. The fall fashion and the winter fashion are of no use where it is hot.   4. If she feels cold, she ought not to wear such a short dress.   5. That beautiful hat is too big for that lady, but such is the fashion.   6. It's cold, the wind is blowing, and you will catch a cold.   7. Does the necktie really warm your chest, or do you wear it because [the] others wear it?   8. When one is on the beach, one should have a beautiful parasol.   9. He thinks only of parties and dances, but he ought to think of work.   10. Let us admire beautiful clothes, beautiful hats, and beautiful girls.

WORD LIST [1]

NOUNS

abito *m.* dress
bottone *m.* button
camicia *f.* shirt
cappello *m.* hat
cravatta *f.* necktie
fazzoletto *m.* handkerchief
festa *f.* party
foglia *f.* leaf
giacca *f.* coat (*of suit*), jacket
manica *f.* sleeve
mano *f.* hand
moda *f.* fashion
mostra *f.* display
Natale *m.* Christmas
natura *f.* nature
parasole *m.* parasol
passeggio *m.* walk, stroll
petto *m.* chest
raffreddore *m.* cold

signorina *f.* young lady, Miss
taschino *m.* breast pocket
vento *m.* wind
vestito *m.* suit
volta *f.* time; **una volta** once

ADJECTIVES

alto, –a tall
corto, –a short
severo, –a severe, cruel

VERBS

ammirare to admire
guardarsi to look at oneself
riscaldare to warm, heat
seguire to follow
tenere to hold

OTHER WORDS

se if

CURRENT USAGE

In un negozio

— Che bella giornata oggi!   Ideale per far delle compre.
Vuoi accompagnarmi, Alma?

— Sì, Margherita, con piacere.   Mi piace molto girare per
i negozi e vedere quel che c'è di nuovo.

[1] The idioms which are given under "Useful Expressions" are not repeated in the "Word List."

— Che borsetta elegante in quella vetrina. <u>Vediamola</u>!

— Entriamo. Signorina, ci mostri quella borsetta nera in vetrina.

— Veramente bella, signora Bertoldi, specialmente per
5 una serata di gala.

— Che te ne pare, Alma?

— Sì, è bella. Quanto ne vuole?

— <u>Domandiamole</u>. Signorina, qual è il prezzo?

— Gliela posso dare per dodicimila lire, signora.

10 — Mi sembra un po' cara. Mi mostri la bianca, lì accanto.

— Certo, signora. Bellissima anche quella. Le prenda
tutte e due; gliele posso dare per ventimila lire.

— Mi lasci vedere. Quale va meglio col mio cappello?

— Tutte e due vanno bene, signora. Se mi permette,
15 però, abbiamo un cappello che va proprio a perfezione con
le due borsette.

— Me lo lasci provare. Dimmi, Alma, che te ne pare?
Ti piace?

— Sì, il cappello mi piace, e mi piacciono anche le due
20 borsette. Direi, però, che farebbero più effetto con un paio
di scarpe rosse.

— Signora, abbiamo appunto un paio di scarpe eleganti,
fatte proprio per Lei. Gliele faccio venire subito.

— Sono eleganti davvero. Però, quanto costa il tutto?

25 — Vediamo: borsette, ventimila; cappello, settemila;
scarpe, diciottomila; totale, quarantacinque mila. Non è
affatto caro.

— Eh, è caro abbastanza. Alma, tu che faresti?

— Io comprerei tutto. Ti va tutto a perfezione.

30 — Va bene. Me li faccia mandare a casa, signorina.

— Non dubiti, signora Bertoldi. Mille grazie, e tornino
presto un'altra volta.

Useful Expressions

far delle compre to do some shopping
girare per i negozi to go around the shops
quel che c'è di nuovo what is new
in vetrina in the (shop) window

serata di gala gala evening
Che te ne pare? What do you think of it?
lì accanto next to it
a perfezione perfectly
fare effɛtto to be effective
Quanto cɔsta il tutto? How much is everything?
Non dubiti! Don't worry! By all means!
un'altra vɔlta again

Questions. 1. Ɛ̀ ideale la giornata per far delle compre?
2. Che piace fare ad Alma? 3. Le due amiche che cɔsa vedono in
vetrina? 4. Qual è il prezzo della borsetta nera? 5. Che altro
vuɔl vedere la signora? 6. Piacciono alla signora la borsetta e
il cappɛllo? 7. Che altro ci vuɔle dopo la borsetta e il cappɛllo?
8. Ci sono scarpe rosse nel negɔzio? 9. Quanto cɔsta il tutto?
10. Le sembra caro questo prɛzzo?

STRUCTURE

75. Table of Pronouns

SUBJECT PRONOUNS	CONJUNCTIVE OBJECT PRONOUNS			DISJUNCTIVE PRONOUNS
	Direct	*Indirect*	*Reflexive*	
io, I	**mi**	**mi**	**mi**	**me**
tu, you (*fam. sing.*)	**ti**	**ti**	**ti**	**te**
egli, he	**lo**	**gli**	**si**	**lui (esso,** it)
essa, she, it	**la**	**le**	**si**	**lɛi (essa)**
Lɛi (*or* **Ella**), you (*polite sing.*)	**La**	**Le**	**Si**	**Lɛi**
noi, we	**ci**	**ci**	**ci**	**noi**
voi, you (*fam. pl.*)	**vi**	**vi**	**vi**	**voi**
essi, they (*m.*)	**li**	**loro**	**si**	**loro (essi)**
esse, they (*f.*)	**le**	**loro**	**si**	**loro (esse)**
Loro, you (*polite pl.*)	**Li, Le**	**Loro**	**Si**	**Loro** (*reflexive third person* — **sè**)

76. Position of Object Pronouns (Cont.)

1. All conjunctive object pronouns come after the verb and are attached to it (except **loro**) when the verb is in the affirmative imperative (**tu, noi,** and **voi** forms only).

> Domandiamole !   *Let's ask her.*
> Scrivi loro più tardi.   *Write to them later.*

2. All conjunctive object pronouns (except **loro**) come before the verb if these same three imperative forms are in the negative.

> Non mi lasciare qui sola.   *Don't leave me here alone.*
> Non li compriamo adesso.   *Let's not buy them now.*

3. When a verb is monosyllabic (one syllable) or ends in an accented vowel, the conjunctive pronoun doubles its initial consonant before it is attached.   (This rule does not apply to **gli** and **loro**.)

> Dammi quella bianca.   *Give me that white one.*
> Dicci quando arriveranno.   *Tell us when they will arrive.*

4. With the adverb **ecco** the pronouns follow and are attached (except **loro**).

> Eccomi pronto.   *Here I am ready.*

5. When an infinitive depends upon another verb such as **potere, volere, dovere, sapere, cominciare, finire, mandare,** etc., the object pronoun may either come before the first verb or be attached to the infinitive.

> Lo voglio provare *or* Voglio provarlo.   *I want to try it.*

6. If the infinitive depends on **vedere, udire, sentire, fare,** or **lasciare,** the pronoun comes before this verb (or is attached to it if the form is in the affirmative imperative).

> L'abbiamo sentito cantare.   *We heard him sing.*
> Lasciami scegliere.   *Let me choose.*

77. Infinitive with *fare*. When followed by an infinitive, **fare** expresses the idea of causing someone else to do an action.

Glielo faccio venire subito. *I'll have it brought immediately.*
Me li faccia mandare. *Have them sent to me.*

78. Possessive Pronouns. In Lesson 5, on page 33, we studied the possessive adjectives. When a noun does not follow the possessive immediately, the possessive is a pronoun and not an adjective. The forms of the possessive pronouns are the same as those of the adjectives, except for the use of the article.
The forms of the possessive pronouns are as follows:

SINGULAR		PLURAL	
il mio, etc.	mine	il nostro, etc.	ours
il tuo, etc.	yours (*fam.*)	il vostro, etc.	yours (*fam.*)
il suo, etc.	his, hers	il loro, etc.	theirs
il Suo, etc.	yours (*pol.*)	il Loro, etc.	yours (*pol.*)

The possessive pronoun is of the same gender and number as the noun to which it refers. Remember that the word **loro** does not change.

I suoi amici e i nostri. *His friends and ours.*
La loro casa e la Sua. *Their house and yours.*

The article is not omitted with possessive pronouns, even when they refer to members of the family.

Suo cugino e il mio. *His cousin and mine.*

The possessive pronoun drops the article after **essere** if possession only is implied. The article is retained even after **essere** if the possessive is used to distinguish one thing from another rather than show possession.

Quella borsetta è Sua. *That handbag is yours.*
BUT Questo cappello è il mio; tu trovati il tuo. *This hat is mine; you find yours.*

LANGUAGE PRACTICE

Si legga senza tradurre:

Milano

Milano è la più grande città industriale e commerciale d'Italia. È il centro delle ferrovie [1] e delle línee aeree [2] d'Europa. La stazione ferroviaria [3] è una delle più grandi del mondo. L'aeroporto è uno dei più importanti d'Europa, con aeroplani che vanno in Germania, Francia,
5 Inghilterra,[4] e in tutti i continenti. Le migliori autostrade [5] d'Italia passano per Milano.

Le ditte [6] principali d'Italia sono di Milano. Le case editrici,[7] i grandi negozi, le grandi fabbriche [8] — tutti hanno o la sede [9] o succursali [10] importanti in questa città.
10 Milano poi è un gran centro di arte e di cultura. Il Duomo è una delle più belle chiese del mondo. La Pinacoteca [11] di Brera ha opere d'arte famosíssime. Santa Maria delle Grazie possiede [12] il famoso *Cenacolo,* [13] dipinto [14] da Leonardo da Vinci. Al Teatro della Scala si danno le più belle rappresentazioni di opere del mondo.
15 Milano è certo una delle più importanti città d'Italia.

Si risponda senza tradurre:

1. Quale città italiana è il centro delle ferrovie e delle línee aeree d'Europa? 2. In che paesi vanno gli aeroplani che partono da Milano? 3. A che serve un'autostrada? 4. Ci sono ditte importanti a Milano? 5. Che cosa è il Duomo di Milano? 6. Quale pinacoteca famosa è a Milano? 7. Chi dipinse il famoso *Cenacolo* che si trova in Santa Maria delle Grazie? 8. Perchè è rinomato il Teatro della Scala?

ESERCIZI

I. Si traducano le seguenti proposizioni (Translate the following sentences):

A. 1. They saw us and spoke to us. 2. I did not see him, but I shall write to him. 3. If he does not buy it, she will not go to dinner. 4. We have done it (*f.*). 5. I have seen them, but I have not spoken to them.

---

[1] railroads. [2] airways. [3] railroad station. [4] England. [5] highways.
[6] firms. [7] publishing houses. [8] factories. [9] home office. [10] branch offices.
[11] art gallery. [12] possesses. [13] Last Supper. [14] painted.

The Duomo of Milano is the masterpiece of Italian Gothic. Along with it you see modern developments in the Piazza della Repubblica.

6. Have you seen the girls? Yes, I saw them this morning. 7. Show me that hat in the window. 8. Let's see it (*f.*). Bring it here. 9. Will you write to them later or are you writing to them now? 10. Take it and show it to your husband.

B. 1. We cannot do it now. 2. They must not see us. 3. Must we go to the store? Must we go there now? 4. She will not be able to eat it tonight. 5. When may I see you? 6. He wishes to speak to you, boys. 7. Will she want to see it before buying it? 8. We were not able to see you this morning. 9. I want to try it (on) now. 10. Let her choose what (**quel che**) she wants.

II. Si traducano le parole inglesi (Translate the English words):

1. (My) scarpe e (theirs). 2. (Our) amici e (yours, *fam. pl.*). 3. (Your) pranzo e (ours). 4. (Her) borsetta e (mine). 5. (Their) vetrine e (ours). 6. (His) negozio e (mine). 7. (Its) prezzo; (its) moda. 8. (My) serata di gala e (yours, *fam. sing.*). 9. (Their) cappelli e (yours, *fam. pl.*). 10. (Her) marito e (yours, *fam. sing.*).

11. (Those) amici sono (ours). 12. (That) mano è (hers). 13. (That) giacca è (his). 14. (This) pranzo è (yours). 15. (Those) cappelli sono (ours). 16. (That) amica è elegante. 17. (Those) alberi sono altissimi. 18. (This) volta non torno. 19. (Those) prezzi (*of yours*) sono troppo alti. 20. (That) cappello (*on you*) e (that) borsetta vanno a perfezione.

III. Use a pronoun instead of the nouns in italics:

1. Vedrai *Margherita* domani. 2. Compriamo *i cappelli* subito. 3. Voglio trovare *un marito* presto. 4. Comprate *la casa* subito. 5. Prenda *la borsetta e il cappello*. 6. Vediamo *la cravatta*. 7. Lascia venire *Antonio*. 8. Voglio sapere *il prezzo*. 9. Vendi *la casa* a tuo fratello. 10. Non finire *il lavoro* troppo presto. 11. Vuol venire con *Alberto?* 12. Sei stato da *gli amici?* 13. Avete trovato *la camicia?* 14. Cosa ne

dice di *Alma e Maria?*   15. Parleremo *al ragazzo* stasera.   16. Ha passato la serata con *gli zii*.   17. Fate venire *il professore*.   18. Facciamo partire *gli studenti*. 19. Non faccia cantare *la ragazza*.   20. Non facciamo scrivere *le lettere*.

IV. Si traduca in italiano (Translate into Italian):

1. We have seen them and we cannot forget them. 2. It's almost three o'clock and he still cannot go to dinner.   3. That handbag is really elegant, especially in the shop window.   4. Let's ask her what the price is before buying it.   5. This hat and this handkerchief go very well together.   6. I want to try it and then we can go home.   7. If you do not buy them, I shall buy them with your money.   8. I cannot understand a word of it and I want to understand it. 9. Would these things be more effective with a pair of white shoes? She wants to buy them.   10. She wants to buy them all, but she does not want to spend too much money.

WORD LIST

NOUNS

borsetta *f.* handbag
compra *f.* purchase
effetto *m.* effect
grazie *f. pl.* thanks
Margherita Margaret
paio *m.* (*pl.* **paia** *f.*) pair
perfezione *f.* perfection
prezzo *m.* price
scarpa *f.* shoe
serata *f.* evening
totale *m.* total
vetrina *f.* (shop) window

ADJECTIVES

bellissimo, –a very beautiful
bianco, –a white
caro, –a dear, expensive
diciottomila eighteen thousand
dodicimila twelve thousand
elegante elegant
ideale ideal
nero, –a black
nuovo, –a new
quarantacinque mila forty-five thousand
rosso, –a red
settemila seven thousand
ventimila twenty thousand

VERBS

accompagnare to accompany
andare bene to go well, agree

dubitare to doubt
entrare to enter (takes ɛssere)
girare to go around
mandare to send
mostrare to show
parere to seem (takes ɛssere)
provare to try on
tornare to return, come back
   (takes ɛssere)

OTHER WORDS

abbastanza *adv.* enough,
   sufficiently
adɛsso now
appunto exactly
davvero really
prɔprio *adv.* exactly
veramente really

CURRENT USAGE

Le bɛlle arti

L'Italia è la culla delle bɛlle arti. Nessuna nazione del mondo ha prodotto tanti compositori, pittori, scultori, e architɛtti famosi come l'Italia. Nell'ɔpera non c'è nazione che le si pɔssa paragonare, a eccezione forse della Germania.
5 Chi può dubitare che Verdi [1] e Puccini abbiano avuto ispirazione quasi divina nel comporre le loro melodie? Ma molti credono che questi siano i soli compositori importanti, dimenticando che l'Italia ha avuto anche un Mascagni, un Rossini, un Donizetti, un Leoncavallo, un Bellini, e tanti
10 altri . . . tutti compositori inimitabili.

Nella pittura, chi non ha sentito parlare di Michelangelo, Leonardo da Vinci, e Raffaɛllo? Eppure non sono affatto i soli grandi pittori che l'Italia abbia prodotti. Bisogna

---

[1] The full name and dates of important figures are given in the end vocabulary.

The Teatro della Scala, in Milano, has presented many great operas to the musical world.

Need we introduce Arturo Toscanini?

imparare a conoscere i capolavori di Giotto, Fra Angelico,
Andrea del Sarto, Botticelli, Tiziano, e tanti altri i cui quadri
si trovano in ogni grande museo del mondo. La pittura
moderna ebbe le sue origini in Italia più di sette secoli fa,
5 ma anche nei nostri giorni non c'è artista che non abbia
l'ambizione di studiare in quel bel paese.

Gli scultori e architetti famosi sono meno conosciuti dal
pubblico, ma sono nondimeno importantissimi nella storia
dell'arte. Forse tutti hanno sentito parlare di Michelangelo
10 e di Benvenuto Cellini, ma non molti conoscono Donatello,
Giambologna, Ghiberti, Bernini, Brunelleschi, e altri ugualmente famosi. Non fa meraviglia che non li si conosca,
perchè in fin dei conti non si può sapere tutto. Ma chi va
in Italia troverà che ogni città è un vero museo, perchè
15 l'arte fa parte dello spirito e del temperamento italiano.

Useful Expressions

a eccezione di with the exception of
sentir parlare di to hear about, hear mentioned
nei nostri giorni in our times
non fa meraviglia it is not surprising
non li si conosca one does not know them
in fin dei conti after all

Questions. 1. Perchè l'Italia è chiamata la culla delle belle
arti? 2. Quale nazione le si può paragonare nell'opera? 3. Si
può dubitare che Verdi e Puccini abbiano avuto ispirazione quasi
divina? 4. Sono questi i soli compositori importanti italiani?
5. Quali pittori famosi conosce Lei? 6. Dove si trovano i quadri
di questi grandi artisti? 7. Qual è l'ambizione di ogni artista nei
nostri giorni? 8. Sono ben conosciuti i grandi scultori e architetti? 9. Fa meraviglia che non li si conosca? 10. Che cosa
troverà chi va in Italia?

STRUCTURE

79. Present Subjunctive: Formation. The tenses studied
so far are called indicative because they indicate a period of time
when an action takes place. In Italian it is also necessary to

indicate the relation of one action to another in terms of the mood of the speaker, as well as other circumstances attending the action. This secondary type of relation is expressed by the subjunctive, divided into four tenses.

The forms of the present subjunctive for the regular conjugations are as follows:

I	II	III	
parl–**i**	vend–**a**	fin–**isca**	dɔrm–**a**
parl–**i**	vend–**a**	fin–**isca**	dɔrm–**a**
parl–**i**	vend–**a**	fin–**isca**	dɔrm–**a**
parl–**iamo**	vend–**iamo**	fin–**iamo**	dorm–**iamo**
parl–**iate**	vend–**iate**	fin–**iate**	dorm–**iate**
parl–**ino**	vend–**ano**	fin–*iscano*	dɔrm–**ano**

The present perfect subjunctive is formed by the present subjunctive of **essere** or **avere,** followed by the past participle of the verb conjugated. You will learn the forms in the next lesson.

For short cuts in learning the present subjunctive, notice that the three persons in the singular are always alike, and the third person plural simply adds –**no** to the singular form. The first person plural of regular verbs is the same as that of the present indicative, and the second person plural always ends in –**iate.**

80. Uses of the Subjunctive: Noun Clauses. The subjunctive, when used in subordinate clauses, denotes something uncertain, possible, or indeterminate. It shows that the idea represented by the clause is a wish, an opinion, a thought, or an expectation of the subject of the main clause. The subjunctive is used in clauses depending on:

1. Expressions of wish or desire. *Change of subject NECESSARY!*

Vɔglio che Lei impari tutto. *I want you to learn everything.*

2. Verbs of requesting, urging, advising, permitting, or commanding.

Digli che non faccia tardi. *Tell him not to be late.*

3. Expressions of fear or doubt.

Chi può dubitare che abbiano avuto ispirazione? *Who can
doubt that they had inspiration?*

4. Expressions of belief, opinion, or supposition.

Credono che questi siano i soli compositori. *They think that
these are the only composers.*

5. Expressions of surprise or emotion of any sort.

Non fa meraviglia che non li si conosca. *It is not surprising
that one does not know them.*

81. Uses of the Subjunctive: Adjective Clauses. The
subjunctive is used in the following types of adjective clauses:

1. A relative clause depending on an indefinite antecedent or
expressing a characteristic of the antecedent not yet attained.

Vuole comporre musica che sia perfetta. *He wants to compose
music which is perfect.*

2. A relative clause depending on an antecedent which is in
the negative or the interrogative.

Non c'è nessuno che lo conosca. *There is no one who knows him.*

3. A relative clause depending on a superlative or its equivalent
(such as **unico, solo, ultimo, primo**).

Non sono i soli grandi pittori che l'Italia abbia prodotti. *They
are not the only great painters that Italy has produced.*
È la più bell'aria che io abbia sentita. *It is the most beautiful
aria I have heard.*

82. Present Subjunctive of Irregular Verbs. The present
subjunctive of common irregular verbs follows a set pattern.
Once you have learned the first person singular, the rest of the
forms follow the pattern of regular verbs.

Following is the present subjunctive of some of the most common irregular verbs:

avere   abbia, abbia, abbia, abbiamo, abbiate, abbiano
dare   dia, dia, dia, diamo, diate, diano

andare - vada - andiamo andiate vodano (handwritten)

dire	dica, dica, dica, diciamo, diciate, dicano
ɛssere	sia, sia, sia, siamo, siate, siano
fare	faccia, faccia, faccia, facciamo, facciate, facciano
piacere	piaccia, piacciano
potere	pɔssa, pɔssa, pɔssa, possiamo, possiate, pɔssano
sapere	sappia, sappia, sappia, sappiamo, sappiate, sappiano
volere	vɔglia, vɔglia, vɔglia, vogliamo, vogliate, vɔgliano

LANGUAGE PRACTICE

Si lɛgga senza tradurre:

La serenata

La serenata è la musica che si suɔna di sera o di nɔtte in onore della fidanzata [1] o di una ragazza che piace molto. Il giovane che vuɔle onorare una giovane in questo mɔdo riunisce [2] un gruppo di tre o quattro amici; alcuni cantano ed alcuni suɔnano. Gli strumenti favoriti per la serenata sono mandolini e chitarre, ma si pɔssono usare anche violini, flauti,[3] e 5 altri strumenti soavi.[4] Non hɔ mai sentito parlare di una serenata con cornetta, trombone, tuba, o contrabasso,[5] ma forse altri paesi hanno altre usanze. La giovane ascolta e magari [6] lascia cadere [7] qualche fiore, se non qualche sospiro.[8] Se i genitori non vɔgliono il giovane, i musicanti corrono il pericolo [9] di qualche dɔccia.[10] Ma l'usanza è bɛlla e la gioventù 10 è la migliore età. Peccato che non pɔssa durare [11] per sɛmpre.

Si risponda senza tradurre:

1. Che cɔsa è la serenata? 2. Che fa il giovane che vuɔle onorare una giovane in questo mɔdo? 3. Quali sono gli strumenti favoriti per la serenata? 4. Che cɔsa fa la ragazza? 5. Che pericolo corrono i musicanti? 6. Qual è la migliore età?

ESERCIZI

I. Si dia la forma adatta del vɛrbo tra parɛntesi e si traduca la proposizione (Give the proper form of the verb in parentheses and translate the sentence):

1. Vuɔle che io lo (fare) ɔggi? 2. Vɔgliono che tutti (imparare) questa melodia. 3. Sono contento che Lɛi

[1] fiancée. [2] gathers. [3] flutes. [4] soft. [5] double bass. [6] perhaps. [7] drops, [8] sigh. [9] run the risk. [10] shower. [11] last.

(studiare) l'italiano.   4. È contɛnto che io (ɛssere) il
professore?   5. Dubito che il professore (volere) venire.
6. Abbiamo paura che tu non lo (potere) trovare.
7. Gli dica che non (dimenticarsi).   8. Crede che
questa (ɛssere) musica italiana?   9. Diciamole che
(portare) tutto il necessario.   10. Peccato che (ɛssere)
così piccolo.   11. Credete che essi (volere) accompagnarci?   12. Dubita che loro (conoscere) molti architɛtti famosi.

II. Si dia la forma adatta del vɛrbo tra parɛntesi e si
traduca:

1. Cerchiamo un'ɔpera che (ɛssere) interessante.
2. Come, non avete trovato nessuna ɔpera che vi
(piacere)?   3. Vuɔle comprare un libro che gli (piacere).   4. Non c'è nessuno che non lo (sapere).   5. Mi
fa meraviglia che lui non ne (volere) sentire parlare.
6. Non gli fa meraviglia che vi (ɛssere) tanti buɔni
compositori?   7. Cerco una nazione che (avere) più
cultura.   8. Non c'è niɛnte che le si (potere) paragonare.   9. È la più bɛlla giovane che io (avere) vista.
10. Crede che (volere) accompagnarci al cinema?
11. Non credo che (potere) venire.   12. Vuɔle che lo
(fare) venire?

III. Si facciano delle proposizioni originali con le seguɛnti
parɔle (Form original sentences with the following words):

1. culla, bɛlle, arti.   2. scultori, architɛtti, compositori.   3. meraviglia, conoscere, tutti.   4. compositore,
musica, bellissima.   5. ispirazione, divina, comporre.
6. Michelangelo, Raffaɛllo, pittori.   7. comporre,
melodie, famose.   8. quadri, trovare, musɛo.   9. Donizetti, Mascagni, inimitabili.   10. paragonare, Italia,
Germania.

IV. Si traduca in italiano:

1. I believe that no nation is as important as Italy
in the fine arts.   2. Do you think that every composer
has inspiration?   3. Who can doubt that good com-

posers may come from any (**qualsiasi**) country? 4. We
have forgotten that we do not know anything about
opera. 5. They are the greatest painters that Italy
has produced. 6. He would like to find a melody that
is more beautiful than this one. 7. There is no artist
who does not have the ambition to study in Italy.
8. Architects are nevertheless very important in the
history of art. 9. Do you think that Donatello and
Giambologna are equally famous? 10. Now I understand that art is really a part of the Italian temperament.

WORD LIST

NOUNS

ambizione *f.* ambition
architetto *m.* architect
capolavoro *m.* masterpiece
compositore *m.* composer
culla *f.* cradle
eccezione *f.* exception
Germania *f.* Germany
ispirazione *f.* inspiration
melodia *f.* melody
meraviglia *f.* surprise, mar-
  vel
origine *f.* origin
parola *f.* word
pittore *m.* painter
pittura *f.* painting
pubblico *m.* public
scultore *m.* sculptor
spirito *m.* spirit, soul
temperamento *m.* temperament

ADJECTIVES

alcuni, -e some
importantissimo, -a very
  important
inimitabile inimitable
moderno, -a modern
nessuno, -a no, no one
solo, -a alone, only
vero, -a true, veritable

VERBS

comporre to compose
paragonare to compare
produrre (*p.p.* **prodotto**) to
  produce

OTHER WORDS

eppure and yet
i cui whose
nondimeno nevertheless
ugualmente equally

CURRENT USAGE

In salotto

— Buona sera, signor professore. Si accomodi! Siamo così lieti che sia venuto a visitarci. Avevamo proprio desiderio di vederla.

— Sono tanto gentili! Mi pare di essere a casa mia
5 quando vengo da Loro.

— Permetta un momento che apra le persiane e faccia entrare la luce. Si sta sempre al buio durante il giorno per stare più freschi.

— Infatti fa tanto caldo che sembra che non ci resti
10 nessuno in città. I Fiorentini vanno tutti in villeggiatura. Da noi fa caldo sì, ma non tanto.

— Eh sì, in America si sta bene per tante cose.

— Spero di non incomodare troppo. Ma sospetto che non abbiano finito ancora il pranzo. Vadano a terminare e non
15 facciano cerimonie. Nel frattempo io ascolto la radio o guardo la televisione, giacchè ce le hanno in casa. Ne sento la mancanza da quando sono in Italia.

— La televisione è recente in Italia; data soltanto dal 1953 (mille novecento cinquantatrè). Guardi con tutto il
20 comodo, ma l'assicuriamo che il pranzo è già terminato. Prenderà un caffè con noi? Lo prendiamo sempre in salotto, dopo il pranzo.

— Grazie, l'accetto con piacere. Che bella musica alla radio! Quel violinista è una meraviglia. Peccato che il
25 pezzo stia per finire.

126

— Sì, è il rondò del concerto per violino di Beethoven.

— Mi rammento bene che Lei è pianista, signorina. Suonava divinamente all'università. Mi suoni qualche pezzo al pianoforte, per favore. Gliene sarei così grato.

— È troppo gentile. Se vuole, Le suonerò l'*Appassionata* 5 di Beethoven, che Le piaceva tanto. Dovrà essere indulgente, però, perchè le dita non sono agili.

— Sono sicuro che suonerà a meraviglia. Mi rallegro tanto che mi abbiano invitato a passare una serata con Loro.   10

Useful Expressions

si accomodi come in, make yourself at home
mi pare di essere a casa mia I feel quite at home
avevamo proprio desiderio we were quite anxious
stare al buio to stay in the dark
non facciano cerimonie do not stand on ceremony
nel frattempo meanwhile
ne sento la mancanza I miss them
da quando sono in Italia since I have been in Italy
con tutto il comodo as much as you wish
a meraviglia marvelously
dovrà essere indulgente you will have to bear with me

Questions. 1. Che cosa si dice quando arriva un amico? 2. Fa caldo a Firenze nell'estate? 3. Dove vanno tutti i Fiorentini? 4. Che cosa dice il professore agli amici? 5. È recente la televisione in Italia? 6. Che si prende in salotto dopo il pranzo? 7. Che cosa suonavano alla radio? 8. Sono agili le dita quando non si suona per lungo tempo? 9. Il professore perchè si rallegra? 10. Lei suona il pianoforte?

STRUCTURE

83. Uses of the Subjunctive: Polite Commands. You learned in Lesson 9 that the present subjunctive is used to express commands in the polite form (**Lei** and **Loro**). This is the main use of the present subjunctive in independent clauses.

Permetta un momento. *Allow me for a moment.*
Vadano a terminare. *Go and finish.*

[handwritten margin notes: Indicative / È vero che / È chiaro che / È evidente / Subjunctive / Peccato / È vergogna (it's a shame) / È necessario / Sembra (it seems) / È strano (it's strange) / È possibile (it's possible) / È incredibile (incredible) / È ridicolo (it's ridiculous) / Non è vero (It's not true)]

With these polite commands object pronouns come before the verb, just as they do before most of the verb forms.

Mi suoni qualche pezzo. *Play me a piece.*
Si accomodi! *Make yourself at home.*

84. Uses of the Subjunctive: Impersonal Expressions. An impersonal expression is one beginning with the word *it* followed by a form of the verb *to be* (it is necessary, it was true, etc.). The subjunctive is used in a clause depending on an impersonal verb, unless the expression denotes what is clear, evident, or a matter of fact.

Peccato che il pezzo stia per finire. *It's too bad that the piece is about over.*
Sembra che non ci resti nessuno. *It seems that no one is left.*
BUT È chiaro che si sbaglia. *It is evident that he is mistaken.*

85. Present Perfect Subjunctive. The present perfect subjunctive is formed by the present subjunctive of **avere** or **essere** followed by the past participle of the verb to be conjugated. Following are model verbs:

---

parlare, *to speak;* **vendere,** *to sell;* **finire,** *to finish*

io	abbia	
tu	abbia	} parlato, venduto, finito
egli, essa, Lei	abbia	
noi	abbiamo	
voi	abbiate	} parlato, venduto, finito
essi, esse, Loro	abbiano	

andare, *to go;* **cadere,** *to fall;* **partire,** *to leave*

io	sia	andato(a)	caduto(a)	partito(a)
tu	sia	andato(a)	caduto(a)	partito(a)
egli, Lei	sia	andato	caduto	partito
essa, Lei	sia	andata	caduta	partita
noi	siamo	andati(e)	caduti(e)	partiti(e)
voi	siate	andati(e)	caduti(e)	partiti(e)
essi, Loro	siano	andati	caduti	partiti
esse, Loro	siano	andate	cadute	partite

The present perfect subjunctive is used, when the meaning so requires it, in a dependent clause which follows a verb in the present or future, or an expression which refers to the present time.

Mi rallegro che mi abbiano invitato. *I am glad you invited me.*
Siamo così lieti che sia venuto a visitarci. *We are so happy that you came to visit us.*
Sospetto che non abbiano finito ancora il pranzo. *I suspect you haven't finished dinner yet.*

86. The Infinitive with Expressions of Emotion. When the subject of the dependent clause is the same as that of the main clause, the infinitive is used instead of the subjunctive. This really corresponds to the English use of the infinitive.

Siamo così lieti di vederla. *We are so happy to see you.*
Spero di non incomodare troppo. *I hope I am not disturbing (you) too much.*

omit   important

87. Reflexive for First Person Plural. In Tuscan usage the third person singular reflexive (with adjective in the plural) frequently takes the place of the first person plural of the verb.

Si sta sempre al buio durante il giorno. *We always stay in the dark during the day.*
Si sta più freschi. *We are cooler.*

88. Present Subjunctive of Irregular Verbs. Following are more of the common verbs irregular in the present subjunctive.

andare	vada, vada, vada, andiamo, andiate, vadano
venire	venga, venga, venga, veniamo, veniate, vengano
dovere	debba, debba, debba, dobbiamo, dobbiate, debbano
piacere	piaccia, piacciano
porre	ponga, ponga, ponga, poniamo, poniate, pongano
rimanere	rimanga, rimanga, rimanga, rimaniamo, rimaniate, rimangano
uscire	esca, esca, esca, usciamo, usciate, escano

LANGUAGE PRACTICE

Si legga senza tradurre:

L'università di Bologna

L'università di Bologna è la più antica [1] e una delle più rinomate d'Italia. Ancora non si sa bene quale sia la più antica università del mondo, quella di Bologna o quella di Parigi, ma tutte e due hanno più di settecento anni. All'università di Bologna studiarono San Tommaso
5 d'Aquino, Dante, il Petrarca, e vi insegnarono [2] Carducci, Pascoli e molti altri scrittori famosi. Bologna è stata sempre rinomata per la sua facoltà [3] di legge,[4] ma ha anche varie altre facoltà importantissime, come lettere,[5] scienze, e medicina. Una laurea [6] dell'università di Bologna è riconosciuta [7] dappertutto.[8]
10 La città di Bologna è interessantissima. Ha avuto importanza storica per molti secoli e anche nei nostri giorni rimane uno dei centri più notevoli [9] dell'Italia settentrionale.[10] Le grandi ferrovie che vanno da Roma al nord passano quasi tutte per Bologna. Peccato che molti turisti che visitano Firenze, Venezia, e Milano non si fermino [11] in questa famosa città prima
15 di continuare per la loro destinazione.

Si risponda senza tradurre:

1. Qual è la più antica università italiana? 2. Quali sono alcuni degli scrittori famosi che studiarono o insegnarono a Bologna? 3. Qual è la più rinomata facoltà dell'università? 4. È riconosciuta una laurea dell'università di Bologna? 5. Perchè è importante Bologna nei nostri giorni? 6. Si fermano molti turisti a visitare questa famosa città?

ESERCIZI

I. Si dia la forma adatta del verbo tra parentesi e si traduca all'inglese:

1. (Venire) a vederci qualche giorno. 2. (Accomodarsi) qui, per favore. 3. (Fare) entrare la luce, perchè è buio. 4. La (aprire) un poco di più. 5. Mi sembra che si (stare) bene per tante cose. 6. Bisogna che loro (ascoltare) per capire. 7. Peccato che Lei non (avere) quel pezzo di musica. 8. Ci rallegriamo che essa (suo-

---

[1] ancient.   [2] taught.   [3] faculty.   [4] law.   [5] liberal arts.   [6] degree.
[7] recognized.   [8] everywhere.   [9] notable.   [10] northern.   [11] stop.

*The Torre degli Asinelli and the
Torre Garisenda have been leaning
in this peculiar way in Bologna
since before the time of Dante.*

nare) così bene.   9. Speriamo che essi (aver finito) il
pranzo.   10. È contento che tutti (essere arrivati)?
11. Sospetto che non gli (piacere) restare senza pranzo.
12. Spera che non (essere arrivato) troppo tardi.
13. (Andare) tutti in villeggiatura.   14. Siamo con-
tenti che Lei (volere) stare con noi.

II. Si traduca in italiano:

1. Come.   2. All (of) you come.   3. Do it.   4. Tell
me.   5. Tell your brother.   6. Do not play.   7. Do
not do it now.   8. Make yourself at home.   9. Do as
you wish.   10. Do not stand on ceremony.   11. Listen
to the radio.   12. Try it on the piano.   13. Do not
play on that piano.   14. Listen, the music is beautiful.
15. Play us a piece.   16. We are happy in Florence
(*reflexive*).   17. We sleep until eight o'clock (*reflexive*).
18. We always stay in the dark (*reflexive*).   19. It is
about over.   20. Go and finish.

III. Si facciano delle proposizioni adoprando le seguenti frasi
(Make up sentences using the following expressions):

1. lieto di vedere.   2. un po'.   3. stare al buio.
4. stare freschi.   5. Non ci resta nessuno.   6. in villeggiatura.   7. prendere un caffè.   8. così gentile.
9. essere a casa sua.   10. far cerimonie.   11. peccato
che.   12. star per finire.

IV. Si traduca in italiano:

1. They are so happy to see us tonight because we
like music.   2. It is so warm here in the summer that
everybody goes on vacation.   3. It's a pity that there
isn't a bit of good music on the radio.   4. He feels
quite at home when he goes to their house.   5. We
hope that our child has not inconvenienced you too
much.   6. I think that they have not finished their
dinner, but we cannot go away now.   7. He stays to
listen to the radio and he does not stand on ceremony.
8. I remember that you play well. Why don't you
play that concerto on the piano?   9. She used to play

a great deal when we were at the university.   10. You will have to bear with me because my fingers are not nimble.

WORD LIST

NOUNS

buio *m.* dark, darkness
cerimonia *f.* ceremony
concerto *m.* concert, concerto
dito *m.* (*pl.* **dita** *f.*) finger
luce *f.* light
mancanza *f.* lack
persiana *f.* shutter
pezzo *m.* piece, composition
pianista *m. or f.* pianist
pianoforte *m.* piano
radio *f.* radio
rondo *m.* rondo
televisione *f.* television
violino *m.* violin
visita *f.* visit

ADJECTIVES

agile nimble
lieto, –a happy

VERBS

accomodarsi to make oneself at home, sit down
ascoltare to listen (to)
assicurare to assure
incomodare to inconvenience
rammentarsi to remember
sospettare to suspect
sperare to hope
terminare to end, finish

OTHER WORDS

divinamente divinely
giacchè since
peccato (it's) too bad
stasera this evening

stare
Subjuntive
stia

stiamo
stiate
stiano

CURRENT USAGE

La geografia dell'Italia

Monti e valli e pɔche pianure — ɛcco la geografia generale dell'Itɑlia. Al nɔrd le Alpi circondano la penisola da un lato all'altro; pɔi gli Appennini l'attravɛrsano da capo a piɛdi. L'Itɑlia è quasi tutta montagne. La pianura mag-
5 giore e la più fɛrtile è quella del Pɔ, nell'Itɑlia settentrionale; la seconda è nel Vɛneto, e la tɛrza nelle Puglie, nel sud della penisola. Ci sono parecchie altre pianure, ma sono piccole.

I grandi fiumi d'Itɑlia sono il Pɔ, l'Adige, l'Arno, e il Tevere. Il Pɔ è il più importante per l'industria e l'agricol-
10 tura. L'Adige è pittoresco, nella sua discesa dalle Alpi. L'Arno è famosissimo nella stɔria; sulle sue sponde sono vissuti i maggiori letterati e artisti dell'Itɑlia. Il Tevere è il fiume del famoso impɛro romano.

Le grandi città hanno ciascuna la prɔpria stɔria.
15 Nell'Itɑlia settentrionale si trɔvano Gɛnova, Torino, Milano, Mantova, Verona, Padova, Venɛzia. Nell'Itɑlia centrale troviamo Bologna, Ravenna, Pisa, Firɛnze, Arezzo, Siɛna, Perugia, e Roma, la regina di tutte le città. Nell'Itɑlia meridionale abbiamo Napoli, Bari, Taranto, Rɛggio Cala-
20 bria. Nelle isole pɔi ci sono Palɛrmo, Messina, Catania, Siracusa, Cagliari, Sassari. In Itɑlia ogni città ha le prɔprie caratteristiche che la distinguono dalle altre.

L'Italia è divisa in diciɔtto regioni e novantadue province. È inutile numerarle perchè non le ricordereste. Guardate
25 la carta geografica però, e cominciate a imparɑrne alcune. Ricordate che quando scrivete in Itɑlia bisogna indicare la

134

provincia e non la regione. Il miglior modo d'imparare la geografia è di fare un viaggio. Speriamo che lo possiate fare presto.

Useful Expressions

da un lato all'altro from one side to the other
da capo a piedi from head to foot
fare un viaggio to take a trip
l'Italia settentrionale northern Italy
l'Italia centrale central Italy
l'Italia meridionale southern Italy

Questions. 1. Quali montagne circondano l'Italia al nord? 2. Quali montagne attraversano la penisola? 3. Quali sono le tre grandi pianure d'Italia? 4. Quali sono i grandi fiumi d'Italia? 5. Dove sono questi fiumi? 6. Perchè è famoso l'Arno? 7. Ricordi alcune città dell'Italia settentrionale. 8. Conosce amici che vengono dall'Italia meridionale? 9. Che caratteristiche hanno le città d'Italia? 10. Quando si scrive a un amico in Italia, che cosa bisogna indicare? 11. Qual è il miglior modo per imparare la geografia?

STRUCTURE

89. **Comparison of Adjectives (Cont.).** In Lesson 11 you learned some of the simple rules for the formation of the comparative and superlative of adjectives. Now you can learn the rules more completely.

The following common adjectives have irregular as well as regular forms for the comparative and the superlative. Bear in mind that there are two types of superlatives in Italian: the relative superlative, which relates a quality to the rest of a group, and the absolute superlative, which gives the highest quality irrespective of any group.

POSITIVE	COMPARATIVE	RELATIVE SUPERLATIVE	ABSOLUTE SUPERLATIVE
buono, *good*	migliore	il migliore	ottimo
cattivo, *bad*	peggiore	il peggiore	pessimo
grande, *large*	maggiore	il maggiore	massimo
piccolo, *small*	minore	il minore	minimo
alto, *high*	superiore	il superiore	supremo
basso, *low*	inferiore	l'inferiore	infimo

La pianura maggiore è quella del Po.   *The largest plain is that of the Po.*

I maggiori letterati e artisti.   *The greatest artists and literary men.*

Although these adjectives have a regular comparison as well as the irregular one, some of the forms are more common than others.   The regular comparison frequently carries a different connotation from the irregular one.   For example, the comparatives **maggiore** and **minore** are used to mean *older* and *younger;* **superiore** and **inferiore** are not used in a literal sense, but rather in a figurative sense.

90. **Absolute Superlative.**   The form which corresponds to the English superlative is a relative superlative in Italian.   In addition, Italian has an absolute superlative, which has no corresponding form in English and which can be translated only by words such as *very, exceedingly,* or *enormously.*   This superlative is formed by dropping the last vowel of an adjective and adding **–issimo.**   The word then becomes a four-form adjective.

famoso	famos*i*ssimo
importante	important*i*ssimo

L'Arno è famos*i*ssimo nella storia.   *The Arno is most famous in history.*

If the positive form of the adjective ends in **–co** or **–go,** an **h** is added in the spelling before the **–issimo.**

ricco	ricch*i*ssimo
largo	largh*i*ssimo

91. Comparison of Equality.   The English *as . . . as* expresses a comparison of equality; it is translated by **tanto . . . quanto** or **così . . . come.**

L'Arno è tanto pittoresco quanto l'Adige.   *The Arno is as picturesque as the Adige.*

The correlatives *the more . . . the more* and *the more . . . the less* are expressed by **quanto più . . . tanto più** and **quanto più . . . tanto meno.**

Quanto più studiava, tanto più imparava. *The more he studied, the more he learned.*

Quanto più mi parla, tanto meno lo capisco. *The more he talks to me, the less I understand him.*

92. Comparison of Adverbs. The comparative of an adverb is formed by placing **più** or **meno** before the positive form.

giù, *down*   più giù, *further down*
presto, *quickly*   più presto, *faster*

Mangia più presto perchè è tardi. *Eat faster because it's late.*

The relative superlative of an adverb is formed by adding the word **possibile** after the adverb introduced by **il più.**

Venite il più presto possibile se volete vederlo. *Come as soon as possible if you want to see him.*

The following common adverbs have an irregular comparative:

molto, *very*   più, *more*
poco, *little*   meno, *less*
male, *badly*   peggio, *worse*
bene, *well*   meglio, *better*

93. Translation of "than" (Cont.). The word *than* is usually translated by **che** or **di.**

1. **Di** is used before nouns, pronouns, or numerals.

Il Po è più lungo del Tevere. *The Po is longer than the Tiber.*

2. **Che** is used before all other parts of speech.

Gli Appennini sono più lunghi che larghi. *The Apennines are longer than (they are) wide.*

3. If **di** is ambiguous, **che** is used instead.

Rosa è più gelosa di Maria che di Linda. *Rose is more jealous of Mary than of Linda.*
Rosa è più gelosa che Maria. *Rose is more jealous than Mary.*

4. *Than* introducing a clause is **di quel che** or **che non.**

Ricorda più di quel che dice. *He remembers more than he tells.*

* 5 If comparison is between two nouns & is not based on any distinctive quality — USE che

LANGUAGE PRACTICE

Si legga senza tradurre:

Due Italiani in America

Nei nostri giorni abbiamo avuto l'onore di avere nel nostro paese due dei più grandi uomini che l'Italia abbia generati,[1] l'uno nel campo della musica e l'altro nella scienza.   Alcuni li hanno conosciuti personalmente e hanno apprezzato [2] in loro la semplicità [3] del vero genio.   Arturo Toscanini, considerato da molti il più grande genio musicale, faceva una vita di 5 continuo [4] lavoro in un ristretto [5] circolo di amici.   Era così modesto che non appariva mai in pubblico se non attraverso [6] la sua musica.   Enrico Fermi, il grande genio dell'era atomica, passava giorno e notte nel suo laboratorio.   Ebbi l'onore di conoscerlo alle università di Columbia e di Cicago, e ogni volta entrava in conversazione come se fosse un semplice 10 compagno di scuola.

Gli uomini di vero genio non hanno bisogno di contare sulle apparenze [7] e di darsi un'aria [8] di grandi personaggi.   Sono nobili perchè sono dotati [9] di un cuore [10] nobile, che è il vero segno [11] della loro superiorità.

Si risponda senza tradurre:

1. In che campi erano conosciuti i due grandi uomini di cui si parla? 2. Come è considerato da molti Arturo Toscanini?   3. Toscanini appariva spesso in pubblico?   4. In quali università americane lavorò Enrico Fermi?   5. Si danno molte arie gli uomini di vero genio?   6. Lei ha conosciuto personalmente Toscanini o Fermi?

ESERCIZI

I. Si dia la forma comparativa e la forma superlativa degli aggettivi seguenti (Give the comparative and the superlative forms of the following adjectives):

1. generale   2. fertile   3. grande   4. pittoresco
5. buono   6. importante   7. famoso   8. piccolo
9. alto 10. bello 11. contento 12. lontano 13. agile
14. gentile   15. ricco

---

[1] produced.   [2] have appreciated.   [3] simplicity.   [4] continual.   [5] narrow, close.   [6] through.   [7] depend on appearances.   [8] put on airs.   [9] endowed.   [10] heart.   [11] mark.

II. Si traduca oralmente (Translate orally):

A. 1. The largest cities. 2. The smallest plain.
3. The highest mountain. 4. The most famous river.
5. The greatest artists. 6. The best industry. 7. The
worst descent. 8. The most picturesque region. 9. The
best way. 10. The easiest lesson.

B. 1. An extremely famous artist. 2. An extremely
wide river. 3. An extremely rich nation. 4. An extremely important history. 5. A very large foot. 6. A
very small empire. 7. A very beautiful mountain.
8. An extremely interesting city. 9. An extremely long
train. 10. An extremely short lesson.

III. Si traducano le parole inglesi nelle seguenti proposizioni
(Translate the English words in the following sentences):

1. (The more) la vedo (the more) mi piace. 2. (The
less) cantano (the more) ci divertiamo. 3. Il Po è
(longer than) il Tevere. 4. L'Arno è (more historical
than) l'Adige. 5. Maria è (older than) sua sorella.
6. Roberto è (younger than) suo cugino. 7. Milano è
(the most important city in) l'Italia settentrionale.
8. Angelina è (the most beautiful girl in) la classe.
9. Noi siamo (the best students in) la scuola. 10. Essi
lavorano più presto (than we). 11. Essa impara più
facilmente (than he). 12. Si sentono meglio (than
you). 13. Partiremo da Verona (as soon as possible).
14. Farò il viaggio (easily). 15. L'agricoltura è (extremely good) in quella regione.

IV. Let one student ask a question and another answer it in
round-robin fashion on the geography of Italy. Go around the
class until all the geographical points taken up in this lesson are
covered.

V. Si traduca in italiano:

1. There are many mountains and valleys, but very
few plains in Italy. 2. The Alps divide Italy from the
other countries of Europe and the Apennines cross the
country from head to foot. 3. Do you know which is

the most fertile valley and which is the poorest region?
4. Industry and agriculture make (*rendere*) northern
Italy more wealthy than southern Italy. 5. The
rivers are extremely famous in history, but they are
most important in industry. 6. There are more large
cities in central Italy than in southern Italy. 7. It
would be useless to enumerate all the provinces, because no one would remember them. 8. I shall take a
trip soon because I want to learn my geography in the
best way. 9. When we look at the map we see that
Italy has many interesting cities. 10. Each city has
its own characteristics which distinguish it from other
cities.

WORD LIST

NOUNS

agricoltura *f.* agriculture
Alpi *f. pl.* Alps
Appennini *m. pl.* Apennines
capo *m.* head
caratteristica *f.* characteristic
carta geografica *f.* map
discesa *f.* descent
fiume *m.* river
geografia *f.* geography
impero *m.* empire
industria *f.* industry
lato *m.* side
letterato *m.* literary figure
modo *m.* way
monte *m.* mountain
nord *m.* north
penisola *f.* peninsula
pianura *f.* plain
provincia *f.* province
Puglie *f. pl. region of Italy,
in the southeast*
regina *f.* queen
regione *f.* region
sponda *f.* shore
sud *m.* south

Tevere *m.* Tiber
valle *f.* valley
Veneto *m. region of Italy, in
the northeast*

ADJECTIVES

fertile fertile
generale general
inutile useless
meridionale southern
parecchi, –ie several
pittoresco, –a picturesque
settentrionale northern

VERBS

attraversare to cross
circondare to surround
distinguere to distinguish
dividere (*p.p.* **diviso**) to divide
indicare to indicate
numerare to enumerate
ricordare to remember, mention

OTHER WORDS

ciascuno, –a each

19

CURRENT USAGE

L'arte e i musei

Eravamo venti alunni nel corso d'italiano. Era un bel gruppo, benchè non tutti fossero bravi studenti. Ci piaceva riunirci in classe e conversare. Il professore era buono e ci lasciava fare; bastava soltanto che non facessimo tanto
5 chiasso da disturbare le classi accanto.

Il professore era affezionato all'arte perchè aveva studiato la pittura nella sua gioventù. Ci parlava spesso di musei e di artisti e voleva che trovassimo il tema interessante, ma noi non eravamo affatto d'accordo. Mentre egli parlava
10 gli studenti sbadigliavano; il brav'uomo faceva finta di non accorgersi e seguitava come se tutti lo ascoltassero.

Ci raccontava le sue visite ai grandi musei d'Italia e degli Stati Uniti. Ci diceva, per esempio, che il Museo Nazionale di Washington possiede una famosa collezione dei quadri
15 del Rinascimento italiano, e che il Museo d'Arte di New York è uno dei più grandi del mondo. Ci diceva che in Italia aveva visitato tutti i musei importanti, e voleva che gli facessimo domande sui grandi artisti italiani.

see pg 181

Noi invece, eravamo molto ignoranti. Chi mai aveva
20 sentito parlare degli Uffizi, del Palazzo Pitti, del Museo del Vaticano, ecc., ecc.? Alcuni avevano sentito parlare di Michelangelo, di Raffaello, e di Leonardo da Vinci, ma gli altri nomi erano sconosciuti. Non c'era nessuno che conoscesse Giotto, il Beato Angelico, Andrea del Sarto, Botticelli,

The Annunciation, by Fra Filippo Lippi, and the Portrait of a Youth, by Pintoricchio, are both in our National Gallery.

Tiziano e tanti altri. Per noi i musei facevano parte del passato, e noi volevamo vivere nel presente e nel futuro.

Il professore però non disperava. Sapeva che qualche giorno ci sarebbe venuta la voglia di comprendere l'arte e
5 apprezzare le bellezze che può produrre il genio umano. Ora che siamo grandi comprendiamo che aveva ragione lui e non noi. Gli siamo grati che ci lasciasse sbadigliare e seguitasse a insegnare, colla speranza che un giorno arrivassimo ad apprezzare l'arte anche noi.

Useful Expressions

corso d'italiano Italian class, Italian course
le classi accanto the classes next door
ci lasciava fare he let us do as we wished
affezionato all'arte devoted to art
d'accordo in agreement
far finta di to make believe
museo d'arte art museum
far domande to ask questions
ci sarebbe venuta la voglia we would get the desire,
     we would feel like
aveva ragione he was right
arrivare ad apprezzare to get to appreciate

Questions. 1. Erano tutti bravi studenti nel gruppo? 2. Che cosa ci piaceva fare? 3. Ci lasciava fare il professore? 4. Il professore perchè era affezionato all'arte? 5. Noi trovavamo interessante il tema? 6. Che faceva il brav'uomo? 7. Cosa possiede il Museo Nazionale di Washington? 8. Quali artisti erano sconosciuti dagli studenti? 9. Che sapeva il professore? 10. Perchè gli siamo grati adesso?

STRUCTURE

94. The Imperfect Subjunctive. The imperfect subjunctive of any verb is formed by taking the second person singular of the past definite of the verb, dropping the **–sti,** and adding the following endings: **–ssi, –ssi, –sse, –ssimo, –ste, –ssero.** This rule holds true for all verbs, regular or irregular. Following are the forms of the imperfect subjunctive for the regular conjugations:

Imperfect Subjunctive —

used with Past Abs. Past Desc. Plu perf Cond'l

I	II	III
parlassi	vendessi	finissi
parlassi	vendessi	finissi
parlasse	vendesse	finisse
parlassimo	vendessimo	finissimo
parlaste	vendeste	finiste
parlassero	vendessero	finissero

Notice the imperfect subjunctive for some of the common irregular verbs:

INFINITIVE	2ND SING. PAST DEF.	IMPF. SUBJ.
avere	avesti	avessi, etc.
essere	fosti	fossi, etc.
dare	desti	dessi, etc.
dire	dicesti	dicessi, etc.
fare	facesti	facessi, etc.
stare	stesti	stessi, etc.

95. Subjunctive in Adverbial Clauses. The subjunctive is used in the following types of adverbial clauses:

1. Purpose: **perchè,** *so that;* **affinchè,** *in order that.*

Scrivemmo affinchè venissero a visitarci. *We wrote so that they would come to visit us.*

2. Time: **prima che,** *before* (also **finchè,** *until,* but only when referring to future time).

Uscirono prima che li vedessi. *They went out before I saw them.*

3. Concession: **benchè,** or **sebbene,** *although;* **con tutto che,** *although;* **per quanto,** *no matter how much,* etc.

Benchè fossero soltanto copie, erano belle. *Although they were only copies, they were beautiful.*

4. Condition: **purchè,** *provided that;* **dato che,** *since;* **a meno che . . . non,** *unless;* **se mai, se pure,** *even if;* **a condizione che,** *on condition that,* etc.

L'accompagnerò purchè sia bella. *I'll accompany her provided she is beautiful.*

5. Negation: **senza che** or **che . . . non,** *without.*

Non passa un mese senza che venga a visitarmi. *Not a month goes by without his coming to visit me.*

96. Optative Subjunctive. The present subjunctive is used in an independent clause to express a wish possible of fulfillment or a curse.

> Dio ti salvi ! *May God save you!*
> Maledetto sia quel giorno ! *Cursed be that day!*

The imperfect subjunctive in an independent clause denotes an action which one wishes were complete, regardless of whether it is possible or not.

Non la vedessi mai più ! *I wish that I would never see her again.*

97. Formation of Adverbs. Many adverbs may be derived from the adjectives by adding **–mente** to the feminine form.

solo, *alone*	sola (*f.*)	solamente, *only*
vivo, *lively*	viva (*f.*)	vivamente, *in a lively fashion*

Adjectives ending in **–le** or **–re** generally drop the final vowel before adding **–mente.**

> difficile (*m.* or *f.*)   difficilmente

98. Table of Relative Pronouns

INVARIABLE	**che,** who, whom, which, that **cui,** whom, which **chi,** he who, she who, the one who, him who
VARIABLE	**il quale, la quale, i quali, le quali,** who, whom, which, that **il cui, la cui, i cui, le cui,** whose **colui che,** he who, the one who; **colei che,** she who, the one who; **coloro che,** they who, those who; **ciò che,** that which, what

99. Use of the Relative Pronouns. You learned in Lesson 9 that **che** is the most common relative pronoun, used everywhere except after a preposition, where **cui** is used instead. Let us summarize all the relative pronouns here.

1. **Che** refers to both persons and things and may be used as the subject or direct object of a verb, but it is not used after prepositions. The relative pronoun may *not* be omitted in Italian, as it is frequently in English.

L'arte che studiarono . . . *The art (which) they studied . . .*

2. **Cui** may be used for persons or things in the singular or in the plural, but only after prepositions.

La giovane con cui parlava . . . *The girl with whom he spoke . . .*

3. **Cui** preceded by the article shows possession and corresponds to the English *whose*. The article agrees with the thing possessed.

La scuola i cui alunni . . . *The school whose students . . .*

4. **Il quale** in the appropriate form may be used as subject, direct object, or object of a preposition. It is used primarily for clearness or emphasis, especially when the relative pronoun does not come immediately after the antecedent. It agrees in gender and number with the antecedent.

Vidi il cugino di mia madre, il quale non vedevo da molti anni. *I saw mother's cousin, whom I had not seen for a long time.*

5. **Chi** as a relative pronoun can be used only in the singular. It contains its own antecedent and corresponds to **colui che** or **colei che.**

Chi ama l'arte ama i musei. *He who loves art loves museums.*

6. **Colui che, colei che,** and **coloro che** refer to persons only.

Coloro che vennero erano studenti. *Those who came were students.*

7. **Ciò che** refers only to things or ideas.

Ciò che fa, lo fa per sè. *What he does, he does for himself.*

LANGUAGE PRACTICE

Si legga senza tradurre:

Torino

Torino è il capoluogo [1] e la città più importante del Piemonte. Fu la prima capitale d'Italia nel 1861. Ha strade regolari, con palazzi moderni. La città è caratteristica per [2] i suoi portici.[3] In un giorno di pioggia [4] si può camminare per lunghi tratti [5] senza bagnarsi.[6] Torino è famosa per
5 la Mole Antonelliana,[7] per il suo meraviglioso palazzo reale,[8] e per il suo museo d'antichità,[9] che è uno dei migliori del mondo. In questo museo si trovano tombe egiziane,[10] statue importantissime dei primi secoli delle dinastie dell'Egitto e famosi papiri che conservano i ricordi di quella civiltà.
10 Torino conserva [11] molti ricordi della famiglia reale di Savoia, famiglia che governò l'Italia dal 1861 fino alla seconda guerra mondiale.[12] La città è famosa per le sue industrie automobilistiche e meccaniche. Infatti Torino è la sede della FIAT (Fabbrica [13] Italiana Automobili Torino). Torino è famosa soprattutto per i suoi bei negozi, dove si trovano le ultime
15 novità [14] della moda femminile.

Si risponda senza tradurre:

1. Perchè è importante la città di Torino nella storia d'Italia?
2. Qual è la caratteristica di Torino? 3. C'è un museo importantissimo a Torino? 4. Per quale ragione è così importante questo museo?
5. Ci sono industrie a Torino? 6. Ci sono bei negozi a Torino?

ESERCIZI

1. Si dia la forma adatta del verbo dato all'infinito e si traduca (Supply the correct form of the verb given in the infinitive and translate):

1. Benchè (essere) pochi, volevano fare la gita. 2. Li vedemmo prima che (partire). 3. Gli parlarono affinchè li (lasciare) andare. 4. Basta che non (fare) troppo chiasso, può venire anche lui. 5. Con tutto che (essere) tutti amici, nessuno voleva essere il primo. 6. Benchè il gruppo vi (andare) ogni anno, sembrava sempre una cosa nuova. 7. Partimmo tutti in autobus,

---

[1] capital (of a region). [2] on account of. [3] porticos. [4] rainy day.
[5] stretches. [6] getting wet. [7] the highest building in Italy. [8] royal palace.
[9] antiquities. [10] Egyptian tombs. [11] preserves. [12] Second World War.
[13] factory. [14] novelties.

senza che nessuno vi (mancare). 8. Ci lasciò andare a
condizione che (tornare) tutti alle dodici. 9. Benchè
(essere) pochi, si divertirono molto. 10. Non voleva
che noi (disturbare) le classi accanto. 11. È possibile
che lei (venire) a trovarci. 12. È impossibile che loro
non lo (sapere).

II. Si dia la forma adatta del pronome relativo e si completi la
proposizione (Supply the correct form of the relative pronoun
and complete the sentence):

1. Gli amici (with whom) conversiamo... 2. Il
professore (with whom) studio l'arte... 3. Il fratello
della ragazza (of whom) parlavamo... 4. Le classi
(which) non volevamo disturbare... 5. Il chiasso
(which) fanno gli alunni... 6. La scuola (to which)
andiamo... 7. L'autobus (in which) viaggiarono...
8. La bellezza dei quadri (which) videro... 9. I
nomi degli artisti (whom) conosco... 10. La giovane (whose) bellezza ammirava... 11. Il professore
(whose) classe andò al museo... 12. Ci sono cinquanta alunni (of whom) trenta...

III. Si traduca oralmente:

1. It was we. 2. It is they. 3. It is he. 4. It is
she. 5. We saw him. 6. She called me. 7. I called
her. 8. He wants them. 9. You want us. 10. We
leave them. 11. I tell him. 12. You tell her. 13. Will
you find them? 14. Will he find you? 15. I admire
them. 16. He admires us. 17. They took it. 18. She
did not take it. 19. He sent to them. 20. We sent
to her.

IV. (*Optional*) Three students, A, B, and C, tell about a trip
to the museum.

A wants to know who went on the trip.
B tells who went there and tells about the museum.
C describes some of the things which they saw.

The conversation continues in this fashion with simple questions and answers.

V. Si traduca in italiano:

1. Although they were all good students, they wanted to talk all the time (*sempre*). 2. The teacher let us do as we wished, but he did not like it that we made so much noise. 3. I would like to go to the museum and see the beautiful paintings. 4. The students yawned, but the teacher kept on as if they were all listening. 5. Although he told us about his visits to the great museums, we did not find the subject interesting. 6. He wanted them to ask questions about the great artists and Italian art. 7. There was no one who knew all the paintings of which he spoke. 8. We want to live in the present and not in the past. 9. The paintings seemed extremely beautiful to us and we admired them a great deal. 10. We understand now that he was right and some day we shall get to appreciate art.

WORD LIST

NOUNS

accordo *m.* agreement
alunno *m.* pupil
bellezza *f.* beauty
chiasso *m.* noise
collezione *f.* collection
conversazione *f.* conversation
corso *m.* course, class
domanda *f.* question
futuro *m.* future
gruppo *m.* group
nome *m.* name
Palazzo Pitti *one of the most important museums in Florence*
presente *m.* present
Rinascimento *m.* Renaissance
speranza *f.* hope
Stati Uniti *m. pl.* United States
Uffizi *the largest museum in Florence*
voglia *f.* desire

ADJECTIVES

affezionato, –a devoted
grato, –a grateful
ignorante ignorant
nazionale national
sconosciuto, –a unknown

VERBS

apprezzare to appreciate
comprendere to understand
conversare to converse, talk
disperare to despair
disturbare to disturb
lasciare to leave, let
sbadigliare to yawn
seguitare to continue

OTHER WORDS

benchè although
da from, as to

CURRENT USAGE

Lettera a una compagna di scuola

Napoli, 4 agosto, 1957

Carissima Lucia,

eccoci finalmente nella città dei tuoi genitori. Arrivammo
da Roma quattro giorni fa. Mi ero promessa di scriverti il
giorno dell'arrivo a Napoli, ma è passato così presto il 5
tempo! Stasera ho deciso di non andare a letto se prima
non avrò finito la tua lettera. Sono sicura che tu avresti
fatto lo stesso.

La città di Napoli è più incantevole di quanto immaginassi. Per noi che siamo abituati ai colori grigi delle nostre 10
città americane, questo panorama italiano è fantastico.
Soltanto quando avrai fatto anche tu il viaggio potrai
comprendere la bellezza di questo paese.

Ieri l'altro andammo al porto a ricevere gli amici Speroni,
che arrivavano sul *Giulio Cesare*. Sul molo c'era una 15
grande confusione e non si poteva trovare nessuno. Sapendo
che dovevano sempre passar la dogana, andammo ad
aspettarli lì, e ci incontrammo senza nessuna difficoltà. Ci
dissero che allo scendere dal piroscafo non ci avevano visti
e perciò avevano chiamato un facchino ed erano andati in 20
dogana a prendere le valige.

Anche loro erano rimasti a bocca aperta della meraviglia
nel vedere il golfo di Napoli. Proprio non trovavano le
parole per esprimere la loro gioia. Mentre il piroscafo approdava avevano ammirato il Vesuvio, le isole di Capri e 25

151

d'Ischia, le belle città di Sorrento e di Castellammare di
Stabia, e la bellissima Napoli. Era un incanto che non si
vede nemmeno nelle pellicole di Hollywood.

    Siamo tutti nello stesso albergo. Che veduta ideale che si
5 gode di qui in Via Caracciolo, col panorama di Posillipo e
la baia di Santa Lucia! Quando facciamo colazione sulla
terrazza ci sembra che la natura abbia fatto qui il suo
capolavoro.

    Ma adesso mi sento stanca; ti scriverò più a lungo fra
10 poco. Ho incontrato un giovane alto e biondo che mi fa
da guida e domattina non lo voglio far aspettare. Tanti
affettuosi saluti a tutti.

La tua aff.ma

Beatrice

Useful Expressions

il giorno dell'arrivo on the day of arrival
di quanto immaginassi than I imagined
quando avrai fatto il viaggio when you take the trip
passar la dogana to go through customs
allo scendere on coming down, when they got off
erano andati in dogana they had gone to the customhouse
a bocca aperta gaping, with mouths wide open
ti scriverò più a lungo I'll write you a longer letter
fra poco soon
mi fa da guida acts as my guide

Questions. 1. Beatrice che cosa si era promessa? 2. Quando
andrà a letto? 3. È incantevole il golfo di Napoli? 4. Lucia
quando potrà comprendere la bellezza del paese? 5. Chi arrivava
sul Giulio Cesare? 6. Dove andammo ad aspettarli? 7. Che
cosa avevano fatto allo scendere dal piroscafo? 8. Che cosa
avevano ammirato mentre il piroscafo approdava? 9. Dove si
trova l'albergo? 10. Quale impressione abbiamo quando facciamo colazione sulla terrazza? 11. Beatrice chi ha incontrato?
12. Quando scriverà più a lungo?

STRUCTURE

    100. Compound Tenses of the Indicative. In Lesson 6
you learned the present perfect, which is formed by the present

What a grand city Pompeii must have been if it retains so much beauty in ruins.

of the auxiliary and the past participle of the verb to be conjugated. The present perfect is one of the various compound tenses
of the indicative. Every simple tense can be joined with a past
participle to form a compound tense. The imperfect indicative,
followed by a past participle, forms the first pluperfect. The
past definite, followed by the past participle, forms the second
pluperfect. The future, followed by a past participle, forms the
future perfect. And the conditional, followed by a past participle,
forms the conditional perfect.

Following are the compound tenses of the indicative of regular
verbs conjugated with **avere:**

PRESENT PERFECT		FIRST PLUPERFECT		SECOND PLUPERFECT	
hɔ		avevo		ɛbbi	
hai		avevi		avesti	
ha	parlato	aveva	parlato	ɛbbe	parlato
abbiamo	venduto	avevamo	venduto	avemmo	venduto
avete	finito	avevate	finito	aveste	finito
hanno		avevano		ɛbbero	

FUTURE PERFECT		CONDITIONAL PERFECT	
avrɔ́		avrɛi	
avrai		avresti	
avrà	parlato	avrɛbbe	parlato
avremo	venduto	avremmo	venduto
avrete	finito	avreste	finito
avranno		avrɛbbero	

Following are the compound tenses of the indicative of verbs
conjugated with **ɛssere:**

PRESENT PERFECT		FIRST PLUPERFECT		SECOND PLUPERFECT	
sono	andato (a)	ɛro	andato (a)	fui	andato (a)
sɛi	caduto (a)	ɛri	caduto (a)	fosti	caduto (a)
è	partito (a)	ɛra	partito (a)	fu	partito (a)
siamo	andati (e)	eravamo	andati (e)	fummo	andati (e)
siɛte	caduti (e)	eravate	caduti (e)	foste	caduti (e)
sono	partiti (e)	ɛrano	partiti (e)	furono	partiti (e)

FUTURE PERFECT		CONDITIONAL PERFECT	
sarò	andato (a)	sarɛi	andato (a)
sarai	caduto (a)	saresti	caduto (a)
sarà	partito (a)	sarɛbbe	partito (a)
saremo	andati (e)	saremmo	andati (e)
sarete	caduti (e)	sareste	caduti (e)
saranno	partiti (e)	sarɛbbero	partiti (e)

101. Auxiliary with Reflexive Verbs. When a verb becomes reflexive it is conjugated with ɛssere.

Aveva promesso di venire prɛsto. *He had promised to come soon.*
Mi ɛro promessa di scriverti. *I had promised myself to write to you.*

102. Uses of the Compound Tenses of the Indicative. The compound tenses correspond, in general, to their equivalent tenses in English. Notice the meanings for the verb **parlare:**

PRES. PERF.	hɔ parlato	I *have spoken*
FIRST PLUP.	avevo parlato	I *had spoken*
SECOND PLUP.	ɛbbi parlato	I *had spoken*
FUTURE PERF.	avrɔ parlato	I *shall have spoken*
COND. PERF.	avrɛi parlato	I *should (would) have spoken*

The only difficulty comes between the first and second pluperfect. Remember that the second pluperfect is used only after conjunctions of time such as: **quando,** *when;* **appena che** or **tɔsto che,** *as soon as;* **dopo che,** *after.*

Quando tutto fu terminato... *When everything was over...*

103. *Sapere* and *conoscere*. There are two verbs which mean *to know:*

1. **Sapere** means to know a fact, to know something through acquired knowledge.

Sappiamo che gli piace Napoli. *We know he likes Naples.*

2. **Conoscere** means to know people, to be acquainted with people, or to know things through natural instinct.

Conosce la mia amica Rosina? *Do you know my friend Rose?*
Conosce bɛne quel paese. *He knows that country well.*

3. **Sapere,** when followed by an infinitive, means *to know how to.*

Sa suonare il pianoforte. *He knows how to play the piano.*

LANGUAGE PRACTICE

Si legga senza tradurre:

Il Boccaccio

Il Boccaccio fu il vero iniziatore [1] della prosa italiana. Nacque a Parigi di padre italiano e madre francese, ma fu portato presto in Italia e ivi [2] passò la maggior parte della sua vita. Scrisse molti libri in latino e in italiano. Era uomo molto colto [3] ed erudito,[4] come si vede soprattutto
5 nelle opere latine. Fu grande ammiratore di Dante; ci ha lasciato non soltanto una delle più importanti biografie del Poeta, ma anche uno dei migliori commenti sui primi diciassette canti dell'Inferno. La sua opera [5] più conosciuta è il *Decameron*, una raccolta [6] di cento novelle che non è mai stata sorpassata [7] in qualsiasi lingua. Il Boccaccio fu lo scrittore che
10 portò a perfezione l'arte di raccontare novelle per puro diletto.[8] Ebbe imitatori in tutte le lingue principali d'Europa, specialmente in inglese e in francese. Anche ora, dopo sei secoli, le sue novelle servono di ispirazione ai grandi novellieri dei nostri giorni.

Si risponda senza tradurre:

1. Chi fu il vero iniziatore della prosa italiana? 2. Dove passò la maggior parte della sua vita il Boccaccio? 3. Come sappiamo che fu grande ammiratore di Dante? 4. Che cosa è il *Decameron*? 5. Che arte portò a perfezione il Boccaccio? 6. Ci sono stati molti imitatori del Boccaccio?

ESERCIZI

I. Si traduca in italiano e si facciano proposizioni complete (Translate into Italian and use in complete sentences):

1. We had arrived. 2. After we had arrived. 3. He had promised. 4. When he had promised. 5. We have promised ourselves. 6. He will not have finished.

---

[1] initiator.　[2] there.　[3] cultured.　[4] learned.　[5] work.　[6] collection.
[7] surpassed.　[8] pleasure, delight.

7. He would have finished. 8. You will have made.
9. They had called. 10. I had put them (*f.*).

II. Si facciano proposizioni complete coi seguenti gruppi di parole (Form original sentences containing the following groups of words):

1. giovane, aspettare, domattina. 2. scrivere, lungo, fra poco. 3. sentirsi, stanco, dormire. 4. colazione, terrazza, incantevole. 5. prendere, valige, albergo. 6. facchino, dogana, andare. 7. piroscafo, approdare, ammirare. 8. bocca, meraviglia, golfo. 9. comprendere, bellezza, paese. 10. panorama, fantastico, Italia. 11. colori, grigi, città. 12. sicuro, fare, lo stesso.

III. Si dia un pronome o una particella pronominale al posto delle parole in corsivo (Substitute an object pronoun or a particle for the italicized words):

1. Arrivammo *a Roma* due giorni fa. 2. Avevo promesso molte cose *a Lucia*. 3. Quando avremo finito *la lettera*, spediremo *la lettera*. 4. Siamo abituati *ai colori grigi*. 5. Potrà comprendere *la difficoltà*. 6. Fecero approdare *il piroscafo*. 7. Conoscono bene *il paese*. 8. Lei sa *la lezione?* 9. Conoscete *i facchini?* 10. Andammo a prendere *le valige* in dogana. 11. Aveva insegnato l'italiano *ai ragazzi*. 12. Hanno preso *un tassì* e sono andati *all'albergo*. 13. Scriverai *a tuo fratello* quando arriverai? 14. Hanno lasciato *Antonio* a bocca aperta. 15. Quando chiuderà *la bocca?*

IV. One student asks another a question in Italian about his arrival in Naples. The second student answers that question and asks a third student another question on the hotel. Go around the class in this fashion until each student has asked and answered at least one question.

V. Si traduca in italiano:

1. The time has gone by so fast that I have not had time to write the letter which I had promised you. 2. Do you think I can go to bed without first finishing that letter? 3. Since they are accustomed to the gray

colors of their city, they find the view really enchanting.
4. While the ship was docking we could enjoy the gulf
of Naples. 5. We had not seen islands like these even
in Hollywood films. 6. As they came (*translate* On
coming) down from the ship they could not find a porter
and they had to wait. 7. Who had taken the bags and
carried them from the ship? 8. What an ideal view
from the terrace, especially when breakfast is ready
and the coffee is hot! 9. Will you write although you
are tired or will you rest before you write? 10. She
had met a tall, blond young man and she did not
want to keep him waiting.

WORD LIST

NOUNS

arrivo *m.* arrival
baia *f.* bay
Beatrice Beatrice
bocca *f.* mouth
confusione *f.* confusion
difficoltà *f.* difficulty
dogana *f.* customhouse
facchino *m.* porter
gioia *f.* joy
golfo *m.* bay, gulf
guida *f.* guide
incanto *m.* enchantment
letto *m.* bed
meraviglia *f.* amazement
molo *m.* wharf
panorama *m.* view, panorama
piroscafo *m.* ship, ocean liner
porto *m.* harbor
terrazza *f.* terrace
valigia *f.* bag, suitcase

ADJECTIVES

affettuoso, –a affectionate
aff.ma = affezionatissima
most affectionate
biondo, –a blond
carissimo, –a dearest
fantastico, –a fantastic
grigio, –a gray
sicuro, –a sure
stanco, –a tired

VERBS

approdare to dock
esprimere to express
godere to enjoy
immaginare to imagine
incontrare to meet
promettere (*p.p.* **promesso**) to promise
scendere to come down (takes **essere**)
sentirsi to feel

OTHER WORDS

domattina tomorrow morning
ieri l'altro the day before yesterday

CURRENT USAGE

Una passeggiata

L'altro giorno volli fare una passeggiata prima di colazione. Era una bellissima giornata di primavera, che faceva venir la voglia di uscire all'aria aperta. Mio fratello mi domandò a che ora sarei tornato; gli risposi che tornavo fra una mezz'oretta. Mi chiese di comprargli delle sigarette ₅ dal tabaccaio.

Poco lontano da casa incontrai l'amico Giannini, che usciva anche lui, e decidemmo di fare due passi insieme. Giannini è un bravo meccanico che lavora in un'autorimessa in Piazza Cavour. Mi domandò se volessi accompagnarlo ₁₀ alla mostra industriale che si teneva poco lontano dalla sua casa. Vi andammo insieme per vedere gli ultimi modelli della meccanica.

C'erano delle belle FIAT di varie grandezze, dalla piccola seicento alle macchine di gran lusso. A me piacque soprat- ₁₅ tutto la mille e cento, nella quale possono viaggiare comodamente quattro persone. C'erano delle Lancia e delle bellissime Alfa Romeo, rinomate automobili da corsa.

Inoltre vedemmo gli ultimi apparecchi di radio e di televisione. Oramai la radio si trova in quasi ogni casa, e la ₂₀ televisione comincia a diffondersi. È curioso trovare gli ultimi apparecchi in case che datano dal medioevo, ma l'Italia non è più la nazione del passato; dopo le guerre è diventata la nazione del futuro.

159

Passai un paio d'ore passeggiando con l'amico. Quando
finalmente guardammo l'orologio erano già passate le dodici
e mezzo. Dovemmo salutarci in fretta e prendere ognuno
la sua strada. Quando giunsi a casa trovai alcuni amici
5 che mi aspettavano da parecchio tempo. Feci le mie scuse
e mi misi a conversare con loro delle solite cose che si dicono
sempre e che non interessano mai.

Useful Expressions

faceva venir la voglia made one feel like
all'aria aperta in the open air
una mezz'oretta about half an hour
poco lontano not far
fare due passi to take a stroll
la seicento the smallest FIAT model
la mille e cento the small FIAT sedan
macchina di gran lusso *f.* very luxurious model
automobile da corsa *f.* racing car
comincia a diffondersi is beginning to become popular
in fretta hurriedly
prendere la sua strada to go one's way
feci le mie scuse I made my apologies
mi misi a conversare I started to talk

Questions. 1. Che cosa volle fare Lei l'altro giorno prima di
colazione? 2. Che voglia faceva venire la giornata di primavera?
3. Cosa le chiese Suo fratello? 4. Chi incontrò poco lontano da
casa? 5. Sa che cosa è una mostra industriale? 6. Ha mai
visto una mille e cento? 7. Si trova in molte case la radio in
Italia adesso? 8. L'Italia è sempre la nazione del passato?
9. Che ora era quando guardammo l'orologio? 10. Che fece Lei
quando trovò gli amici in casa?

STRUCTURE

104. Irregular Verbs: Past Definite. All verbs (except
essere) which are irregular in the past definite may be formed
from the 1st and 2nd persons singular of this tense as follows:

1. Take the 1st person singular, drop the **-i,** and add **-e** for
the 3rd person singular and **-ero** for the 3rd person plural.

venn**i,** venn**e,** venn**ero**

2. Take the 2nd person singular, drop the –**sti**, and add –**mmo** for the 1st person plural and –**ste** for the 2nd person plural.

veni**sti**, veni**mmo**, veni**ste**

Notice how this formula works with some of the common verbs and notice the forms of ɛssere:

dire	dissi, dicesti, disse, dicemmo, diceste, dissero
fare	feci, facesti, fece, facemmo, faceste, fecero
scrivere	scrissi, scrivesti, scrisse, scrivemmo, scriveste, scrissero
ɛssere	fui, fosti, fu, fummo, foste, furono

You can now derive the past definite of all the following common irregular verbs, and learn their irregular past participles at the same time. The verbs with an asterisk (*) are conjugated with ɛssere.

INFINITIVE	PAST DEFINITE	PAST PARTICIPLE
bere, *to drink*	bevvi, bevesti, etc.	bevuto
cadere, *to fall*	caddi, cadesti, etc.	*caduto
chiɛdere, *to ask*	chiɛsi, chiedesti, etc.	chiɛsto
chiudere, *to close*	chiusi, chiudesti, etc.	chiuso
conoscere, *to know*	conobbi, conoscesti, etc.	conosciuto
correre, *to run*	corsi, corresti, etc.	*corso (also with **avere**)
dare, *to give*	diɛdi, desti, etc.	dato
decidere, *to decide*	deçisi, decidesti, etc.	deciso
giungere, *to reach*	giunsi, giungesti, etc.	*giunto
lɛggere, *to read*	lessi, leggesti, etc.	lɛtto
mettere, *to put*	misi, mettesti, etc.	messo
porre, *to put*	posi, ponesti, etc.	posto
prɛndere, *to take*	presi, prendesti, etc.	preso
rimanere, *to remain*	rimasi, rimanesti, etc.	*rimasto
rispondere, *to answer*	risposi, rispondesti, etc.	risposto
sapere, *to know*	sɛppi, sapesti, etc.	saputo
scendere, *to go down*	scesi, scendesti, etc.	*sceso
stare, *to be, stay*	stɛtti, stesti, etc.	*stato
tradurre, *to translate*	tradussi, traducesti, etc.	tradotto
vedere, *to see*	vidi, vedesti, etc.	visto
volere, *to want*	vɔlli, volesti, etc.	voluto

105. Distinction between Present Perfect, Past Definite, and Imperfect. All three of these tenses express an action which took place in past time, and frequently all three are translated the same way in English. However, they are not interchangeable in Italian because each tense expresses a specific shade of meaning.

The present perfect expresses an action or event which has taken place recently in the past and is connected mentally with the present by the speaker. If the speaker refers to events of the same day or specifically qualifies the period of time by the word *this* (*this week, this month*), the tense to be used is the present perfect.

Ha visto la mostra industriale?   *Have you seen the industrial show (recently)?*

The past definite expresses an action which took place at a definite time in the past and is now completely over. It is used to express historical events. With verbs implying mental action, the past definite signifies that a decision was made.

L'altro giorno volli fare una passeggiata.   *The other day I decided to take a walk.*

The imperfect expresses a continued, customary, or repeated action in the past. If a certain action was continued and the end of the action is not implied, the imperfect is used.

Gli amici mi aspettavano.   *The friends were waiting for me.*

If an action took place repeatedly in the past as a matter of custom, the verb is in the imperfect.

Uscivamo con loro.   *We used to go out with them.*

If a verb implies a state of mind in the past, the imperfect tense is used.

Voleva accompagnarci.   *He wanted to accompany us.*

If an action in the past comes to interrupt another action which was going on, the former is in the past definite and the latter in the imperfect.

Incontrai l'amico Giannini, che usciva anche lui.   *I met my friend Giannini, who was going out, too.*

106. Uses of the Gerund. What is commonly referred to as
a present participle is grammatically a gerund. The form ends in
–ndo, is invariable, and may be used either in the present or in
the past.

	I	II	III
PRESENT	parlando, *speaking*	vendɛndo, *selling*	finɛndo, *finishing*
PAST	avɛndo parlato, *having spoken*	avɛndo venduto, *having sold*	avɛndo finito, *having finished*

If a verb is conjugated with **ɛssere** the gerund is **essɛndo** and the
past participle agrees with the subject, as for example, **essɛndo
arrivata, essɛndo partiti,** etc.

1. The gerund is frequently used to express the manner in
which an action is done.

Studiando s'impɑrano molte cɔse. *By studying one learns many
things.*

2. The gerund, being a verb, may take an object.

Vedɛndolo, lo comprai subito. *When I saw it, I bought it immediately.*

3. The gerund, used with the verb **stare,** expresses an action
in progress.

Stavamo conversando quando arrivɔ. *We were conversing when
he arrived.*

LANGUAGE PRACTICE

Si lɛgga senza tradurre:

Galilɛo Galilɛi

Galilɛo Galilɛi fu uno dei maggiori scienziati del mondo. Ɛra sommo
matemɑtico,[1] fisico,[2] astrɔnomo, e filɔsofo. Scoprì,[3] fra molte altre cɔse,
la legge del pɛndolo,[4] che è pɔi divenuta così importante nella fisica
modɛrna.

[1] mathematician. [2] physicist. [3] He discovered. [4] pendulum.

The Leaning Tower of Pisa reminds us primarily of Galileo's scientific discoveries. Yet the Tower is quite beautiful, even though it tips a bit.

Si racconta che una volta alcuni operai [1] che lavoravano a una fontana vennero a chiedergli consiglio. Il problema consisteva nel fatto che non potevano far salire [2] l'acqua in un tubo al di sopra di [3] una certa altezza.[4]

— Eppure — dicevano — la natura aborre dal vuoto.[5]

— Sì — disse il grande scienziato, — ma aborre dal vuoto soltanto fino all'altezza di trentatrè metri.* 5

L'allievo [6] Torricelli continuò gli studi sulla pressione atmosferica [7] e arrivò all'invenzione del barometro.

Si risponda senza tradurre:

1. Che legge scoprì Galileo Galilei? 2. A che cosa lavoravano alcuni operai? 3. Che vuol dire che la natura aborre dal vuoto? 4. Quali studi continuò l'allievo Torricelli? 5. È importante la legge del pendolo?

ESERCIZI

I. Si dia la forma adatta del passato remoto dei verbi fra parentesi (Supply the correct form of the past definite of the verbs in parentheses):

1. Egli (volere, rispondere, fare, decidere).
2. Noi (dire, stare, chiedere, vedere).
3. Essi (sapere, leggere, prendere, rimanere).
4. Io (scrivere, volere, conoscere, divenire).
5. Tu (bere, cadere, chiudere, porre).

II. Si adopri il passato prossimo, imperfetto, o passato remoto, secondo il significato (Use the present perfect, imperfect, or past definite, according to the sense):

1. (We wanted to) fare una passeggiata, ma (we did not have) il tempo. 2. (They went out) stamattina e (they wanted to) visitare un museo. 3. (I asked him) perchè (he could not) venire a fare due passi. 4. (She has gone) via perchè non le piace quel che Lei (have said). 5. Chi (has seen) la mostra industriale che (was) nella nostra città? 6. L'altro giorno (they stopped) a vedere le automobili ed ora (they have al-

---

[1] workmen. [2] raise. [3] above. [4] height. [5] abhors a vacuum. [6] pupil. [7] atmospheric pressure.

* Whoever made up this story forgot that the meter did not come into being until a century and a half after Galileo's death.

ready bought) la loro nuɔva macchina. 7. (We saw) gli *u*ltimi apparecchi di televisione e ne (bought) uno. 8. (I could not) paragonare le automɔbili perchè (there was) soltanto una. 9. Quando (he arrived) tutti lo (were waiting). 10. Ne (they remained) contɛnti e (they accepted) l'invito.

III. Si traduca oralmente:

1. While buying. 2. By taking. 3. Having waited. 4. Having arrived. 5. By accepting them. 6. By asking. 7. Upon meeting her. 8. While going out from the house. 9. Having remained. 10. Having decided.

11. They told him. 12. She asked us. 13. We asked her. 14. You spoke to me. 15. You invited him. 16. You (*fam. pl.*) saw them. 17. Will you accept it? 18. Will they take them? 19. I answered her. 20. He answered them.

IV. One student invites another to go for a walk. They discuss the places they want to visit and what they want to do. Both students are interested in cars, television, radio, and similar subjects and they bring them into the conversation.

V. Si traduca in italiano:

1. He wanted me to take a walk with him before dinner, but I was too tired. 2. Not far from the school they met the professor and they took a walk together. 3. If you are not well, why don't you go home instead of going to the exhibition? 4. Shall we go there together and see the latest models? 5. She stopped to see the new hats because she wanted to compare them with those of last year. 6. Television is new and many still think that it is not worth while to buy a set. 7. Look at your watch and tell me what time it is, please. 8. When it is late we do not stop to talk with our friends. 9. She had been waiting for him for some time when he finally arrived. 10. We began to converse with them about the usual things, but they do not interest me.

WORD LIST

NOUNS

Alfa Romeo *make of car*
apparecchio *m.* set
autorimessa *f.* garage
corsa *f.* race
grandezza *f.* size
Lancia *make of car*
macchina *f.* car
meccanica *f.* mechanics
meccanico *m.* mechanic
medioevo *m.* Middle Ages
mostra *f.* show, exhibition
orologio *m.* watch, clock
passeggiata *f.* walk, stroll
passo *m.* step
scusa *f.* excuse, apology
sigaretta *f.* cigarette
tabaccaio *m.* tobacco vendor, tobacco store

ADJECTIVES

curioso, –a curious
industriale industrial
solito, –a usual

VERBS

aspettare to wait for
datare (da) to date back to
diffondersi to become popular
diventare to become (takes essere)
domandare to ask
giungere to reach, arrive at (takes essere)
salutarsi to say good-by; greet
tornare to get back (takes essere)
viaggiare to travel

OTHER WORDS

comodamente comfortably
inoltre moreover
ognuno each one
oramai now, nowadays

CURRENT USAGE

Nella pensione

In una pensione di famiglia si sta bene e si spende meno che in un albergo. Parecchi anni fa la pensione accettava

soltanto ospiti che stessero a mese, o almeno a settimane intere, ma adesso li accettano anche per un giorno solo. In pensione non solo si dorme, ma si prendono tutti i pasti del giorno; mentre in un albergo generalmente si va soltanto
5 per dormire.

Quando ero in pensione facevo una bella vita. Appena sveglio chiamavo la cameriera e mi facevo portare il caffè e latte. A casa mia posso chiamare quanto voglio, chè nessuno me lo porta. Avrei preferito una buona colazione con
10 spremuta d'arancia e due uova fritte, ma in Italia bisogna contentarsi di panini con burro.

C'erano in pensione due altri Americani che erano venuti a studiare in Italia. Appena vestiti ci riunivamo in salotto per fare i piani per la giornata. Andavamo a visitare le
15 chiese, i musei, ed i quartieri storici della città. Non ci mancava mai qualche cosa da fare. Verso la mezza tornavamo alla pensione.

Facevamo colazione all'una, o alle tredici, come si dice ora in Italia. Ce la servivano nella sala da pranzo, dove
20 tutti ci riunivamo per scambiare le notizie del giorno o le impressioni della città. Gl'Italiani che abitavano in pensione preferivano discorrere dei fatti del giorno, mentre noi turisti parlavamo di capolavori d'arte o delle compre che avevamo fatte. Queste conversazioni erano la parte più
25 interessante della nostra giornata. Verso le due e mezzo o le tre andavamo tutti a fare un sonnellino, secondo l'usanza del paese. È bello riposare un poco dopo il pranzo e fa bene alla salute. Verso le quattro si andava di nuovo a visitare qualche museo o qualche chiesa, o a fare delle compre.
30 Si tornava alla pensione verso le sette (o le diciannove), pronti per la cena, che non si faceva prima delle otto. Dopo la cena facevamo un giro in piazza, dove ci fermavamo a prendere un caffè e a sentire la musica. Era bella la vita in pensione, senza pensieri e senza lavoro. Peccato che durasse
35 soltanto per le vacanze.

*Country life and city life: A woman washing in any one of a
host of little towns, and people walking in the streets of Livorno.*

Useful Expressions

a mese by the month
facevo una bɛlla vita I led a nice life
caffɛ e latte coffee with milk
quanto vɔglio all I want
spremuta d'arancia orange juice
qualche cɔsa da fare something to do
fatti del giorno happenings of the day, events of the day
fare un sonnellino to take a nap
fa bɛne alla salute it's good for the health
far delle compre to go shopping
far un giro to take a walk around

Questions. 1. Come si sta in una pensione? 2. In una pensione accɛttano ɔspiti per pɔchi giorni? 3. Quando chiedeva il caffɛ e latte, chi glielo portava? 4. Cɔsa preferisce Lɛi per la colazione? 5. C'ɛrano altri Americani in pensione? 6. Quali ɛrano i piani per la giornata? 7. A che ora si faceva colazione? 8. Dove gliela servivano? 9. Di che cɔsa parlavano gl'Italiani? 10. Di che cɔsa parlavano i turisti? 11. Qual è l'usanza dopo il pranzo? 12. Che cɔsa si faceva dopo cena?

STRUCTURE

107. Double Object Pronouns (Cont.). As you learned in Lesson 12, when two object pronouns depend on the same verb, the indirect always comes before the direct and they are both placed where one pronoun object would be placed.

Subito me lo pɔrta. *She brings it to me immediately.*

1. Before another object pronoun **mi, ti, ci, vi, si** change the **i** to **e** and become **me, te, ce, ve, se.**

Ce la servivano nella sala da pranzo. *They used to serve it to us in the dining room.*

2. **Gli** and **le** (indirect objects) both become **glie** before another pronoun and the two pronouns are generally joined.

La camerièra glielo pɔrta lì. *The maid brings it to her there.*

3. The pronoun **loro** generally comes after the verb. If a direct object pronoun comes after the verb together with **loro,** then **loro** is introduced by the preposition **a.**

Lo abbiamo portato loro stamattina. *We took it to them this morning.*

Portalo a loro. *Take it to them.*

108. Definite Article with Possessives. You learned in Lesson 5 that the possessive adjectives or pronouns are generally preceded by the definite article in Italian and that there are some instances where the definite article is not used. It is not used when speaking of a member of the family in the singular and unmodified by an adjective or a suffix. The article, however, is used when the word is in the plural or is modified.

> i miei genitori, *my parents*
> il mio caro fratello, *my dear brother*
> il mio fratellino, *my little brother*

The words **babbo, mamma, nonno, nonna,** and the possessive **loro** retain the definite article.

The article is not used when the possessive comes after **essere** and simply implies possession.

> Questo libro è mio. *This book is mine.*

However, when the possessive is used to distinguish as well as to show possession, the article must be used.

Questo è il mio; non so dove sia il Suo. *This one is mine; I don't know where yours is.*

109. Object Pronouns with *fare* + Infinitive. When an object pronoun depends on a verb which is used as an infinitive complementing **fare,** the pronoun comes before the verb **fare.** Double object pronouns are placed where the single pronoun would go.

> Me lo faccio portare. *I have it brought to me.*

110. Metric System. For weights and measures Italian uses the metric system, which is used for scientific measurements throughout the world. The most common units are:

mɛtro, *meter* = 39.37 inches
chilɔmetro, *kilometer* = 1000 meters ($\frac{5}{8}$ of a mile)
centɨmetro, *centimeter* = $\frac{1}{100}$ of a meter (1 inch = 2.34 centimeters)
grammo, *gram*, unit of small weight
chilogrammo, *kilogram* = 1000 grams ($2\frac{1}{5}$ lbs.)
litro, *liter* = about 1 quart (1.026 quart)

LANGUAGE PRACTICE

Si lɛgga senza tradurre:

La famiglia

In Italia la famiglia è la base della società. Il padre di famiglia è il
direttore e mɛrita ¹ il rispetto di tutti. La madre è direttrice e il cɛntro
di tutto l'amore familiare. È lɛi l'interpetre della volontà ² del padre e
dei desidɛri dei figli. In Italia il comune ³ è un gruppo di famiglie piuttɔsto
5 che un gruppo di individui. Il paese è un gruppo di famiglie più numeroso,
e la città è un gruppo di famiglie che non si conoscono più fra di loro.⁴ In
Italia i legami di famiglia ⁵ non si pɛrdono mai ⁶ e le relazioni familiari
pɔrtano sempre un ɔbbligo.⁷ Nè matrimɔni,⁸ nè impegni,⁹ nè distanze
riɛscono ¹⁰ a rompere i vɨncoli ¹¹ che legano ¹² la famiglia italiana. Questi
10 vɨncoli sɛmbrano eccessivi alle famiglie di altre nazioni, ma in Italia si
riconosce che la famiglia è la base della civiltà.

Si risponda senza tradurre:

1. È importante la famiglia in Italia? 2. Che funzione ha il padre di
famiglia? 3. Sono importanti i figli nel concɛtto della famiglia? 4. Che
relazione ha la città rispɛtto alla famiglia? 5. Sono facili a rɔmpere i
vɨncoli della famiglia italiana? 6. È d'accɔrdo Lɛi con questo concɛtto
della famiglia?

ESERCIZI

I. Substitute the proper conjunctive pronouns for the nouns
in italics or for those given in English. Notice that each sentence
contains two object pronouns.

1. Ha parlato (of it) *a suo padre.* 2. Porteranno *il
caffè alla mamma.* 3. Faccio portare *la cena* (to me).

---

¹ deserves, commands. ² will. ³ commune, community. ⁴ among themselves. ⁵ family ties. ⁶ are never lost. ⁷ obligation. ⁸ marriages. ⁹ obliga-
tions, duties. ¹⁰ succeed. ¹¹ links. ¹² bind.

4. Spedirete *le lettere a Roberto* domattina? 5. Serviranno *la colazione* (to him) in camera. 6. Scambiamo *le notizie* (with them) al pranzo. 7. Scriverai *la lettera* (to them) quando arriverai? 8. Abbiamo dato *le uova* (to you, *fam. pl.*) stamattina. 9. Non posso dire *il fatto ad Alberto* perchè non mi capirebbe. 10. Portate *il pranzo* (to us) subito, per favore!

II. Si traduca, adoprando pronomi personali (Translate, using conjunctive object pronouns):

A. 1. We bring it to you (*pol.*). 2. They send it to us. 3. I shall speak of it to her. 4. She gives it (*m.*) to them. 5. We have brought them to him. 6. They have written it to me. 7. They will bring it to you (*fam.*). 8. I have given it (*f.*) to her. 9. I speak of it to you. 10. She was sending it to him.

B. (*Familiar*) 1. Speak to me; do not speak to him. 2. Give the book to us; do not give it to them. 3. Learn the lesson, boys; learn it well. 4. Understand me well. 5. Speak of it to us tomorrow; do not speak of it to us today.

III. Si traduca oralmente e si facciano proposizioni complete (Translate orally and use in complete original sentences):

1. My sister. 2. His dad. 3. Her grandfather. 4. Our grandmother. 5. Your (*fam.*) mother. 6. Your (*fam.*) mama. 7. Their brothers. 8. Their sister. 9. Their parents. 10. Your (*fam. pl.*) cousin. 11. Your (*fam. pl.*) cousins. 12. Our dear brother. 13. Your dear sister. 14. His young cousin. 15. Her young aunt. 16. His good wife. 17. My sisters. 18. Their dad. 19. Your grandfather. 20. My dear father.

IV. Ask questions using each of the following idioms and have someone else answer the questions:

1. fare un sonnellino. 2. fare un giro. 3. caffè e latte. 4. far delle compre. 5. fra poco tempo. 6. fare da guida. 7. lasciare a bocca aperta. 8. far bene alla salute. 9. valer la pena. 10. in fretta.

V. Si traduca in italiano:

1. If you want to spend less than in a hotel, you should go to a "pensione." 2. We take all our daily meals there and we lead a fine life. 3. I want my breakfast, but I don't know if they will bring it to my room. 4. They will bring it to you because that is the custom. 5. When you are at home no one brings it to you in your room; you go in the kitchen, like everybody else (*tutti gli altri*). 6. Italians prefer to discuss the events of the day, while tourists talk about purchases which they have made. 7. Which is longer, a meter or a yard?[1] Which is larger, a liter or a quart?[1] 8. We all go (*use reflexive*) to take a nap in the afternoon, although we are not sleepy. 9. My grandfather and my grandmother go to bed at about eight o'clock. 10. When we are at the table, we exchange the news of the day during dinner.

WORD LIST

NOUNS

bɛne *m.* good
burro *m.* butter
cameriɛra *f.* maid
cena *f.* supper
impressione *f.* impression
mɛzza *f.* half-past twelve
ɔspite *m.* guest
panino *m.* bun, roll
pasto *m.* meal
pensiɛro *m.* worry
pensione di famiglia *f.* family-style boarding house
piano *m.* plan
piazza *f.* square
quartiɛre *m.* quarter, section
sonnellino *m.* nap

spremuta d'arancia *f.* orange juice
tavola *f.* table; **a tavola** at the table
tredici thirteen; **alle tredici** at one in the afternoon
uɔvo *m.* (*pl.* **uɔva** *f.*) egg
vacanze *f. pl.* vacation

ADJECTIVES

americano, –a American
fritto, –a fried
intero, –a whole
pronto, –a ready
solo, –a single
sveglio, –a awake
vestito, –a (*p.p.*) dressed

[1] Do not translate *yard* or *quart*.

VERBS

alzarsi to get up
bere to drink
contentarsi to be satisfied
discorrere to discuss
dormire to sleep
durare to last, take (takes ɛssere)

riposare to rest
riunirsi to get together
scambiare to exchange

OTHER WORDS

chè (= **perchè**) for, because
generalmente generally
vɛrso toward, about

CURRENT USAGE

Una gita a Castɛl Gandɔlfo

Eravamo stati parecchie vɔlte a Roma, ma non avevamo mai fatto una gita a Castɛl Gandɔlfo, sɛde estiva del Papa. Una domenica mattina ci decidemmo a fare il viaggio e chiedemmo all'albɛrgo dove si prendesse l'autobus per Castɛl Gandɔlfo. Il gerɛnte ci disse di andare alla Stazione 5 Tɛrmini, dove a dɛstra dell'entrata principale avremmo trovato l'autobus che faceva quel servizio.

Infatti lo trovammo senza difficoltà. Domandammo quanto durasse la gita e ci dissero che in meno di due ore saremmo arrivati. Domandammo anche a che ora saremmo 10 potuti tornare e se ci fossero autobus di ritorno tutto il pomeriggio. Dovevamo sɛmpre assicurarci del ritorno perchè avevamo il nɔstro piccino di sɛtte anni, il quale spesso si stancava e voleva tornare all'albɛrgo, che per lui ɛra casa sua. 15

Castel Gandolfo has beautiful gardens.

Swiss guards watch over the Pope's regular residence, the Vatican.

La gita fu incantevole. L'*a*utobus lasciò la pianura di Roma e cominciò a salire la cresta degli Appennini. Ogni svolta ci offriva un nuovo panorama della Città Eterna. I pini lungo l'autostrada ci rammentavano la musica dei « Pini di Roma », di Ottorino Respighi. Al piccino, però, il 5 viaggio gli rammentava che sentiva appetito, e voleva sapere quando si facesse colazione.

Finalmente l'*a*utobus arrivò alla piccola piazza del villaggio chiamato Castel Gandolfo. Sembrava un mondo in cui il tempo si fosse fermato molti secoli fa. Il castello del 10 Papa mostrava la grandiosa bellezza di una vecchia signora dell'alta aristocrazia. E noi, coll'apparecchio cinematografico, giravamo pellicole per poi mostrare agli amici in America l'incanto di quel paesello nelle montagne.

Useful Expressions

ci decidemmo a we decided to
a destra dell'entrata to the right of the entrance
faceva quel servizio made that run
(gli) *a*utobus di ritorno return busses
sentiva appetito he felt hungry
apparecchio cinematografico movie camera
giravamo pellicole we made movies

Questions. 1. Qual è la sede estiva del Papa? 2. Dove si prende l'*a*utobus per andare a Castel Gandolfo? 3. Che cosa fa il gerente di un albergo? 4. Quanto dura la gita da Roma a Castel Gandolfo? 5. Perchè dovevamo assicurarci del ritorno? 6. È nella pianura o nelle montagne il Castello? 7. Ha mai sentito la musica dei « Pini di Roma », di Respighi? 8. Sente appetito Lei quando viaggia per lungo tempo in *a*utobus? 9. A che cosa può paragonare la bellezza del Castello? 10. Lei ha un apparecchio cinematografico?

STRUCTURE

111. Sequence of Tenses. The sequence of tenses determines only the tense of the subjunctive that is to be used in subordinate clauses.

1. If the main verb is in the present or the future indicative or in the imperative, the subjunctive verb is in the present or present perfect.

> Vuole che tutti lo sappiano. *He wants everybody to know it.*
> Mi dispiace che non sia arrivato. *I am sorry he has not arrived.*

2. If the main verb is in any other tense of the indicative (except the present perfect), the subjunctive verb is in the imperfect or pluperfect.

> Domandammo quanto durasse la gita. *We asked how long the trip might last.*
> Non sapeva che essa fosse stata qui. *He did not know that she had been here.*

3. If the main verb is in the present perfect indicative, the subjunctive verb may be in the present, present perfect, or imperfect subjunctive, according to the sense.

> Ha creduto che l'affare non sia serio. *He thought the matter was not serious (Now or at any time).*
> Non abbiamo capito perchè non sia arrivato. *We did not understand why he did not arrive (Recently).*
> Non hanno permesso che lui partisse. *They did not allow him to leave (Some time ago).*

112. Compound Tenses of the Subjunctive. You learned in Lesson 17 that the present perfect subjunctive is formed by the present subjunctive of the auxiliary and the past participle. The pluperfect subjunctive is formed by the imperfect subjunctive of the auxiliary followed by the past participle. These two are the only compound tenses of the subjunctive in Italian. Following are the forms for regular verbs.

Verbs Conjugated with **avere**

PRESENT PERFECT SUBJUNCTIVE		PLUPERFECT SUBJUNCTIVE	
abbia		avessi	
abbia		avessi	
abbia	comprato	avesse	comprato
abbiamo	venduto	avessimo	venduto
abbiate	finito	aveste	finito
abbiano		avessero	

Verbs Conjugated with εssere

sia	andato (a)		fossi	andato (a)
sia	caduto (a)		fossi	caduto (a)
sia	partito (a)		fosse	partito (a)

siamo	andati (e)		fossimo	andati (e)
siate	caduti (e)		foste	caduti (e)
siano	partiti (e)		fossero	partiti (e)

The present perfect subjunctive is used in the same way as the corresponding tense of the indicative, but in clauses requiring the subjunctive, of course.

Non sappiamo se la pellicola sia arrivata o no. *We don't know whether the film has arrived or not.*

The pluperfect subjunctive corresponds to either the first or the second pluperfect of the indicative, because there is no second pluperfect in the subjunctive.

Non si ricordava se avesse fatto colazione. *He did not remember whether he had had breakfast.*

113. Subjunctive in Indirect Questions. An indirect question is a subordinate clause introduced by an interrogative word. The most common interrogative words are: **se,** *whether;* **chi,** *who;* **che, che cɔsa,** or **cɔsa,** *what;* **quale,** *what;* **quando,** *when;* **come,** *how.*

1. An indirect question takes the subjunctive if the subordinate clause precedes the main clause.

Quale fosse la sua sorpresa, non si puɔ immaginare. *One cannot imagine his surprise.*

2. An indirect question takes the subjunctive to show uncertainty or a tendency to believe the contrary of the statement of the clause.

Mi domandɔ se potesse venire. *He asked me whether he might come.*

114. Subjunctive with Indefinite Words. The subjunctive may be used after certain indefinite words or phrases such as

chiunque, *whoever;* **qualunque,** *whichever;* **dovunque,** *wherever;* **comunque,** *however;* **per quanto,** *no matter how much;* etc.

Chiunque venga, non sono in casa. *Whoever comes, I am not at home.*

115. Summary of Plural of Nouns. Besides the plurals taken up in Lesson 2, there are additional forms which do not follow the general rules.

1. Masculine nouns other than those ending in an accented vowel or in a consonant normally end in an **i** in the plural, regardless of the ending in the singular.

l'artista *m.*, gli artisti (l'artista *f.*, le artiste)

2. Nouns ending in **co, go, ca, ga** normally add an **h** before the **i** or **e** of the plural (exceptions: **amici, medici, nemici, porci, teologi, Greci, Magi,** and several others).

il tabacco, i tabacchi   la strega (*witch*), le streghe

3. Many nouns are masculine in the singular and feminine in the plural. Many of these have also a masculine plural form, which is slightly different in meaning from the normal, feminine plural.

il braccio, *the arm*	le braccia	(bracci)
il centinaio, *the hundred*	le centinaia	
il dito, *the finger*	le dita	(diti)
il ginocchio, *the knee*	le ginocchia	(ginocchi)
il grido, *the cry*	le grida	(gridi)
il labbro, *the lip*	le labbra	(labbri)
il lenzuolo, *the (bed) sheet*	le lenzuola	(lenzuoli)
il membro, *the limb*	le membra	(membri)
il migliaio, *the thousand*	le migliaia	
il miglio, *the mile*	le miglia	
il muro, *the wall (outside)*	le mura	(muri)
l'osso, *the bone*	le ossa	(ossi)
l'uovo, *the egg*	le uova	

When the above words refer to parts of the body, the feminine plural refers to parts belonging to the same person.

Giulia aveva le labbra tinte. *Julia had painted lips.*

LANGUAGE PRACTICE

Si legga senza tradurre:

La Città del Vaticano

La Città del Vaticano è la sede del Papa.　È una piccola città indipendente al centro della grande città di Roma.　Il suo governo [1] dipende direttamente dalla Chiesa e non dal governo italiano.　Ha la propria ferrovia, il proprio ufficio postale,[2] le proprie guardie, e le proprie funzioni.　Quel che c'è di più bello sono i suoi giardini.　　　　　　　　　5

Le guardie della Città del Vaticano sono svizzere; sono completamente fedeli [3] alla Chiesa e guardano la piccola città con uno zelo [4] straordinario. Hanno i propri costumi, che sono caratteristici e pittoreschi.　Una volta l'anno, con una funzione speciale, le nuove guardie vengono ammesse [5] alla guardia regolare.　In questa funzione solenne prestano giuramento [6] 10 di essere fedeli alla loro missione.　D'allora in poi [7] restano nella guardia del Vaticano, la maggior parte per tutta la vita.　La Città del Vaticano è simbolo dell'Impero della Chiesa sulla terra.

Si risponda senza tradurre:

1. Da quale governo dipende la Città del Vaticano?　2. Che cosa ha la Città del Vaticano?　3. Sono belli i giardini del Vaticano?　4. Portano costumi speciali le guardie del Vaticano?　5. Che funzione c'è una volta l'anno?　6. Che giuramento prestano le nuove guardie?

ESERCIZI

I. Si adoperi la forma adatta dell'indicativo o del congiuntivo nelle seguenti proposizioni e si dicano ad alta voce (Use the correct form of the indicative or the subjunctive in the following sentences and say aloud):

1. (They asked) al gerente dove (they might find) un albergo migliore.　2. Il gerente (was not) contento che essi (wanted to) andar via.　3. (He wanted to) sapere come (he had arrived) così presto.　4. (He asked) a che ora (they had breakfast) in quella pensione.　5. (It seems impossible) che Lei (have never been) a Castel Gandolfo.　6. (We asked) quanto (would last) il viaggio da Napoli a Roma.　7. (It seemed)

---

[1] government.　[2] post office.　[3] faithful.　[4] zeal.　[5] are admitted.　[6] they take an oath.　[7] from then on.

curioso che tutti (were) americani. 8. (It will seem) che tutti (want to) essere i primi a partire. 9. (She wanted) un marito che (would know how to) preparare un bel pranzo. 10. Dite a Roberto che (he should not forget) che noi l'aspettiamo.

II. Si dia il plurale delle seguenti frasi e si adoperino in proposizioni complete (Give the plural of the following expressions and use in complete sentences):

1. l'apparecchio cinematografico. 2. il medico greco. 3. il labbro rosso. 4. il dito lungo. 5. il mio ginocchio. 6. il suo nemico. 7. il migliaio di dollari. 8. il lenzuolo bianco. 9. l'osso grande. 10. il grido forte. 11. l'artista italiano. 12. il tabacco greco. 13. il viaggio lungo. 14. lo zio povero. 15. il negozio di abiti. 16. il nostro amico. 17. la nostra amica. 18. la lunga gita. 19. il braccio buono. 20. l'uovo giallo.

III. Si traduca in italiano:

1. Whoever comes. 2. Wherever they go. 3. No matter how he says it. (However he may say it.) 4. They wanted us to leave. 5. He wishes you to stay. 6. I wish you to speak. 7. Provided they sell. 8. In order that you learn. 9. Although she finishes. 10. Without his knowing it. 11. Without his knowing him. 12. Before you (*fam. pl.*) return. 13. He wanted us to think. 14. We were looking for a man who knew how to cook. 15. They wanted a maid who knew French.

IV. Write a composition of about a hundred words on a trip which you have taken recently. The teacher will have the compositions read and discussed in class.

V. Si traduca in italiano:

1. Although we had been to Rome several times, we had never taken a trip to the Pope's summer residence. 2. After we had decided to take the trip, we had to ask where we might get the bus. 3. The man-

ager told us to go to the Termini station, because almost all the busses leave from there. 4. There were hundreds of cars and thousands of people near the entrance. 5. They wanted to assure themselves of the return trip because their little boy got tired easily. 6. Too bad there wasn't more time so that we could spend a few days in that little town. 7. Every turn offered a beautiful view of the crest of the Apennines. 8. The trip reminded me that I felt hungry and I wanted to know when I could eat. 9. It seems like a world where time stopped several centuries ago. 10. When you have a movie camera you can put on film the charm of that panorama.

WORD LIST

NOUNS

apparecchio *m.* set, camera
aristocrazia *f.* aristocracy
autostrada *f.* highway
castɛllo (castɛl) *m.* castle; **Castɛl Gandɔlfo** *the Papal summer residence*
cresta *f.* crest
gerɛnte *m.* manager
Papa *m.* Pope
pellicola *f.* film
pino *m.* pine
ritorno *m.* return
sɛde *f.* residence
servizio *m.* service
svɔlta *f.* turn
villaggio *m.* village

ADJECTIVE

estivo, –a summer *adj.*

VERBS

decidersi (a) to decide (to)
girare to turn
offrire to offer
salire to go up (takes ɛssere)
stancarsi to get tired

OTHER WORDS

dɛstra: a dɛstra to the right
pɔi afterwards
quanto how long

CURRENT USAGE

Il pranzo

È veramente un'arte apparecchiare la tavola. Nel disporre i posti degli invitati bisogna tener conto delle loro amicizie e simpatie, ma io mi occuperò soltanto della tavola stessa.

⁵ Prima di stendere la tovaglia bisogna mettere un feltro sulla tavola. Poi si mettono le posate: il coltello, i cucchiai ed i cucchiaini, a destra del piatto e le forchette a sinistra. Il tovagliolo va a sinistra del piatto o anche sul piatto stesso; poi quando si comincia, ogni invitato lo mette sulle ginocchia.

¹⁰ I bicchieri si mettono davanti al piatto, uno per l'acqua e l'altro per il vino, poichè in Italia non si pranza senza vino.

Per una colazione o un pranzo modesto, ecco alcune pietanze: prima viene una minestra, che può essere pasta asciutta al sugo di pomodoro, pasta in brodo, spaghetti al ¹⁵ burro, o qualche minestrone. Poi si serve un piatto di carne, come ad esempio pollo arrosto con patatine fritte, vitello arrosto con spinaci, agnello al forno, o manzo ai ferri. Il pranzo si può servire con una buona insalata di lattuga o di pomodori. Poi c'è sempre del formaggio: bel paese, romano, ²⁰ svizzero, parmigiano, gorgonzola, provolone, ecc. Alla fine c'è frutta e caffè espresso, senza i quali nessun pranzo può essere completo.

Per un pranzo di lusso potete scegliere voi stessi le pietanze che vi piacciono. Eccone un lungo elenco:

184

Cibi e Bevande — Foods and Drinks

JUICES: **spremuta d'arancia** *f.* orange juice
spremuta d'ananasso *f.* pineapple juice
spremuta di limone *f.* lemon juice
spremuta di pomodoro *f.* tomato juice

FRUIT: **albicocca** *f.* apricot   **pera** *f.* pear
ananasso *m.* pineapple   **pesca** *f.* peach
ciliegia *f.* cherry   **pompelmo** *m.* grapefruit
fico *m.* fig   **popone (melone)** *m.* melon
fragola *f.* strawberry   **uva** *f.* grapes
mela *f.* apple

SOUPS: **brodo** *m.* broth
brodo ristretto *m.* consommé
minestra di cipolla *f.* onion soup
minestra di fagioli *f.* bean soup
minestra di piselli *f.* pea soup
minestra di pollo *f.* chicken soup
minestrone *m.* thick vegetable soup

FISH: **anguilla** *f.* eel   **salmone** *m.* salmon
aragosta *f.* lobster   **tonno** *m.* tuna fish
merluzzo *m.* cod   **trota** *f.* trout

MEATS: **agnello** *m.* lamb
coscia d'agnello *f.* leg of lamb
costoletta di vitello *f.* veal cutlet *or* chop
manzo ai ferri *m.* (*or* **bistecca** *f.*) broiled steak
pollo arrosto *m.* roast chicken
polpetta *f.* meat ball
rosbiffe *m.* roast beef
salsiccia *f.* sausage
scaloppine *f. pl.* small veal cutlets

VEGETABLES: **carciofo** *m.* artichoke
carota *f.* carrot
cavolfiore *m.* cauliflower
fagiolini *m. pl.* string beans
granturco *m.* corn
lattuga *f.* lettuce
melanzana *f.* eggplant
patata lessa *f.* boiled potato
patate al forno *f. pl.* oven baked potatoes
patatine fritte *f. pl.* French fried potatoes
purè di patate *m.* mashed potatoes
peperone *m.* pepper
piselli *m. pl.* peas
pomodoro *m.* tomato

	spinaci *m. pl.* spinach
	zucchini *m. pl.* Italian squash
SALADS:	**insalata mista** *f.* mixed salad
	insalata di cicoria *f.* chicory salad
	insalata di lattuga *f.* lettuce salad
	insalata di pomodɔri *f.* tomato salad
DRINKS:	*a*cqua **minerale** *f.* mineral water
	birra *f.* beer
	caffè *m.* coffee
	caffè con panna *m.* coffee with cream
	caffè esprɛsso *m.* strong black coffee
	caffè nero *m.* black coffee
	cioccolata *f.* chocolate
	latte *m.* milk
	tè *m.* tea
DESSERTS:	**gelato di cioccolata** *m.* chocolate ice cream
	gelato di crɛma *m.* vanilla ice cream
	gelato di fragole *m.* strawberry ice cream
	gelato di pɛsche *m.* peach ice cream
	spumone *m.* spumone ice cream
	tɔrta *f.* cake
	tɔrta di frutta *f.* fruit pie
EGGS:	**frittata** *f.* omelette
	uɔva affogate *f. pl.* poached eggs
	uɔva fritte *f. pl.* fried eggs
	uɔva strapazzate *f. pl.* scrambled eggs
	uɔvo bazzɔtto *m.* soft-boiled egg
	uɔvo sɔdo *m.* hard-boiled egg
BREAD:	**pane** *m.* bread
	pane di granturco *m.* corn bread
	pane di segale *m.* rye bread
	pane fresco *m.* fresh bread
	pane raffermo *m.* stale bread
	panino *m.* roll
WINES:	**vino bianco** *m.* white wine
	vino fɔrte *m.* strong-bodied wine
	vino leggiɛro *m.* light wine
	vino moscato *m.* muscatel
	vino rosso (nero) *m.* red wine
	vino spumante *m.* sparkling wine

STRUCTURE

116. Compound Tenses of Verbs Followed by the Infinitive. To form the compound tenses of a verb followed by an

*Family life in an Italian home.
Television has not become so popular as to break up the family unit.*

infinitive you use the auxiliary which the verb in the infinitive would normally take.

Non ha voluto lavorare. *He did not want to (would not) work.*
Siamo dovuti partire alle sette. *We had to leave at seven.*

117. The Infinitive as a Substantive. An infinitive may be used as a noun, that is, as subject, object, or predicate nominative. When used as subject or object the infinitive normally takes the definite article.

L'apparecchiare una tavola è facile. *Setting a table is easy.*
Amiamo il cucinare. *We love cooking.*

When used as a predicate nominative, the infinitive takes no article.

È facile sbagliarsi. *It's easy to be mistaken.*

118. The Infinitive with Prepositions. After prepositions Italian uses an infinitive, whereas English uses a gerund (*–ing*).

Nel disporre le posate ... *In setting the places ...*

119. The Infinitive with Adjectives. When an infinitive depends on an adjective it is usually preceded by **a** (unless the infinitive is a predicate nominative).

Fu il primo a venire. *He was the first to come.*
BUT → È necessario partire. *It's necessary to leave.*

120. The Infinitive with Nouns. When an infinitive depends on a noun it is preceded by **da** if the infinitive expresses the purpose or intention for which the object in question serves; otherwise **di** is used.

acqua da bere, *drinking water (water for drinking)*
BUT → la gioia di vederla, *the joy of seeing you*

121. Complementary Infinitives

Common verbs which govern an infinitive without a preposition:

bastare (*impers.*), *to suffice*   potere, *to be able*
bisognare (*impers.*), *to need*   preferire, *to prefer*

desiderare, *to desire*

dovere, *to owe, ought*

fare, *to make*

giovare (*impers.*), *to be advantageous*

lasciare, *to allow*

sapere, *to know how to*

sembrare, *to seem*

sentire, *to hear*

udire, *to hear*

vedere, *to see*

volere, *to want*

Common verbs which take **a** before a following infinitive:

aiutare, *to help*

andare, *to go*

cominciare, *to begin*

imparare, *to learn*

incoraggiare, *to encourage*

insegnare, *to teach*

mandare, *to send*

mettersi, *to begin, start*

prendere, *to begin*

seguitare, *to continue*

stare, *to stand*

Common verbs which take **di** before a following infinitive:

comandare, *to command*

credere, *to think, believe*

dire, *to tell*

finire, *to finish*

importare (*impers.*), *to be of importance*

permettere, *to permit*

piacere (*impers.*), *to please*

pregare, *to beg*

proibire, *to prohibit*

promettere, *to promise*

stabilire, *to resolve*

toccare (*impers.*), *to be one's turn*

LANGUAGE PRACTICE

Si legga senza tradurre:

Leonardo da Vinci

Una volta nel corso della storia la natura ha voluto raccogliere[1] in un solo uomo tutte le facoltà che formano il genio umano — risultato:[2] Leonardo da Vinci. L'uomo può essere ben proporzionato e di forza[3] straordinaria: Leonardo da Vinci era bello, alto, e fortissimo. L'uomo può essere artista: Leonardo era sommo pittore e scultore. L'uomo 5 può costruire[4] bellissimi edifici: Leonardo era architetto. L'uomo può conoscere le leggi della matematica: Leonardo era gran matematico. L'uomo può conoscere le leggi della meccanica: Leonardo era sommo ingegnere. L'uomo può conoscere la natura del corpo umano:[5] Leonardo

[1] gather. [2] result. [3] strength. [4] construct. [5] human body.

fece profondi [1] studi di anatomia. Arrivò finanche [2] a studiare le leggi del volo [3] quattrocento anni prima dell'aviazione.

Come mai questo prodigio? La natura non ci svela [4] i suoi segreti. Ogni essere [5] umano è dotato delle sue facoltà, chi [6] più e chi [6] meno. 5 In questa gradazione [7] ci fu un essere che ebbe più facoltà di qualsiasi altro nella storia. Ammiriamolo per il suo genio e contentiamoci di essere individualmente dotati di qualche facoltà che ci distingue dagli altri.

Si risponda senza tradurre:

1. Aveva molte grandi facoltà Leonardo da Vinci? 2. Era alto, forte, e bello? 3. Conosce qualche quadro famoso di Leonardo? 4. Leonardo conobbe le leggi della matematica e della meccanica? 5. Che studi fece Leonardo sull'aviazione? 6. Sa Lei in che secolo visse Leonardo da Vinci?

ESERCIZI

I. Si traduca oralmente:

A. 1. Learning is difficult. 2. Teaching is still more difficult. 3. I prefer sleeping to working. 4. Knowledge (*use infinitive*) is good for the mind. 5. Studying grammar is easy. 6. To get up early is important. 7. To speak Italian is a pleasure. 8. Setting a table is easy. 9. I told her to leave. 10. He promised to come.

B. 1. That apple is good to eat. 2. He was the first to enter. 3. Were you the last to arrive? 4. I have a great deal to do. 5. This is drinking water. 6. Have you work to do? 7. Has she potatoes to sell? 8. We have a dinner to serve. 9. This is a cup for drinking. 10. You have some books to read.

II. Ask questions using the following expressions and have someone else answer the questions:

1. pasta asciutta al sugo di pomodoro. 2. minestrone. 3. spaghetti al burro. 4. piatto di carne. 5. pollo arrosto. 6. patatine fritte. 7. vitello ar-

---

[1] deep. [2] even. [3] flight. [4] reveal. [5] being. [6] some. [7] gradation.

rosto. 8. agnello al forno. 9. manzo ai ferri. 10. formaggio bel paese. 11. formaggio parmigiano. 12. caffè espresso. 13. pasta in brodo. 14. acqua e vino. 15. frutta fresca.

III. Si risponda in italiano:

1. È facile apparecchiare la tavola per un pranzo? 2. Di che cosa si deve tener conto quando si apparecchia? 3. Come si mettono poi le posate? 4. Dove si mette il tovagliolo quando si comincia a mangiare? 5. Quanti bicchieri si mettono a tavola e dove si mettono? 6. Con che pietanza si comincia un pranzo italiano? 7. Che carne piace di più a Lei? 8. Conosce Lei molti formaggi? 9. Che cosa ci vuole per fare un pranzo completo?

IV. Let each student prepare a dinner menu, including juices, soups, meat or fish, vegetables, fruit, drink, and dessert. Let the students ask each other in Italian what they have included at every point in their menus.

V. Si traduca in italiano:

1. When one sets a table, one has to keep in mind the friendships and likings of the guests. 2. In setting the places one should put the knife and spoons on the right of the plate and the forks on the left. 3. Put the napkin on your knees when the dinner begins. 4. Did you know that in Italy they do not dine without wine? 5. For fruit I like strawberries, peaches, and pears; I do not like pineapple or apricots. 6. For a meat course (**piatto**), do you prefer lamb, broiled steak, or roast chicken? 7. What vegetables do you wish, corn, string beans, spinach, or eggplant? 8. What does the little fellow want, oven baked potatoes, mashed potatoes, a boiled potato, or French fried potatoes? 9. It is not easy to choose between veal chops, small veal cutlets, sausage, and roast beef. Isn't there any lamb? 10. I don't know (my) wines; I know only white wine, red wine, light wine, and strong-bodied wine.

WORD LIST

agnɛllo al forno *m.* roast lamb

amicizia *f.* friendship

bɛl paese *m. a type of cheese*

bicchiɛre *m.* glass

caffè esprɛsso *m.* strong, black coffee; demi-tasse

carne *f.* meat

coltɛllo *m.* knife

conto *m.* account; **tener conto di** to keep in mind

cucchiaino *m.* teaspoon

cucchiaio *m.* spoon

feltro *m.* pad

forchetta *f.* fork

ginɔcchio *m.* (*pl.* **ginɔcchia** *f.*) knee

gorgonzola *m. a type of blue cheese*

invitato *m.* guest (*at dinner*)

manzo ai fɛrri *m.* (broiled) steak

minɛstra *f.* soup, first course

minestrone *m.* thick vegetable soup

parmigiano *m.* Parmesan, *a type of cheese*

pasta asciutta *f.* macaroni

pasta in brɔdo *f.* soup with noodles (macaroni)

patatine fritte *f. pl.* French fried potatoes

piatto *m.* plate, dish

pietanza *f.* course

pollo arrɔsto *m.* roast chicken

posata *f.* place setting (*for a table*)

posto *m.* place

provolone *m. a type of cheese*

romano *m. a type of cheese*

simpatia *f.* liking

spaghetti al burro *m. pl.* spaghetti with butter

spinaci *m. pl.* spinach

sugo *m.* sauce; **sugo di pomodɔro** tomato sauce

svizzero *m.* Swiss, *a type of cheese*

tovaglia *f.* tablecloth

tovagliɔlo *m.* napkin

vitɛllo arrɔsto *m.* roast veal

complɛto, –a complete

apparecchiare to set (*a table*)

disporre to set (*places*)

occuparsi di to deal with

stɛndere to lay

davanti a in front of

poichè since

sinistra: a sinistra, to the left

CURRENT USAGE

A zonzo per la città

— Siamo molto stanchi stasera. Abbiamo girato dappertutto perchè ci occorrevano molte cose. Arrivati alla fine del viaggio volevamo comprare ricordi per i nostri amici. Prima, però, abbiamo dovuto cercare parecchi articoli che ci servivano per la toletta. ⁵

— Dimmi un po'? Se si vuol comprare del profumo, dove si può trovare?

— Si può trovare in una profumeria. Ne abbiamo trovato di una qualità eccellente all'angolo di Via Calzaiuoli e Via degli Speziali. Se cercassi in tutta Firenze, non ne troveresti ¹⁰ di qualità migliore. Hanno anche ciprie di tutti i tipi e di tutti i colori. Se avessimo avuto più denaro con noi, avremmo comprato dei profumi ottimi, ma costavano un occhio.

— Che altro avete comprato oggi? ¹⁵

— Di oggetti personali abbiamo comprato degli spazzolini da denti e del dentifricio. Il nostro piccino aveva adoperato i nostri spazzolini per pulirsi le scarpe e il dentifricio per decorare i mobili.

— Bravo piccino! E che regali? ²⁰

— In un negozio vicino al Ponte Vecchio abbiamo trovato delle borsette di cuoio fiorentino. Ne abbiamo comprato sei di vari colori; sono ottime come regali perchè non prendono molto spazio nelle valige. C'erano anche delle belle

spille in filigrana, e ne abbiamo comprate sei. Poi anche
una mezza dozzina di portagioielli, che sono così apprezzati
come ricordi.

— Avete molti amici?

5 — Sì, molti. Fatto sta che se fossi ricca avrei comprato
il negozio intero. Bisogna limitarsi quando si comprano
regali, altrimenti non ci resta denaro per il ritorno.

— Se io potessi, resterei per sempre qui a Firenze. Ma
il nostro lavoro è in America e, finite le vacanze, bisogna
10 riprendere le nostre occupazioni. Beato chi può viaggiare
sempre, senza preoccuparsi del lavoro.

Useful Expressions

a zonzo at random
ci occorrevano molte cose we needed many things
ci servivano we needed
dimmi un po' tell me
costavano un occhio they cost a fortune
spazzolino da denti toothbrush
fatto sta the fact is
per sempre forever

Questions. 1. Se Lei avesse molto denaro, comprerebbe
ricordi per tutti gli amici? 2. Se Le servissero articoli per la
toletta, in che negozio andrebbe? 3. Dove si possono comprare
profumi e ciprie? 4. Perchè non si possono comprare molti ottimi
profumi? 5. Che oggetti personali avete comprato? 6. Se il
piccino adoperasse lo spazzolino da denti per pulirsi le scarpe,
cosa direbbe la madre? 7. Se Lei trovasse delle borsette di cuoio
fiorentino, ne comprerebbe una dozzina? 8. Se Sua sorella volesse
un portagioielli, dove lo comprerebbe? 9. Se fossimo ricchi,
viaggeremmo molto? 10. Se Lei potesse, resterebbe per sempre
a Firenze?

STRUCTURE

122. Contrary-to-fact and Should-would Sentences. A
contrary-to-fact sentence assumes a condition which cannot be
true under the circumstances and draws a conclusion from it.

In Italian the if-clause takes the imperfect or pluperfect sub-junctive and the result clause takes the conditional or the conditional perfect.

Se io potessi, resterei per sempre qui a Firenze. *If I could, I would remain forever here in Florence.*

Notice that in the above sentence the simple tenses are used when referring to the present. When referring to past time the compound tenses are used, as in the following sentence:

Se avessimo avuto più denaro con noi, avremmo comprato dei profumi ottimi. *If we had had more money with us, we would have bought some excellent perfumes.*

The simple and compound tenses can be used together if the sense so requires.

Se fossi ricca, avrei comprato il negozio intero. *If I were rich, I would have bought out the store.*

A should-would sentence implies that if certain conditions were true in the future, certain results would follow. This type is treated like a contrary-to-fact sentence.

Se venisse presto, andremmo insieme. *If he should come early, we would go together.*

123. Past Participle. The past participle may be used alone in an absolute construction. It agrees with the word it modifies and may be translated by a participial phrase or by a clause.

Arrivati alla fine del viaggio . . . *Having reached the end of our trip . . .*
Finite le vacanze . . . *Since the vacation was over . . .*

124. Object Pronouns with Participles. When a pronoun depends on a participle (past or present) used independently in an absolute construction, it is attached to the participle.

Trovatili in casa, li salutò. *Having found them at home, he greeted them.*
Invitandolo, gli farai onore. *By inviting him you will honor him.*

Picturesque Taormina lies at the foot of Mt. Etna, of which we give you a glimpse. This is Sicily in its splendor.

LANGUAGE PRACTICE

Si legga senza tradurre:

La Conca d'Oro [1]

Palermo è il capoluogo della Sicilia e la sua città principale. Ha un porto importante per l'industria e il commercio dell'Italia. La città è situata in una delle valli più fertili, dove si coltivano olivi, aranci, limoni, fichi, e tanti altri alberi da frutta.[2] In questa valle ci sono vigne [3] che producono un vino famoso, chiamato Marsala. La valle è così fertile che 5 si chiama Conca d'Oro.

Palermo però, è rinomata non solo per il suo clima e i prodotti agricoli, ma per l'importanza storica. Fin dai tempi greci e romani, Palermo fu una delle città più importanti del Mediterraneo. Nel secolo decimoterzo [4] la città fu sede del famoso impero di Federico II. Nella sua corte cominciò 10 a svilupparsi la letteratura italiana, che poi continuò in Toscana. Senza la Scuola Poetica Siciliana forse l'italiano non sarebbe mai arrivato alla perfezione che raggiunse [5] coi poeti del Dolce Stil Nuovo.

Si risponda senza tradurre:

1. Che importanza ha Palermo per l'Italia? 2. Quali sono alcuni dei prodotti agricoli della Conca d'Oro? 3. Ha importanza storica la città di Palermo? 4. In che secolo fu l'impero di Federico II? 5. Dove cominiciò a svilupparsi la letteratura italiana? 6. In che secolo e dove raggiunse la più alta perfezione la letteratura italiana?

ESERCIZI

I. Si dia la forma adatta del verbo fra parentesi e si dica ad alta voce (Give the proper forms of the verbs in parentheses and say aloud):

1. Se noi non (essere) stanchi, non (potere) dormire stasera. 2. Se non (avere avuto) bisogno di parecchie cose, non (aver girato) dappertutto. 3. Se Lei (volere) comprare dei ricordi, ne (trovare) molti in quel negozio. 4. Se essi (cercare) in tutta Roma, non ne (potere) trovare di migliore qualità. 5. Se io (desiderare) ciprie di tutti i tipi, ne (comprare) nella profumeria all'angolo di questa strada. 6. Se i portagioielli (costare) meno,

---

[1] gold bowl. [2] fruit trees. [3] vineyards. [4] thirteenth. [5] reached.

ne (prendere) per tutti. 7. Se noi (aver comprato) uno spazzolino da denti, ora ne (avere) due. 8. Se il dentifricio (essere) buono, (pulire) i denti. 9. Se Lei (comprare) delle spille in filigrana, tutte le amiche ne (volere). 10. Lei (restare) a Firenze se (potere)?

II. Si traduca oralmente:

1. Having finished the work. 2. Having seen the city. 3. Having done many things. 4. The vacation being over. 5. The letter having been written. 6. Having read everything. 7. Having entered the house. 8. Having come out of the theater. 9. Having produced the wine. 10. Having sold the products. 11. Having arrived there. 12. Having found him at home. 13. Having bought the shoes. 14. Having limited himself. 15. Having worried for a long time.

III. Si facciano delle proposizioni complete adoperando i seguenti gruppi di parole (Form complete sentences in Italian using the following groups of words):

1. riprendere, occupazioni, dovere. 2. profumo, cipria, profumeria. 3. profumo, occhio, costare. 4. regalo, borsetta, cuoio. 5. valigia, spazio, poco. 6. portagioielli, apprezzare, ricordo. 7. valige, molte, viaggiare. 8. altrimenti, restare, denaro. 9. negozio, angolo, strada. 10. mobili, decorare, dentifricio.

IV. Two students stage a conversation in which one is a clerk in a store and the other is a customer. Vary the type of store and discuss the many different articles which may be bought in an Italian city.

V. Si traduca in italiano:

1. Having reached the end of our trip, we want to buy souvenirs for our friends in the United States. 2. The articles which we needed for our toilette are sold in different stores. 3. If we wanted to buy everything, we would have to go around everywhere. 4. At the corner of our street we found some articles of excellent

quality.   5. We would have bought more personal objects if we had not used up our money.   6. If he had wanted to clean his shoes, he could have used something else.   7. Do these filigree pins take up too much room in your bags?   Can we buy a dozen of them? 8. These Florentine leather handbags cost a fortune, but they are really beautiful, otherwise we would not buy them.   9. Do you have many friends?   It would seem so, because you are buying many souvenirs. 10. When the vacation is over, we shall be glad to take up our duties again.

WORD LIST

NOUNS

angolo *m.* corner
articolo *m.* article
cipria *f.* face powder
cuoio *m.* leather
dentifricio *m.* toothpaste
filigrana *f.* filigree
mobili *m. pl.* furniture
occhio *m.* eye
occupazione *f.* occupation, job
portagioielli *m.* (*invar.*) jewel box
profumeria *f.* perfume shop
profumo *m.* perfume
qualità *f.* quality
regalo *m.* gift

ricordo *m.* souvenir
scarpa *f.* shoe
spazio *m.* space
spilla *f.* pin
tipo *m.* type, kind
toletta *f.* toilette

ADJECTIVES

eccellente excellent
fiorentino, –a Florentine
ottimo, –a excellent
personale personal

VERBS

adoperare to use
apprezzare to appreciate
decorare to decorate
riprendere to take up again

CURRENT USAGE

In ferrovia

Stiamo per lasciare la nostra cara Italia. Siamo sul direttissimo Milano-Zurigo, il quale ci porterà oltre le Alpi. Il treno fila rapidamente. Io ed Angelina stiamo lì a guardare da un finestrino dello scompartimento di seconda classe. Il
5 nostro piccino dorme placidamente sul sedile, perchè siamo soltanto noi tre nello scompartimento. Lontano lontano, sulle montagne, si vedono tante casette circondate da alberetti. A noi che siamo lontani sembrano alberini di Natale, ma da vicino saranno alberoni altissimi.
10 Passando vicino a un'autostrada vediamo automobili che sembrano indietreggiare invece di andare avanti. Quando passiamo per qualche villaggio, vediamo giovanotti che passeggiano a braccetto delle fidanzate, donnette che portano ragazzini per la mano, ometti che sembrano così buffi con
15 quei baffoni che coprono le guance. Ora passiamo lungo un ruscelletto con un bel ponticello. Poi si vedono dei villini così graziosi, e delle casacce da far paura. Alle stazioni dove il direttissimo non si ferma ci sono sempre tanti a guardare il treno: bambini, ragazzini, signorine, giovanotti, vecchietti,
20 tutti a guardare il treno e salutare i viaggiatori.

Però non vediamo l'ora di arrivare alla nostra destinazione. Abbiamo due amici che ci aspettano a Zurigo, una mia segretaria col marito svizzero. Non li vediamo da un anno perchè vennero in Europa subito dopo sposati. Abbiamo spedito un bigliettino per annunziare il nostro arrivo e siamo sicuri che ci aspetteranno a braccia aperte, perchè vogliamo loro molto bene. Così il nostro viaggio finirà con una visita ai nostri cari amici. 5

Useful Expressions

in ferrovia on the train
lontano lontano far away
da vicino from nearby
a braccetto di arm in arm with
portano per la mano lead by the hand
da far paura frightful
non vediamo l'ora di we are very anxious to
a braccia aperte with open arms
vogliamo loro molto bene we like them very much

Questions. 1. Dove ci porterà il direttissimo Milano-Zurigo? 2. Che cosa facciamo tutti e tre nello scompartimento di seconda classe? 3. Che cosa si vede lontano lontano? 4. Saranno grandi gli alberi che vediamo? 5. Che sembrano fare le automobili che vediamo? 6. Che vediamo quando passiamo per qualche villaggio? 7. Sono buffi gli uomini che hanno baffoni? 8. Che altro si vede dal treno? 9. Ci sono molti alle stazioni dove il direttissimo non si ferma? 10. Ci sembra lungo il viaggio? 11. Chi ci aspetta a Zurigo? 12. Come finirà il nostro viaggio?

STRUCTURE

125. Suffixes. Italian can express many different shades of the meaning of a noun (and less commonly of an adjective) by means of suffixes. The proper use of these suffixes is one of the most delicate points in the language. The student should not use any suffix without first finding that particular form of the word in the text, or in a good Italian dictionary such as Petrocchi, Zingarelli, or Cappuccini-Migliorini. In adding the suffix, the final vowel of the word is dropped; if that vowel is preceded by a c or g sound, the original sound must be retained.

quadro + etto = quadretto, *small picture*
buco + ino = buchino, *small hole*

*Cortina d'Ampezzo, in the Dolomites, is
a luxurious summer and winter resort.
Don't be surprised if your funds give out.*

126. Augmentatives. The following suffixes convey the idea of increase in size or quality.

1. **–one, –ona** denotes extraordinary size.

> uno stradone, *a very large street*

2. **–ɔtto, –ɔtta** denotes something halfway between large and small.

> un ragazzɔtto, *a sturdy young man*

3. **–accio, –accia** conveys a strong disparaging or disdaining tone.

> un tempaccio, *some terrible weather*
> un ragazzaccio, *a terrible youngster*

4. **–astro, –astra** conveys the idea of something that doesn't quite succeed in being what it wants to be.

> un poetastro, *a poetaster, a would-be poet*
> giallastro, *yellowish*

127. Diminutives. The following suffixes denote smallness of size or quality.

1. **–ino, –ina; –ɛllo, –ɛlla; –etto, –etta** denote smallness and grace.

> una stanzina, *a pretty little room*
> una vecchietta, *a neat old lady*

2. **–uccio, –uccia; –uzzo, –uzza** denote smallness and endearment, but sometimes also disparagement.

> un monelluccio, *a cute little rascal*

3. Nouns may take more than one suffix at a time.

> casa — casetta — casettina — casettuccia

128. Suffixes with Adjectives. Adjectives as well as nouns may take suffixes.

grande, *large*	grandetto, *somewhat large*
bɛllo, *beautiful*	bellino, *rather cute*

LANGUAGE PRACTICE

Read the following sonnet aloud and memorize it.

Sonetto di Petrarca (LXI)*

Benedetto sia 'l [1] giorno e 'l mese e l'anno
  E la stagione e 'l tempo e l'ora e 'l punto
  E 'l bel paese e 'l loco [2] ov'io [3] fui giunto
  Da duo [4] begli occhi che legato m'hanno;
5 E benedetto il primo dolce affanno
  Ch'i' [5] ebbi ad esser con Amor congiunto,
  E l'arco e le saette ond'io fui punto
  E le piaghe che 'n [6] fin al cor mi vanno.
Benedette le voci tante ch'io
10 Chiamando il nome di mia donna ho sparte,
  E i sospiri e le lagrime e 'l disio;
E benedette sian tutte le carte
  Ov'io fama le acquisto, e 'l pensier mio
  Ch'è sol di lei sí ch'altra [7] non v'ha [8] parte.

ESERCIZI

I. Si traduca oralmente, adoperando suffissi (Translate orally, using suffixes):

1. A little-boy. 2. A little-girl. 3. A little-book.
4. A little-table. 5. A neat-little-woman. 6. A pretty-little-child. 7. A pretty-little-brook. 8. A cute-little-house. 9. A cute-little-room. 10. A sturdy-young-man. 11. An enormous-tree. 12. An enormous-mustache. 13. Some tiny-trees. 14. A dirty-old-house.
15. An awful-boy. 16. Greenish. 17. Yellowish.
18. A would-be-poet. 19. Some little-old-men. 20. A neat-little-note.

II. Si spieghi mediante aggettivi il significato delle seguenti parole con suffissi (Explain with adjectives in Italian the approximate meaning of the following words with suffixes):

[1] 'l = il. [2] loco = luogo. [3] ov'io = dove io. [4] duo = due. [5] Ch'i' = Che io. [6] 'n = in. [7] ch'altra = che altra. [8] v'ha = vi ha.
* This sonnet is printed without phonetic symbols.

1. Un trenino. 2. Un finestrone. 3. Un villaggetto.
4. La manina. 5. Le guanciacce. 6. Un ponticelluc-
cio. 7. Due amiconi. 8. Un viaggetto. 9. Un ragaz-'
zino. 10. Un articoletto. 11. Verdastro. 12. Un
regaluccio. 13. Uno spillone. 14. Una visitina.
15. Un lavoretto. 16. Dei pensieracci. 17. Il col-
tellino. 18. Il bicchierino. 19. Un ponticello. 20. Un
poetastro.

III. Si traduca oralmente:

1. We did not see them. 2. They were waiting for
him. 3. I like her very much. 4. Will you greet him?
5. Will he stop? 6. They cover them. 7. She leads
them by the hand. 8. Let's look at him. 9. We are
leaving it (*f.*). 10. Can he carry it? 11. Look at it
well (*fam.*). 12. They were about to leave. 13. Take
it (*m.*) now. 14. Did you send it (*f.*)? 15. He would
send them. 16. Announce me (*fam. pl.*). 17. They
had announced them. 18. Stop (*fam. pl.*). 19. Let's
end it (*f.*). 20. Write it (*f.*) immediately.

IV. Write a composition of about one hundred words on a train
trip, describing what you saw from the train. The teacher will
have the compositions read in class and let other students ask
questions on the topics.

V. Si traduca in italiano:

1. We are about to leave the country and the express
from Milano to Zurich is speeding along. 2. The compartment has two windows from which we can see the
mountains far away. 3. There are so many pretty-
little-houses surrounded by enormous-trees which look
like tiny-little-trees. 4. Can you see those cars which
seem to be going backwards because the train is speeding so rapidly? 5. If those sturdy-young-men are
strolling arm in arm with their fiancées they must be
very happy. 6. Those neat-little-women who are leading the little-children by the hand are going toward the
school. 7. When we were passing alongside the pretty-

little-stream I saw a beautiful little-bridge which I liked
very much. 8. Have you ever seen any really frightful
houses when you were traveling through Italy? 9. If
everybody stopped to watch the train, nobody would
be left at home. 10. Our trip ends with a visit to our
friends and our book ends with greetings to all.

WORD LIST

NOUNS

alberetto *m.* tiny tree
alberino *m.* little tree
alberone *m.* great big tree
baffoni *m. pl.* big mustache
bambino *m.* child
bigliettino *m.* little note
braccio *m.* (*pl.* **braccia** *f.*)
  arm
casaccia *f.* awful house
casetta *f.* tiny house
destinazione *f.* destination
direttissimo *m.* express
  train
donnetta *f.* neat little
  woman
ferrovia *f.* railway
fidanzata *f.* fiancée
finestrino *m.* car window
giovanotto *m.* sturdy young
  man
guancia *f.* cheek
ometto *m.* little man
paura *f.* fear
ponticello *m.* neat little
  bridge
ragazzino *m.* little boy, child
ruscelletto *m.* pretty little
  brook

scompartimento *m.* compartment
segretaria *f.* secretary
sedile *m.* seat
vecchietto *m.* neat little old
  man
viaggiatore *m.* traveler
villino *m.* neat little house
Zurigo Zurich

ADJECTIVES

buffo, –a funny
svizzero, –a Swiss

VERBS

annunziare to announce
coprire to cover
filare to speed along
indietreggiare to go backwards (takes **essere**)
spedire to send
sposarsi (**con**) to get married (to)

OTHER WORDS

avanti forwards
placidamente peacefully
rapidamente rapidly

VERB APPENDIX AND VOCABULARIES

I have bought - ho comprato
I had   "   avevo   "
  "   "   "   — ebbi   "
      (use only after —
         appena dopo quando)
I will have bought - avrò   "
I would have   "   — avrei

Accent marks   { Oggi giorno –
\ grave.   now - a - days
               { Tempo fa –
                days ago

Past Definite

mettere   vedere

misi   vidi
mettesti   vedesti
            vide
mise   vedemmo
mettemmo   vedeste
metteste   videro
misero

Present Participle –
   1. ando   –   2 & 3 endo

REGULAR VERBS AND AUXILIARIES

Regular Conjugations			Auxiliary Verbs	
I	II	III	avere	εssere

Infinitive (Infinito)

parlare	vendere	finire *and* dormire	avere	εssere

Present Participle (Partic*i*pio presεnte)

parlando	vendεndo	finεndo dormεndo	avεndo	essεndo

Past Participle (Partic*i*pio passato)

parlato	venduto	finito dormito	avuto	stato

Indicative Mood (Indicativo)

PRESENT (PRESεNTE)

parlo	vendo	finisco	dɔrmo	hɔ	sono
parli	vendi	finisci	dɔrmi	hai	sεi
parla	vende	finisce	dɔrme	ha	è
parliamo	vendiamo	finiamo	dormiamo	abbiamo	siamo
parlate	vendete	finite	dormite	avete	siεte
p*a*rlano	vendono	fin*i*scono	dɔrmono	hanno	sono

IMPERFECT *or* PAST DESCRIPTIVE (IMPERFεTTO) *time not definite*

parlavo	vendevo	finivo	avevo	εro
parlavi	vendevi	finivi	avevi	εri
parla*v*a	vendeva	finiva	aveva	εra
parlavamo	vendevamo	finivamo	avevamo	eravamo
parlavate	vendevate	finivate	avevate	eravate
parl*a*vano	vend*e*vano	fin*i*vano	avevano	εrano

PAST DEFINITE *or* PAST ABSOLUTE (PASSATO REMɔTO) *Preterite*

parlai	vendei (εtti)	finii	εbbi	fui	*volli*
parlasti	vendesti	finisti	avesti	fosti	*volesti*
parlɔ	vendè (εtte)	finì	εbbe	fu	*volle*
parlammo	vendemmo	finimmo	avemmo	fummo	*volemmo*
parlaste	vendeste	finiste	aveste	foste	*voleste*
parlarono	vend*e*rono (εttero)	fin*i*rono	εbbero	furono	*vollero*

FUTURE (FUTURO)

parlerɔ	venderɔ	finirɔ	avrɔ	sarɔ
parlerai	venderai	finirai	avrai	sarai
parlerà	venderà	finirà	avrà	sarà
parleremo	venderemo	finiremo	avremo	saremo
parlerete	venderete	finirete	avrete	sarete
parleranno	venderanno	finiranno	avranno	saranno

CONDITIONAL (CONDIZIONALE PRESÉNTE)

parlerɛi	venderɛi	finirɛi	avrɛi	sarɛi
parleresti	venderesti	finiresti	avresti	saresti
parlerɛbbe	venderɛbbe	finirɛbbe	avrɛbbe	sarɛbbe
parleremmo	venderemmo	finiremmo	avremmo	saremmo
parlereste	vendereste	finireste	avreste	sareste
parlerɛbbero	venderɛbbero	finirɛbbero	avrɛbbero	sarɛbbero

PRESENT PERFECT (PASSATO PRƆSSIMO)

hɔ parlato	hɔ venduto	hɔ finito	hɔ avuto	sono stato(a)

FIRST PLUPERFECT (TRAPASSATO PRƆSSIMO)

avevo parlato	avevo venduto	avevo finito	avevo avuto	ɛro stato(a)

SECOND PLUPERFECT (TRAPASSATO REMƆTO)

ɛbbi parlato	ɛbbi venduto	ɛbbi finito	ɛbbi avuto	fui stato(a)

FUTURE PERFECT (FUTURO ANTERIORE)

avrɔ parlato	avrɔ venduto	avrɔ finito	avrɔ avuto	sarɔ stato(a)

CONDITIONAL PERFECT (CONDIZIONALE PASSATO)

avrɛi parlato	avrɛi venduto	avrɛi finito	avrɛi avuto	sarɛi stato(a)

Subjunctive Mood (Congiuntivo or Soggiuntivo)

PRESENT (PRESÉNTE)

parli	venda	finisca	dɔrma	abbia	sia
parli	venda	finisca	dɔrma	abbia	sia
parli	venda	finisca	dɔrma	abbia	sia
parliamo	vendiamo	finiamo	dormiamo	abbiamo	siamo
parliate	vendiate	finiate	dormiate	abbiate	siate
parlino	vendano	finiscano	dɔrmano	abbiano	siano

IMPERFECT or PAST (IMPERFÉTTO)

parlassi	vendessi	finissi	avessi	fossi
parlassi	vendessi	finissi	avessi	fossi
parlasse	vendesse	finisse	avesse	fosse
parlassimo	vendessimo	finissimo	avessimo	fossimo
parlaste	vendeste	finiste	aveste	foste
parlassero	vendessero	finissero	avessero	fossero

PRESENT PERFECT (PASSATO)

abbia parlato	abbia venduto	abbia finito	abbia avuto	sia stato(a)

PAST PERFECT (TRAPASSATO)

avessi parlato   avessi venduto   avessi finito   avessi avuto   fossi stato(a)

Imperative (Imperativo)

| parla | vendi | finisci | dɔrmi | abbi | sii |
| parli | venda | finisca | dɔrma | abbia | sia |

parliamo	vendiamo	finiamo	dormiamo	abbiamo	siamo
parlate	vendete	finite	dormite	abbiate	siate
parlino	vendano	finiscano	dɔrmano	abbiano	siano

(Second person singular negative)

non parlare   non vendere   non finire   non dormire   non avere   non ɛssere

IRREGULAR VERBS

In this section we have given all the irregular verbs which are likely to be needed by a first-year student. We have not included verbs of a purely literary nature or verbs which are very uncommon. Only the irregular forms are given, and only enough of those to leave no doubt as to what the full conjugation would be. The asterisk (*) indicates that a verb is conjugated with ɛssere. The small circle (°) indicates that a verb is conjugated sometimes with ɛssere and sometimes with **avere**. The abbreviations used are as follows and in the following order:

p.i.	present indicative	*p.d.*	past definite
p.s.	present subjunctive	*p.p.*	past participle
f.	future	*pres. p.*	present participle
i.	imperfect	*impve.*	imperative

*accadere, to happen (*impersonal*); *see* cadere
accɛndere, to light; *p.d.* accesi, accendesti; *p.p.* acceso
accludere, to enclose; *p.d.* acclusi, accludesti; *p.p.* accluso
*accɔrgersi, to notice; *see* scɔrgere
accrescere, to increase; *see* crescere
aggiungere, to add; *see* giungere
ammettere, to admit; *see* mettere
*andare, to go; *p.i.* vado *or* vɔ, vai, va, andiamo, andate, vanno; *p.s.* vada; *f.* andrɔ; *impve.* va'
*apparire, to appear; *p.i.* appaio *or* apparisco, appari *or* apparisci, appare *or* apparisce, appariamo, apparite, appaiono *or* appariscono; *p.s.* appaia *or* apparisca; *p.d.* apparsi *or* apparvi *or* apparii, apparisti; *p.p.* apparso *or* apparito; *impve.* appari *or* apparisci
°appartenere, to belong; *see* tenere
appɛndere, to hang; *p.d.* appesi, appendesti; *p.p.* appeso
apprɛndere, to learn; *see* prɛndere
aprire, to open; *p.d.* apɛrsi *or* aprii, apristi; *p.p.* apɛrto
ardere, to burn; *p.d.* arsi, ardesti; *p.p.* arso

*__ascendere__, to ascend; *see* __scendere__
__ass*i*stere__, to assist, be present; *p.p.* assistito
__ass*u*mere__, to assume; *p.d.* assunsi, assumesti; *p.p.* assunto
*__avvedersi__, to perceive, notice; *see* __vedere__
*__avvenire__, to happen (*impersonal*); *see* __venire__
__avvɔlgere__, to wrap; *see* __vɔlgere__
__benedire__, to bless; *see* __dire__
__bere__, to drink; *p.i.* bevo, bevi; *f.* berrɔ̀; *i.* bevevo; *p.d.* bevvi *or* bevei *or* bevɛtti, bevesti; *p.p.* bevuto
*__cadere__, to fall; *f.* cadrɔ̀; *p.d.* caddi, cadesti
__chiɛdere__, to ask; *p.d.* chiɛsi, chiedesti; *p.p.* chiɛsto
__chiudere__, to close; *p.d.* chiusi, chiudesti; *p.p.* chiuso
__cɔgliere__, to gather; *p.i.* cɔlgo, cɔgli, cɔglie, cogliamo, cogliete, cɔlgono; *p.d.* cɔlsi, cogliesti; *p.p.* cɔlto
__commettere__, to commit; *see* __mettere__
__commuɔvere__, to move, affect; *see* __muɔvere__
*__comparire__, to appear; *see* __apparire__
__comporre__, to compose; *see* __porre__
__comprɛndere__, to comprehend, include; *see* __prɛndere__
__concɛdere__, to concede; *p.d.* concɛssi *or* concedei *or* concedɛtti, concedesti; *p.p.* concɛsso *or* conceduto
__conchiudere__ *or* __concludere__, to conclude; *see* __chiudere__ *and* __accludere__
__condurre__, to conduct, lead; *f.* condurrɔ̀; *i.* conducevo; *p.d.* condussi, conducesti; *p.p.* condotto
__confondere__, to confuse; *p.d.* confusi, confondesti; *p.p.* confuso
__conoscere__, to know; *p.d.* conobbi, conoscesti; *p.p.* conosciuto
*__cons*i*stere__, to consist; *p.p.* consistito
__contradire__, to contradict; *see* __dire__
__contrarre__, to contract; *see* __trarre__
__convenire__, to agree; *see* __venire__
__conv*i*ncere__, to convince; *see* __v*i*ncere__
__coprire__, to cover; *see* __aprire__
__corrɛggere__, to correct; *p.d.* corrɛssi, correggesti; *p.p.* corrɛtto
°__c*o*rrere__, to run; *p.d.* corsi, corresti; *p.p.* corso
__corrisp*o*ndere__, to correspond; *see* __risp*o*ndere__
__costr*i*ngere__, to force; *see* __str*i*ngere__
__costruire__, to construct, build; *p.d.* costrussi *or* costruii, costruisti; *p.p.* costrutto *or* costruito
°__crescere__, to grow; *p.d.* crebbi, crescesti; *p.p.* cresciuto
__cucire__, to sew; *p.i.* cucio; *p.s.* cucia
__cuɔcere__, to cook; *p.i.* cuɔcio, cuɔci, cuɔce, cociamo, cocete, cuɔciono; *p.s.* cuɔcia; *p.d.* cɔssi, cocesti; *p.p.* cɔtto
__dare__, to give; *p.i.* dɔ, dai, dà, diamo, date, danno; *p.s.* dia; *f.* darɔ̀; *p.d.* dɛtti *or* diɛdi, desti; *impve.* da'
__dec*i*dere__, to decide; *p.d.* decisi, decidesti; *p.p.* deciso
__descr*i*vere__, to describe; *see* __scr*i*vere__
__difɛndere__, to defend; *p.d.* difesi, difendesti; *p.p.* difeso
__diff*o*ndere__, to diffuse; *p.d.* diffusi, diffondesti; *p.p.* diffuso
*__dipɛndere__, to depend; *see* __appɛndere__
__dip*i*ngere__, to paint; *p.d.* dipinsi, dipingesti; *p.p.* dipinto
__dire__, to say, tell; *p.i.* dico, dici, dice, diciamo, dite, d*i*cono; *p.s.* dica; *f.* dirɔ̀; *i.* dicevo; *p.d.* dissi, dicesti; *p.p.* detto; *impve.* di', diciamo, dite
__dir*i*gere__, to direct; *p.d.* dirɛssi, dirigesti; *p.p.* dirɛtto

*__discendere__, to descend; *see* __scendere__
__discorrere__, to converse; *see* __correre__
__discutere__, to discuss; *p.d.* discussi, discutesti; *p.p.* discusso
*__dispiacere__, to be displeasing; *see* __piacere__
__disporre__, to dispose; *see* __porre__
__distinguere__, to distinguish; *p.d.* distinsi, distinguesti; *p.p.* distinto
__distrarre__, to distract; *see* __trarre__
__distruggere__, to destroy; *p.d.* distrussi, distruggesti; *p.p.* distrutto
*__divenire__, to become; *see* __venire__
__dividere__, to divide; *p.d.* divisi, dividesti; *p.p.* diviso
*__dolere__, to ache, pain; *p.i.* dɔlgo, duɔli, duɔle, doliamo, dolete, dɔlgono; *p.s.* dɔlga; *f.* dorrɔ̀; *p.d.* dɔlsi, dolesti
°__dovere__, to have to, be obliged to, must; *p.i.* dɛvo *or* dɛbbo, dɛvi, dɛve, dobbiamo, dovete, dɛvono *or* dɛbbono; *p.s.* dɛva *or* dɛbba; *f.* dovrɔ̀
*__esistere__, to exist; *p.p.* esistito
__esplodere__, to explode; *p.d.* esplɔsi, esplodesti; *p.p.* esplɔso
__esprimere__, to express; *p.d.* esprɛssi, esprimesti; *p.p.* esprɛsso
*__evadere__, to evade; *p.d.* evasi, evadesti; *p.p.* evaso
__fare__, to do, make; *p.i.* faccio *or* fɔ, fai, fa, facciamo, fate, fanno; *p.s.* faccia; *f.* farɔ̀; *i.* facevo; *p.d.* feci, facesti; *p.p.* fatto; *pres. p.* facɛndo; *impve.* fa', facciamo, fate
__fingere__, to pretend; *p.d.* finsi, fingesti; *p.p.* finto
__friggere__, to fry; *p.d.* frissi, friggesti; *p.p.* fritto
*__giacere__, to lie; *p.i.* giaccio, giaci, giace, giaciamo, giacete, giacciono; *p.s.* giaccia; *p.d.* giacqui, giacesti
°__giungere__, to arrive; join (*of hands*); *p.d.* giunsi, giungesti; *p.p.* giunto
__godere__, to enjoy; *f.* godrɔ̀
__imporre__, to impose; *see* __porre__
__imprimere__, to imprint, impress; *p.d.* imprɛssi, imprimesti; *p.p.* imprɛsso
__insistere__, to insist; *p.p.* insistito
__intɛndere__, to intend, understand; *p.d.* intesi, intendesti; *p.p.* inteso
__interrompere__, to interrupt; *see* __rompere__
*__intervenire__, to intervene; *see* __venire__
__introdurre__, to introduce; *p.i.* introduco, introduci; *p.s.* introduca; *f.* introdurrɔ̀; *i.* introducevo; *p.d.* introdussi, introducesti; *p.p.* introdotto
*__intrudersi__, to intrude; *p.d.* m'intrusi, t'intrudesti; *p.p.* intruso
__involgere__, to wrap; *see* __vɔlgere__
__lɛggere__, to read; *p.d.* lɛssi, leggesti; *p.p.* lɛtto
__mantenere__, to maintain; *see* __tenere__
__mettere__, to put; *p.d.* misi, mettesti; *p.p.* messo
__mɔrdere__, to bite; *p.d.* mɔrsi, mordesti; *p.p.* mɔrso
*__morire__, to die; *p.i.* muɔio, muɔri, muɔre, moriamo, morite, muɔiono; *p.s.* muɔia; *f.* morrɔ̀; *p.p.* mɔrto
__muɔvere__ *or* __mɔvere__, to move; *p.i.* muɔvo, muɔvi, muɔve, moviamo, movete, muɔvono; *p.d.* mɔssi, movesti; *p.p.* mɔsso
*__nascere__, to be born; *p.d.* nacqui, nascesti; *p.p.* nato
__nascondere__, to hide, conceal; *p.d.* nascosi, nascondesti; *p.p.* nascosto
__nuɔcere__ *or* __nɔcere__, to hurt, harm; *p.i.* nɔccio, nuɔci, nuɔce, nociamo, nocete, nɔcciono; *p.s.* nɔccia; *p.d.* nɔcqui, nocesti; *p.p.* nociuto
*__occɔrrere__, to be necessary (*impersonal*); *see* __correre__
__offɛndere__, to offend; *see* __difɛndere__
__offrire__, to offer; *p.d.* offɛrsi *or* offrii, offristi; *p.p.* offɛrto
__omettere__, to omit; *see* __mettere__

opporre to oppose; *see* **porre**

opprimere, to oppress; *p.d.* oppressi, opprimesti; *p.p.* oppresso

ottenere, to obtain; *see* **tenere**

*__parere__, to seem, appear; *p.i.* paio, pari, pare, paiamo *or* pariamo, parete, paiono; *p.s.* paia; *f.* parrò; *p.d.* parvi *or* parsi, paresti; *p.p.* parso

percorrere, to run over; *see* **correre**

percuotere, to strike; *see* **scuotere**

perdere, to lose; *p.d.* persi *or* perdei *or* perdetti, perdesti; *p.p.* perso *or* perduto

permettere, to permit; *see* **mettere**

persuadere, to persuade; *p.d.* persuasi, persuadesti; *p.p.* persuaso

*__piacere__, to be pleasing; *p.i.* piaccio, piaci, piace, piacciamo, piacete, piacciono; *p.s.* piaccia; *p.d.* piacqui, piacesti; *p.p.* piaciuto

piangere, to cry, weep; *p.d.* piansi, piangesti; *p.p.* pianto

°**piovere**, to rain (*impersonal*); *p.d.* piovve

porgere, to present, offer, extend; *p.d.* porsi, porgesti; *p.p.* porto

porre, to put, place; *p.i.* pongo, poni, pone, poniamo, ponete, pongono; *p.s.* ponga; *f.* porrò; *p.d.* posi, ponesti; *p.p.* posto

posporre, to postpone; *see* **porre**

possedere, to possess, own; *see* **sedere**

°**potere**, to be able, may, can; *p.i.* posso, puoi, può, possiamo, potete, possono; *p.s.* possa; *f.* potrò

prediligere, to prefer; *p.d.* predilessi, prediligesti; *p.p.* prediletto

prendere, to take; *p.d.* presi, prendesti; *p.p.* preso

pretendere, to pretend; *see* **tendere**

prevedere, to foresee; *see* **vedere**

prevenire, to anticipate, prevent, forewarn; *see* **venire**

produrre, to produce; *see* **condurre**

promettere, to promise; *see* **mettere**

proporre, to propose; *see* **porre**

proteggere, to protect; *p.d.* protessi, proteggesti; *p.p.* protetto

provvedere, to provide; *see* **vedere**

pungere, to prick, sting; *p.d.* punsi, pungesti; *p.p.* punto

raccogliere, to gather; *see* **cogliere**

radere, to shave; *p.d.* rasi, radesti; *p.p.* raso

raggiungere, to overtake; *see* **giungere**

redimere, to redeem; *p.d.* redensi, redimesti; *p.p.* redento

reggere, to support; *p.d.* ressi, reggesti; *p.p.* retto

rendere, to render; *p.d.* resi, rendesti; *p.p.* reso

reprimere, to repress; *see* **opprimere**

resistere, to resist; *p.p.* resistito

respingere, to push back; *see* **spingere**

richiedere, to request; *see* **chiedere**

riconoscere, to recognize; *see* **conoscere**

ricoprire, to cover again; *see* **aprire**

*__ricorrere__, to have recourse, refer; *see* **correre**

ridere, to laugh; *p.d.* risi, ridesti; *p.p.* riso

ridurre, to reduce; *see* **condurre**

rifare, to do again, make (*a bed*); *see* **fare**

riflettere, to reflect; *p.p.* riflesso *or* riflettuto

*__rimanere__, to remain; *p.i.* rimango, rimani, rimane, rimaniamo, rimanete, rimangono; *p.s.* rimanga; *f.* rimarrò; *p.d.* rimasi, rimanesti; *p.p.* rimasto

rimettere, to replace; *see* **mettere**
rimpiangere, to regret; *see* **piangere**
rimuovere, to remove; *see* **muovere**
*****rinascere,** to be born again; *see* **nascere**
rinchiudere, to shut in, enclose; *see* **chiudere**
*****rincrescere,** to regret *(impersonal)*; *see* **crescere**
riprendere, to take back, recover; *see* **prendere**
riprodurre, to reproduce; *see* **condurre**
riscuotere, to collect; *see* **scuotere**
risolvere, to resolve; *p.d.* risolsi *or* risolvei *or* risolvetti, risolvesti; *p.p.* risolto *or* risoluto
rispondere, to answer; *p.d.* risposi, rispondesti; *p.p.* risposto
ritenere, to retain; *see* **tenere**
ritrarre, to draw; *see* **trarre**
*****riuscire,** to succeed; *see* **uscire**
rivolgere, to turn, turn again; *see* **volgere**
rodere, to gnaw; *p.d.* rosi, rodesti; *p.p.* roso
rompere, to break; *p.d.* ruppi, rompesti; *p.p.* rotto
*****salire,** to ascend, climb, go up; *p.i.* salgo, sali, sale, saliamo, salite, salgono; *p.s.* salga
sapere, to know, know how; *p.i.* so, sai, sa, sappiamo, sapete, sanno; *p.s.* sappia; *f.* saprò; *p.d.* seppi, sapesti; *impve.* sappi, sappiamo, sappiate
*****scadere,** to fall due; *see* **cadere**
scegliere, to choose; *p.i.* scelgo, scegli, sceglie, scegliamo, scegliete, scelgono; *p.s.* scelga; *p.d.* scelsi, scegliesti; *p.p.* scelto
*****scendere,** to descend, go down; *p.d.* scesi, scendesti; *p.p.* sceso
schiudere, to open; *see* **chiudere**
sciogliere, to untie, dissolve; *p.i.* sciolgo, sciogli, scioglie, sciogliamo, sciogliete, sciolgono; *p.s.* sciolga; *p.d.* sciolsi, sciogliesti; *p.p.* sciolto
scommettere, to bet; *see* **mettere**
scoprire, to discover; *see* **aprire**
scorgere, to perceive; *p.d.* scorsi, scorgesti; *p.p.* scorto
scrivere, to write; *p.d.* scrissi, scrivesti; *p.p.* scritto
scuotere, to shake; *p.i.* scuoto, scuoti, scuote, scotiamo, scotete, scuotono; *p.s.* scuota; *f.* scuoterò; *p.d.* scossi, scotesti; *p.p.* scosso
sedere, to sit; *p.i.* siedo *or* seggo, siedi, siede, sediamo, sedete, siedono *or* seggono; *p.s.* sieda *or* segga
seppellire, to bury; *p.p.* sepolto *or* seppellito
smettere, to cease, stop; *see* **mettere**
smuovere, to move, displace; *see* **muovere**
soccorrere, to aid, assist; *see* **correre**
soddisfare, to satisfy; *see* **fare**
soffrire, to suffer; *see* **offrire**
soggiungere, to add; *see* **giungere**
*****solere,** to be accustomed; *p.i.* soglio, suoli, suole, sogliamo, solete, sogliono; *p.s.* soglia; *p.p.* solito
sommergere, to submerge; *p.d.* sommersi, sommergesti; *p.p.* sommerso
sopprimere, to suppress; *see* **esprimere**
*****sorgere,** to arise; *p.d.* sorsi, sorgesti; *p.p.* sorto
sorprendere, to surprise; *see* **prendere**
sorreggere, to support; *see* **reggere**
sorridere, to smile; *see* **ridere**
sospendere, to suspend; *see* **appendere**

216 BEGINNING ITALIAN GRAMMAR

sostenere, to support; *see* **tenere**
sottintɛndere, to imply; *see* **tɛndere**
sottomettere, to subdue; *see* **mettere**
sottrarre, to subtract; *see* **trarre**
spɑndere, to spread; *p.d.* spasi, spandesti; *p.p.* spaso
spɑrgere, to spread, scatter; *p.d.* sparsi, spargesti; *p.p.* sparso
*****sparire,** to disappear; *p.i.* sparisco; *p.d.* sparii *or* sparvi, sparisti
spɛndere, to spend; *p.d.* spesi, spendesti; *p.p.* speso
spengere *or* **spɛgnere,** to extinguish; *p.d.* spɛnsi, spengesti; *p.p.* spɛnto
*****spɛrdersi,** to disappear, get lost; *see* **pɛrdere**
spingere, to push; *p.d.* spinsi, spingesti; *p.p.* spinto
*****spɔrgersi,** to lean out; *see* **pɔrgere**
*****stare,** to stay, stand, be; *p.i.* stɔ, stai, sta, stiamo, state, stanno; *p.s.* stia; *f.* starɔ; *p.d.* stɛtti, stesti; *p.p.* stato; *impve.* sta'
stɛndere, to stretch out; *see* **tɛndere**
stringere, to tighten; *p.d.* strinsi, stringesti; *p.p.* stretto
*****succɛdere,** to succeed, happen; *see* **concɛdere**
supporre, to suppose; *see* **porre**
*****svenire,** to faint; *see* **venire**
svɔlgere, to unfold; *see* **vɔlgere**
tacere, to be silent; *p.i.* taccio, taci, tace, taciamo, tacete, tacciono; *p.s.* taccia; *p.d.* tacqui, tacesti; *p.p.* taciuto
tɛndere, to tend; *p.d.* tesi, tendesti; *p.p.* teso
tenere, to hold, have; *p.i.* tɛngo, tiɛni, tiɛne, teniamo, tenete, tɛngono; *p.s.* tɛnga; *f.* terrɔ; *p.d.* tenni, tenesti
tingere, to dye; *p.d.* tinsi, tingesti; *p.p.* tinto
tɔgliere *or* **tɔrre,** to take from; *p.i.* tɔlgo, tɔgli, tɔglie, togliamo, togliete, tɔlgono; *p.s.* tɔlga; *f.* togglierɔ *or* torrɔ; *p.d.* tɔlsi, togliesti; *p.p.* tɔlto
tɔrcere, to twist; *p.d.* tɔrsi, torcesti; *p.p.* tɔrto
tradurre, to translate; *see* **condurre**
trarre, to draw, pull; *p.i.* traggo, trai, trae, traiamo, traete, traggono; *p.s.* tragga; *f.* trarrɔ; *p.d.* trassi, traesti; *p.p.* tratto
trascorrere, to spend (*time*); *see* **correre**
trasmettere, to transmit; *see* **mettere**
trattenere, to detain; *see* **tenere**
uccidere, to kill; *p.d.* uccisi, uccidesti; *p.p.* ucciso
udire, to hear; *p.i.* ɔdo, ɔdi, ɔde, udiamo, udite, ɔdono; *p.s.* ɔda
ungere, to grease, anoint; *p.d.* unsi, ungesti; *p.p.* unto
*****uscire,** to go out; *p.i.* ɛsco, ɛsci, ɛsce, usciamo, uscite, ɛscono; *p.s.* ɛsca
*****valere,** to be worth; *p.i.* valgo, vali, vale, valiamo, valete, vɑlgono; *p.s.* valga; *f.* varrɔ; *p.d.* valsi, valesti; *p.p.* valso
vedere, to see; *f.* vedrɔ; *p.d.* vidi, vedesti; *p.p.* visto *or* veduto
*****venire,** to come; *p.i.* vɛngo, vieni, viɛne, veniamo, venite, vɛngono; *p.s.* vɛnga; *f.* verrɔ; *p.d.* venni, venisti; *p.p.* venuto
vincere, to win; *p.d.* vinsi, vincesti; *p.p.* vinto
°**vivere,** to live; *f.* vivrɔ; *p.d.* vissi, vivesti; *p.p.* vissuto
°**volere,** to will, wish, want; *p.i.* vɔglio, vuɔi, vuɔle, vogliamo, volete, vɔgliono; *p.s.* vɔglia; *f.* vorrɔ; *p.d.* vɔlli, volesti; *impve.* vɔgli, vogliamo, vogliate
vɔlgere, to turn, revolve; *p.d.* vɔlsi, volgesti; *p.p.* vɔlto**

Vocabulary

ITALIAN–ENGLISH

Articles, contractions, numerals, identical cognates, and words and expressions translated in the grammar sections are generally omitted from this vocabulary. The asterisk (*) before a verb indicates that it is conjugated with **εssere**; the sign (°) indicates that the verb sometimes takes **εssere** and sometimes **avere**, according to the meaning. Tonic open **e** is indicated by the symbol ε; tonic open **o,** by ɔ; these two symbols, italicized vowels, and the grave accent indicate stress. In words in which the stress is not indicated, it comes on the next to the last vowel. Italicized *s* and *z* are voiced. Only the grave accent is used.

A

a, ad to, at, about, in, for
abbastanza *adv.* enough, sufficiently
abitare (*pres.* **abito**) to live, dwell
abito *m.* dress
abituato, –a accustomed
aborrire (da) (*pres.* **aborro**) to abhor
accanto (a) next to; next door; **lì —,** next to it
accettare (*pres.* **accεtto**) to accept
acciuga *f.* anchovy
*accomodarsi (*pres.* **mi accɔmodo**) to make oneself comfortable, make oneself at home, sit down
accompagnare to accompany
accɔrdo *m.* agreement; **d'—,** in agreement
*accɔrgersi to notice
acqua *f.* water
acquistare to acquire, obtain
adatto, –a suitable
adεsso now
adoperare (*pres.* **adɔpero**) to use
adorare (*pres.* **adoro**) to adore
Adriatico *m.* Adriatic Sea
aεreo, –a *adj.* air; **linea aεrea** *f.* airline
aeroplano *m.* airplane
aeropɔrto *m.* airport
affanno *m.* care, anxiety
affatto at all
affettuoso, –a affectionate

affinchè so that, in order that
aff. mo, –a = affezionatissimo, –a most affectionate
affezionato, –a devoted
agile nimble
agnεllo *m.* lamb; **— al forno** *m.* roast lamb
agosto *m.* August
agricola (*invar. in sing.*) agricultural
agricoltura *f.* agriculture
ah! oh!
alberetto *m.* tiny little tree
albεrgo *m.* hotel
alberino *m.* little tree
albero *m.* tree; **— da frutta** fruit tree
alberone *m.* great big tree
Alberto Albert
alcuni, –e some
Alfa Romεo *make of car*
Alighiεri, Dante (1265–1321) *greatest Italian poet*
alliεvo *m.* pupil
allɔggio *m.* lodging
allora then; **d'— in pɔi** from then on
almeno at least
Alpi *f. pl.* Alps
alpinismo *m.* Alpinism, mountain climbing
altezza *f.* height
alto, –a tall, high
altro, –a other; **che altro** what else; **non altro che** nothing but
alunno *m.* (**alunna** *f.*) pupil

*alzarsi to get up
Amalfi *a city near Naples, on the famous Amalfi drive*
ambizione *f.* ambition
Amεrica *f.* America
americano, –a American
amica *f. (pl.* amiche) friend
amicizia *f.* friendship
amico *m. (pl.* amici) friend
ammalato, –a ill, sick
ammettere *irr.* to admit
ammirare to admire
ammiratore *m.* admirer
amore *m.* love
anatomia *f.* anatomy
anche also, even
ancora yet, still
*andare to go; — a passeggio to go for a walk; — a perfezione to fit perfectly
Andrεa del Sarto (1487–1531) *great Italian painter*
anεddoto *m.* anecdote
Angεlico: Fra — *or* Il Beato —, (1387–1455) *great Italian painter*
angolo *m.* corner
anno *m.* year
*annoiarsi (*pres.* mi annɔio) to get bored
annunziare (*pres.* annunzio) to announce
antichità *f.* antiquity
antico, –a old, ancient
Antɔnio Anthony
apparecchiare (*pres.* apparecchio) to set (*a table*)
apparecchio *m.* appliance, set; — cinematografico movie camera
apparεnza *f.* appearance
*apparire *irr.* to appear
appena hardly; non —, as soon as; — che as soon as
Appennini *m. pl.* Apennines
appetito *m.* appetite; avere —, to be hungry; buɔn —, enjoy your dinner; sentire —, to feel hungry
apprezzare (*pres.* apprεzzo) to appreciate
approdare (*pres.* apprɔdo) to dock, land
appunto exactly
aprire *irr.* to open

arancia *f.* orange; spremuta d'—, orange juice
arancio *m.* orange tree
archeolɔgico, –a archeological
architεtto *m.* architect
arco *m.* bow
aria *f.* air; all'— apεrta in the open air; darsi molte arie, put on airs
aristocrazia *f.* aristocracy
armadio *m.* closet
*arrivare to arrive
arrivederla (*or* arrivederci) goodby, so long
arrivo *m.* arrival
arte *f.* art; le bεlle arti the fine arts
articolo *m.* article
artista *m. or f.* artist
ascensore *m.* elevator
ascoltare (*pres.* ascolto) to listen to
aspettare (*pres.* aspεtto) to wait (for)
assicurare to assure; *assicurarsi to make certain
astrɔnomo *m.* astronomer
atɔmico, –a atomic
attraversare (*pres.* attravεrso) to cross
attravεrso through
aula *f.* classroom
autobus *m.* bus
automɔbile *f.* automobile, car; — da corsa *f.* racing car
automobilistico, –a auto (*adj.*)
autostrada *f.* highway
autunno *m.* autumn
avanti forward
avere *irr.* to have
aviazione *f.* aviation
Avignone *a city in southern France, once the residence of the Popes*
avvocato *m.* lawyer
azzurro, –a blue

B

babbo *m.* dad, father
baffoni *m. pl.* big mustache
*bagnarsi to get wet, bathe
baia *f.* bay
ballo *m.* dancing, dance

bambino *m.* child
barbiere *m.* barber; **fare il** —, to be a barber
Bargello *a famous museum in Florence*
barometro *m.* barometer
base *f.* basis
bastare *imper.* to be enough
battistero *m.* baptistry
beato, –a lucky, happy
Beethoven (1770–1827) *one of the greatest German composers*
bellezza *f.* beauty
Bellini, Giovanni (1426–1516) *early Italian painter*
Bellini, Vincenzo (1801–1835) *famous Italian operatic composer*
bellissimo, –a very beautiful
bello, –a (**bei, begli**) beautiful
bel paese *m. a type of cheese*
benchè although
bene (**ben**) well, fine; **va bene** that's fine
bene *m.* good; **fa — alla salute** is good for the health
benedetto, –a blessed
bere *irr.* to drink
Bernini, Giovanni Lorenzo (1598–1680) *famous Italian painter, sculptor, and architect*
bianco, –a white
bicchiere *m.* glass
bigliettino *m.* little note
biglietto *m.* ticket; **fare il** —, to get a ticket
binario *m.* track
biografia *f.* biography
biondo, –a blond
biscotto *m.* cookie
bisognare *imper.* (*pres.* **bisogna**) to need to, have to
bisogno *m.* need; **aver — di** to need; **far** —, to need
bocca *f.* mouth; **a — aperta** gaping
Boccaccio, Giovanni (1313–1375) *the greatest Italian writer of prose*
Bologna *important city in north central Italy*
borsetta *f.* handbag
bottega *f.* shop
Botticelli, Sandro (1444–1510) *great Italian painter*

bottiglia *f.* bottle
bottone *m.* button
braccetto: a — di arm in arm with
braccio *m.* (*pl.* **braccia** *f.*) arm; **a braccia aperte** with open arms
bravo, –a good, fine; **bravo!** fine!
Brunelleschi, Filippo (1377–1446) *famous Italian sculptor and architect*
brutto, –a bad
buffo, –a funny
buio *m.* dark, darkness; **al** —, in the dark
buono, –a good; good-hearted
burro *m.* butter

C

*****cadere** *irr.* to fall; **lasciar** —, to drop
caffè *m.* coffee; café; **— e latte** coffee with milk; **— espresso** strong black coffee, demi-tasse
calcio *m.* soccer
caldo *m.* heat; **fa** —, it is warm
calzolaio *m.* shoemaker
camera *f.* room; **— da letto** bedroom; **in** —, in my room, in the room
cameriera *f.* maid
cameriere *m.* waiter
camicia *f.* shirt; **in maniche di** —, in shirt sleeves
camminare to walk
cammino *m.* way, road
campanello *m.* bell
Campanile di Giotto *m. famous tower next to the Duomo in Florence*
campo *m.* field
canale *m.* canal
cantare to sing
canto *m.* canto (*of a poem*)
capire (**isco**) to understand
capitale *f.* capital
capo *m.* head
capolavoro *m.* masterpiece
capoluogo *m.* capital (*of a region*)
cappello *m.* hat
Capri *a very picturesque island in the bay of Naples*
Via Caracciolo *one of the pictur-*

esque streets in Naples, running along the bay

caratteristica *f.* characteristic

caratteristico, –a characteristic

carbone *m.* coal

carciofo *m.* artichoke

carissimo, –a dearest

Carlo Charles

carne *f.* meat

caro, –a dear, expensive

carta *f.* paper; **— geografica** *f.* map

casa *f.* house, home; **a —**, home, to the house; **in —**, at home; **— commerciale** *f.* business house; **— editrice** *f.* publishing house

casaccia *f.* awful house

casetta *f.* neat little house

caspita! heavens!

Castellammare di Stabia *city on the bay of Naples*

castello (castel) *m.* castle; **Castel Gandolfo** *Papal summer residence*

cattedrale *f.* cathedral

cattivo, –a bad

causare (*pres.* **causo**) to cause

cavallo *m.* horse

Cellini, Benvenuto (1500–1571) *celebrated sculptor and goldsmith*

cena *f.* supper

Cenacolo *m.* Last Supper

cento one hundred

centrale central

centro *m.* center

cercare (*pres.* **cerco**) to look for, search

cerimonia *f.* ceremony; **far cerimonie** to stand on ceremony

certo certainly

che that; than; who, whom, which; **che . . . non** *conj.* without

che? what? **— cosa?** what? **— altro?** what else?

chè = perchè for, because

chi who, whom; he who, the one who

chi? who? whom?

chiamare to call; ***chiamarsi** to be called; **si chiama** his name is

chiaro, –a clear

chiasso *m.* noise

chiedere *irr.* to ask, ask for

chiesa *f.* church

chitarra *f.* guitar

chiunque whoever

ci there; **c'è** there is; **ci sono** there are

ciarlare to chat

ciascuno, –a each

cibo *m.* food

ciclismo *m.* bicycle riding

cielo *m.* sky

cinematografia *f.* movie industry

cinematografo *m.* movies

cinquanta fifty

cinque five

ciò that; **cioè** that is

cipria *f.* face powder

circolo *m.* club; circle

circondare (*pres.* **circondo**) to surround

città *f.* city; **Città Eterna** Eternal City (*Rome*)

civiltà *f.* civilization

classe *f.* class

clientela *f.* clientele

clima *m.* climate

colazione *f.* breakfast; **seconda —**, lunch; **far —**, to have breakfast

collezione *f.* collection

colore *m.* color

coltello *m.* knife

coltivare to cultivate

colto, –a cultured

come how, what, like, just as, as; **come?** why? how is that? **— mai?** how come?

cominciare (*pres.* **comincio**) to begin

commentare (*pres.* **commento**) to comment, write a commentary

commento *m.* commentary

commerciale commercial, business (*adj.*)

commercio *m.* business

comodamente comfortably

comodo *m.* comfort; **con tutto il —**, as much as one wishes, at complete leisure

comodo, –a comfortable

compagna *f.* companion, friend

compagnia *f.* company

compagno *m.* companion

compito *m.* assignment; *pl.* home-work

completamente completely

completare (*pres.* **compl**ɛ**to**) to complete

complɛ**to, –a** complete

comporre *irr.* to compose

*__comportarsi__ (*pres.* **mi comp**ɔ**rto**) to behave

compositore *m.* composer

composto (*p.p. of* **comporre**) having composed

compra *f.* purchase; **far delle compre** to do some shopping

comprare (*pres.* **compro**) to buy

comprɛ**ndere** *irr.* to understand

comune common

comune *m.* commune, community

comu**nque** however

con with

conca d'ɔ**ro** *f.* gold bowl

concɛ**rto** *m.* concert, concerto

concɛ**tto** *m.* concept, conception

condizione *f.* condition; **a — che** *conj.* on condition that

confusione *f.* confusion

congiu**ngere** *irr.* to be joined to

conoscɛ**nza** *f.* acquaintance

conoscere *irr.* to know

consegnare (*pres.* **consegno**) to turn over

conservare (*pres.* **cons**ɛ**rvo**) to preserve, keep

considerare (*pres.* **cons**i**dero**) to consider

consi**glio** *m.* advice

consi**stere** (*pres.* **consisto**) to consist

contagioso, –a contagious

contare (*pres.* **conto**) to count

*__contentarsi__ (*pres.* **mi cont**ɛ**nto**) to be satisfied

contɛ**nto, –a** happy

continɛ**nte** *m.* continent

continuare (*pres.* **cont**i**nuo**) to continue

conti**nuo, –a** continual

conto *m.* account; **tener — di** to keep in mind; **per — mio** for myself

contrabasso *m.* double bass

conversare (*pres.* **conv**ɛ**rso**) to talk

conversazione *f.* conversation

coprire *irr.* to cover

cɔ**r = cu**ɔ**re** *m.* heart

coraggioso, –a courageous, brave

cordialità *f.* cordiality

cornetta *f.* cornet

cɔ**rpo** *m.* body

°**correre** *irr.* to run

corsa *f.* race; **autom**ɔ**bile da —,** *f.* racing car

corso *m.* course, class

corte *f.* court

cortese courteous

corto, –a short

cɔ**sa** *f.* thing; **c**ɔ**sa?** *or* **che — ?** what?

così thus, so; **così . . . come** as . . . as

costare (*pres.* **c**ɔ**sto**) to cost; **— un** ɔ**cchio** to cost a fortune

costruire (**isco**) to build

costume *m.* costume

cotesto (**codesto**), **–a** that (*near person spoken to*)

cɔ**tto** (*p.p. of* **cu**ɔ**cere**) cooked; **prosciutto —,** *m.* boiled ham

cravatta *f.* necktie

credere (*pres.* **credo**) to believe

cresta *f.* crest

criticare (*pres.* **cr**i**tico**) to criticize

crudo, –a raw; **prosciutto —,** *m.* smoked (Virginia) ham

cucchiaino *m.* teaspoon

cucchia**io** *m.* spoon

cucina *f.* kitchen; **in —,** in the kitchen

cugino *m.* cousin

cui whom; **il —, la —,** *etc.* whose

culla *f.* cradle

cultura *f.* culture

cuɔ**io** *m.* leather

cuɔ**re** *m.* heart

curioso, –a curious

curva *f.* curve

D

da from, by; at the house of

dappertutto everywhere

dare *irr.* to give; *__darsi pensi__ɛ__ro__ to worry

datare (**da**) to date from (back to)

dato che *conj.* since

davanti a in front of

davvero really
dec*i*dere *irr.* to decide; ***dec*i*dersi**
  (a) to decide (to)
decimot*ε*rzo, –a thirteenth
decorare (*pres.* **dec*ɔ*ro**) to decorate
denaro *m.* money
dentifr*i*cio *m.* toothpaste
desiderare (*pres.* **des*i*dero**) to desire, want
desid*ε*rio *m.* desire; **avevamo pr*ɔ*-
  prio —, we were quite anxious
destinazione *f.* destination
d*ε*stra *f.* right hand; **a —**, to the
  right
dettatura *f.* dictation
di of; than; from
di*a*logo *m.* dialogue
diamante *m.* diamond
diann*ɔ*ve nineteen; **le —**, seven
  o'clock
diciass*ε*tte seventeen
dici*ɔ*tto eighteen; **—mila** eighteen
  thousand
di*ε*ci ten
diff*i*cile difficult, hard
difficoltà *f.* difficulty, trouble
***diff*o*ndersi** *irr.* to become popular
dil*ε*tto *m.* delight, pleasure
dimenticare (*pres.* **dimentico**) to
  forget
dimostrare (*pres.* **dimostro**) to
  show
dinastia *f.* dynasty
dintorni *m. pl.* neighborhood, surroundings
Dio *m.* God
dip*ε*ndere (da) *irr.* to depend (on)
dip*i*ngere *irr.* to paint
dire *irr.* to say; **vu*ɔ*l dire** it means
direttamente directly
direttissimo *m.* express (train)
direttore *m.* director
direttrice *f.* director
dirimp*ε*tto (a) opposite
disa*s*tro *m.* disaster
discesa *f.* descent
disc*o*rrere *irr.* to discuss
disio *m.* desire
disperare (*pres.* **disp*ε*ro**) to despair
dispon*i*bile eligible
distante distant, far
distanza *f.* distance

dist*i*nguere *irr.* to distinguish
disturbare to disturb
dito *m.* (*pl.* **dita** *f.*) finger
ditta *f.* firm
***diventare** (*pres.* **divento**) to be-
  come
***divertirsi** (*pres.* **mi div*ε*rto**) to
  have a good time, enjoy oneself
div*i*dere *irr.* to divide
divinamente divinely
divino, –a divine; **Divina Com-
  m*ε*dia** *f.* Divine Comedy
doccia *f.* shower
dodici twelve; **alle —**, at twelve
  o'clock
dodicimila twelve thousand
dogana *f.* customhouse; **andare
  in —**, to go to the customhouse;
  passar la —, to go through
  customs
dolce sweet; **Dolce Stil Nu*ɔ*vo** *a
  style of poetry current at the end of
  the thirteenth century in Italy*
d*ɔ*llaro *m.* dollar
domanda *f.* question; **far una —**,
  to ask a question
domandare to ask
domattina tomorrow morning
domenica *f.* Sunday
Donat*ε*llo (Donato de' Bardi)
  (1386–1466) *one of the greatest
  Italian sculptors*
Donizetti, Gaetano (1797–1848)
  famous Italian operatic composer
d*ɔ*nna *f.* lady
donnetta *f.* neat little woman
dopo after; **— che** *conj.* after
dormire (*pres.* **d*ɔ*rmo**) to sleep
dotato (di) endowed (with)
dottore *m.* doctor
dove where; **di — *ε*?** where are
  you from?
°dovere *irr.* to have to, owe
do*z*zina *f.* dozen
dubitare (*pres.* **d*u*bito**) to doubt;
  non d*u*biti don't worry! by all
  means!
due two
duec*ε*nto two hundred
duetto *m.* duet
du*ɔ*mo *m.* cathedral, duomo
durante during
***durare** to last

E

e, ed and
ebbɛne *adv.* well
eccellɛnte excellent
eccessivo, –a excessive
eccezione *f.* exception
ɛcco here is, here are
econɔmico, –a economical
edifício *m.* building
editrice editorial; **casa —,** *f.* publishing house
effɛtto *m.* effect; **fare —,** to be effective, look better
Egitto *m.* Egypt
egiziano, –a Egyptian
elegante elegant
elettricista *m.* electrician
elɛttrico, –a electrical
***entrare** (*pres.* **entro**) to enter, go in
eppure and yet
ɛra *f.* era, age
Ercolano Herculaneum, *a city covered by lava when Vesuvius erupted in 79 A.D.*
erudito, –a learned
esɛmpio *m.* example; **ad —,** *or* **per —,** for example
esercizio *m.* exercise
esprimere *irr.* to express
***ɛssere** *irr.* to be
estate *f.* summer
estivo, –a summer (*adj.*)
etɛrno, –a eternal
Eurɔpa *f.* Europe
europɛo, –a European

F

fa ago
fabbrica *f.* factory
facchino *m.* porter
facilmente easily
facoltà *f.* faculty
falegname *m.* carpenter; **fare il —,** to be a carpenter
fama *f.* fame
famíglia *f.* family
familiare familiar, family (*adj.*); **fɛsta —,** *f.* party
famoso, –a famous
fanciullo *m. or* **fanciulla** *f.* child
fantastico, –a fantastic

fare *irr.* to make, do, let; **far colazione** to have breakfast; **fare una domanda** to ask a question; **fare un viaggio** to take a trip; **far portare** to have brought; **fare le sue scuse** to make one's apologies; **fare una bɛlla vita** to lead a nice life; ***farsi** to become; ***farsi ricco** to get rich
fatto *m.* fact; happening, event; **fatto sta** the point is, the fact is
favore *m.* favor; **per —,** please
favorito, –a favorite
fazzoletto *m.* handkerchief
fedele faithful
Federico II (1194–1250) *learned king of Sicily, in whose court Italian literature began*
felice happy
feltro *m.* felt pad
femminile feminine
***fermarsi** (*pres.* **mi fermo**) to stop
ferrovia *f.* railway; **in —,** on the train
ferroviario, –a railway (*adj.*); **stazione —a** *f.* railroad station
fɛrtile fertile
fɛsta *f.* feast; **— familiare** party
FIAT = **Fabbrica Italiana Automɔbili Torino**
fico *m.* fig tree; fig
fidanzamento *m.* engagement
fidanzata *f.* fiancée
figlia *f.* daughter
figlio *m.* son
***filare** to speed along
filigrana *f.* filigree
filɔsofo *m.* philosopher
finalmente finally
finanche even, as far as
finchè until
fine *f.* end
finɛstra *f.* window
finestrino *m.* car window
finire (**isco**) to finish; **— per** to end up by
fino a until, up to; **fin(o) da** ever since
finta: far — di to make believe
fiore *m.* flower
fiorentino, –a Florentine
Firɛnze *f.* Florence, *a city in Tuscany, in central Italy*

fisica f. physics
fisico m. physicist
fisso, -a fixed; **orario fisso** m. fixed hours
fiume m. river
flauto m. flute
foglio m. sheet (of paper)
fontana f. fountain; **Fontana di Trevi** Trevi Fountain
forchetta f. fork
formaggio m. cheese
formare (pres. **formo**) to form
Formia a city in Lazio, on the road from Naples to Rome
fornaio m. baker
forse perhaps
forte adj. strong, loud; adv. hard
fortissimo, -a very strong
forza f. strength
fra between, among, within; — **poco** (**tempo**) soon; — **di loro** among themselves
Francia f. France
frase f. phrase, saying
fratello m. brother
frattempo: nel —, meanwhile
freddo m. cold; **fa** —, it's cold
fresco, -a cool
fretta f. hurry; **aver** —, to be in a hurry; **in** —, hurriedly
fritto, -a fried
frutta f. fruit
fruttivendolo m. fruit vendor
fulmine f. lightning (bolt)
funzione f. function
futuro m. future

G

Galileo: Galileo Galilei (1564–1642) one of the world's great scientists, mathematicians, and astronomers
gamba f. leg
geloso, -a jealous
generale general
generalmente generally
generare (pres. **genero**) to generate, produce
generazione f. generation
genio m. genius
genitori m. pl. parents
gentile kind

geografia f. geography
gerente m. manager
Germania f. Germany
Ghiberti, Lorenzo (1378–1455) famous Italian sculptor, painter, and architect
già already
giacca f. coat (of suit), jacket
giacchè since
giallo, -a yellow
Giambologna (Giovanni da Bologna) (1524–1608) famous Italian sculptor
giardino m. garden
ginocchio m. (pl. **ginocchia** f.) knee
gioco m. game
Giorgio George
giornata f. day
giorno m. day
Giotto (di Bondone) (1276–1336) great Florentine painter and architect
giovane adj. young; m. young man; f. young lady
giovanotto m. sturdy young man
gioventù f. youth
girare to turn; go around
giro m. tour; **fare un** —, to walk around
gita f. trip; **fare una** —, to take a trip
giù down
giudizio m. judgment; **con** —, with good sense
Giulio Cesare m. a ship of the Italian Line
***giungere** irr. to arrive at, reach
giuramento m. oath
gli pron. to him
godere (pres. **godo**) to enjoy
Goldoni, Carlo (1707–1793) famous Italian playwright
golfo m. bay, gulf
gondola f. gondola
gorgonzola m. a type of blue cheese
governare (pres. **governo**) to govern
governo m. government
gradazione f. gradation, scale
grande (gran) big, large
grandezza f. size
grandioso, -a grandiose

grato, –a grateful
grattacielo *m.* skyscraper
grazie *f. pl.* thanks; **tante —,** thank you very much
grazioso, –a pretty, graceful
Greco *m.* Greek
grido *m. (pl.* **grida** *f.,* **gridi** *m.)* cry
grigio, –a gray
gruppo *m.* group
guadagnare to earn
guancia *f.* cheek
guardare to look at; *****guardarsi** to look at oneself
guardia *f.* guard
guerra *f.* war
guida *f.* guide; **far da —,** act as a guide
guidare to drive

I

Iddio the Lord
idea *f.* idea
ideale ideal
ieri l'altro the day before yesterday
ignorante ignorant
imbottito, –a stuffed; **panino imbottito** *m.* sandwich
imitatore *m.* imitator
immaginare *(pres.* **immagino)** to imagine
imparare to learn
impegno *m.* obligation, duty
impero *m.* empire
impiegato *m.* clerk, employee
importante important
importantissimo, –a most important
importanza *f.* importance
impressione *f.* impression
incantevole enchanting
incanto *m.* enchantment, charm
incomodare *(pres.* **incomodo)** to inconvenience
incontrare *(pres.* **incontro)** to meet
indi thence, from this
indicare *(pres.* **indico)** to indicate
indietreggiare *(pres.* **indietreggio)** to go backwards
indipendente independent

individualmente individually
individuo *m.* individual
indulgente kind, indulgent
industria *f.* industry
industriale industrial
infatti in fact
Inferno *m.* Hell; *the first* **cantica** *of the Divine Comedy*
infinito *m.* infinitive
influsso *m.* influence
ingegnere *m.* engineer
Inghilterra *f.* England
inglese *adj.* English; *m.* Englishman
inimitabile inimitable
iniziatore *m.* initiator
inoltre moreover
insegnare *(pres.* **insegno)** to teach
insieme together; **— a** together with
insomma after all
intelligenza *f.* intelligence
interessante interesting
interessantissimo, –a most interesting
interessare *(pres.* **interesso)** to interest
intero, –a whole
interpetre *m.* interpreter
inutile useless
inutilmente uselessly
invece instead
invenzione *f.* invention
inverno *m.* winter
invitare to invite
invitato *m.* guest *(at dinner)*
invito *m.* invitation
Ischia *a picturesque island in the bay of Naples*
isola *f.* island
ispirazione *f.* inspiration
Italia *f.* Italy
italiano, –a Italian; *m.* Italian
ivi there

L

la *pron.* her, it
là *adv.* there
labbro *m. (pl.* **labbra** *f.)* lip
laboratorio *m.* laboratory
lagrima *f.* tear
lampeggiare *(pres.* **lampeggia)** to lighten, be lightning

226

BEGINNING ITALIAN GRAMMAR

Lancia *make of car*
largo, –a wide
lasciare to leave, let; **lasciar vedere** to let one see; **lasciar fare** to let one do as he wishes
latino *m.* Latin
lato *m.* side
latte *m.* milk
laurea *f.* degree
lavorare (*pres.* **lavoro**) to work
lavoro *m.* work; **— di casa** housework
le *pron.* them
legame *m.* tie
legare (*pres.* **lego**) to bind
legge *f.* law
lɛggere *irr.* to read
lenzuɔlo *m.* (*pl.* **lenzuɔla** *f.*) (bed) sheet
Leonardo da Vinci (1452–1519) *the greatest genius of all times*
Leoncavallo, Ruggero (1858–1919) *famous Italian operatic composer*
lɛttera *f.* letter
letterato *m.* literary figure
letteratura *f.* literature
lɛttere *f. pl.* liberal arts
lɛtto *m.* bed
lezione *f.* lesson
li *pron.* them
lì *adv.* there
libro *m.* book
Lido *m. famous beach on a reef near Venice*
liɛto, –a happy
limone *m.* lemon tree; lemon
linea *f.* line; **— aɛrea** *f.* airline
lingua *f.* language
lira *f.* lira (*at present one dollar = 625 lire*)
lo *pron.* him, it
Londra *f.* London
lontano far; **— da** far from; **—, far away
Lorɛnzo Lawrence
Loro you; **il Loro, la Loro,** *etc.* your
loro them, they, to them
il loro, la loro, *etc.* their, theirs
luce *f.* light
Lucia Lucy
luglio *m.* July
lui him, he

lungo, –a long; **lungo** *prep.* along; **più a —,** further, more
luɔgo *m.* place
lusso *m.* luxury; **di —,** luxurious, expensive

M

ma but
macchina *f.* car; **— di gran lusso** *f.* very luxurious model
madre *f.* mother
maɛstro *m.* teacher
magari perhaps
maggiore major, greater, larger
mai never; **non ... —,** never; **se —,** even if
malato *m.* sick person
malattia *f.* illness
male *adv.* bad, badly
male *n.m.* evil, ache; **non c'ɛ —,** fairly well
maledetto, –a cursed
mancanza *f.* lack; **sentir la —,** to miss
mancare to lack, be missing
mandare to send
mandolino *m.* mandolin
mangiare to eat; **qualche cɔsa da —,** something to eat
manica *f.* sleeve; **in maniche di camicia** in shirt sleeves
maniɛra *f.* manner, way
mano *f.* hand
mantenere *irr.* to keep
manzo ai fɛrri *m.* broiled beef, steak
mare *m.* sea
Margherita Margaret
Maria Mary
marito *m.* husband
Marsala *m. a well-known Sicilian wine*
Mascagni, Piɛtro (1863–1945) *famous Italian operatic composer*
matematico *m.* mathematician
matrimɔnio *m.* matrimony, marriage
mattina *f.* morning
maturo, –a mature
me me, myself
meccanica *f.* mechanics
meccanico, –a mechanical

medicina *f.* medicine
mɛdico *m.* doctor
medioɛvo *m.* Middle Ages
meditazione *f.* meditation
Mediterraneo *m.* Mediterranean
mɛglio *adv.* better
mela *f.* apple
melodia *f.* melody, aria
meno minus, less; — **di** *or* — **che** less than; **a** — **che** . . . **non** unless
mentre while
meravíglia *f.* surprise, wonder, astonishment; **a** —, marvelously; **non gli fa** —, it doesn't surprise him
*__meravigliarsi__ (*pres.* **mi meravíglio**) to be astonished
meraviglioso, -a marvelous
mercato *m.* shopping district
meridionale southern
meritare (*pres.* **mɛrito**) to command, deserve
mese *m.* month
mestiɛre *m.* trade
mɛtro *m.* meter (*39.37 inches*)
mettere *irr.* to put; — **a luce** to bring to light; — **in mostra** to put on display, display; *__mettersi a__ to start
mɛzzo, -a half; **la mɛzza** half-past twelve; **mɛzz'oretta** *f.* about half an hour
mezzogiorno *m.* noon
mi me, to me, for me, myself
mica at all; **non** . . . —, hardly
Michelangelo Buonarroti (1475–1564) *one of the greatest artistic geniuses of all times*
migliorare (*pres.* **miglioro**) to improve
migliore better; **il** —, the best
mila (*pl.* *of* **mille**) thousands
mille (*pl.* **mila**) thousand; **mille e cɛnto** *f.* small sedan (*FIAT model*)
minɛstra *f.* soup, first course
minestrone *m.* thick vegetable soup
minuto *m.* minute
il mio, la mia, *etc.* my, mine
missione *f.* mission
mobili *m. pl.* furniture
moda *f.* fashion

modɛllo *m.* model
modɛrno, -a modern
modɛsto, -a modest, simple
modista *f.* milliner
modo *m.* way
moglie *f.* wife
Mole Antonelliana *the highest building in Italy* (*in Torino*)
molo *m.* wharf
molto, -a much, a great deal of; *pl.* many; **molto** *adv.* very
momento *m.* moment
mondiale world (*adj.*)
mondo *m.* world
montagna *f.* mountain
monte *m.* mountain
*__morire__ *irr.* to die
mortadɛlla *f.* bologna
mostra *f.* show, exhibition; — **industriale** industrial show; **mettere in** —, to put on display
mostrare (*pres.* **mostro**) to show, present
motoscafo *m.* motorboat
*__muoversi__ *irr.* to move
Murano *an island near Venice, famous for its glass industry*
muratore *m.* mason, bricklayer
musɛo *m.* museum
musica *f.* music
musicale musical
musicante *m.* musician

N

Napoli Naples, *largest city in southern Italy*
*__nascere__ *irr.* to be born
nascondere *irr.* to hide
Natale *m.* Christmas
natura *f.* nature
naturale natural
nazionale national
nazione *f.* nation, country
ne of it, of them, some of it, some of them
nè: non . . . **nè** . . . **nè,** neither . . . nor
necessario, -a necessary
negare (*pres.* **nɛgo**) to deny
negozio *m.* store, shop; — **di abiti** dress shop
nemico *m.* enemy

nemmeno: non ... —, not even
nero, –a black
nessuno, –a no; *pron.* no one
neve *f.* snow
***nevicare** *imper.* (*pres.* **nevica**) to
  snow
niɛnte nothing
nɔbile noble
nome *m.* name
non not
nɔrd *m.* north
il nɔstro, la nɔstra, *etc.* our, ours
notevole notable
notizia *f.* news
nɔto, –a noted, known
nɔtte *f.* night
novantasɛtte ninety-seven
nɔve nine; **alle —,** at nine o'clock
novɛlla *f.* novella, short story
novelliɛre *m.* short-story writer
novità *f.* novelty
numerare (*pres.* **numero**) to enumerate
numero *m.* number
numeroso, –a numerous
nuɔto *m.* swimming
nuɔvo, –a new
nutrimento *m.* nourishment

O

o or; **o ... o** either ... or
ɔbbligo *m.* obligation
ɔcchio *m.* eye; **costare un —,** to
  cost a fortune
***occorrere** *imper., irr.* to need
***occuparsi (di)** to deal (with)
occupazione *f.* job, occupation
offrire *irr.* (*pres.* **ɔffro**) to offer
oggɛtto *m.* object
ɔggi today
ogni every
ognuno, –a each (one); *pron.* each
  one
ɔlio *m.* oil
oliva *f.* olive
olivo *m.* olive tree
ometto *m.* little man
onorare (*pres.* **onoro**) to honor
onore *m.* honor
ɔpera *f.* work, opera; **— d'arte** *f.*
  masterpiece
operaio *m.* workman

ora *adv.* now
ora *f.* hour, time; **a che —?** at
  what time? **che — ɛ?** *or* **che ore
  sono?** what time is it?
oralmente *adv.* orally
oramai now, nowadays
orario *m.* the hours; schedule
oretta *f.* about an hour
originale original
origine *f.* origin
ɔro *m.* gold; **conca d'—,** gold bowl
orolɔgio *m.* watch, clock
ɔspite *m.* guest
ɔsso *m.* (*pl.* **ɔssa** *f.*) bone
ɔttimo, –a excellent
ɔtto eight
ottocɛnto eight hundred

P

padre *m.* father
paese *m.* country, nation; town
paesɛllo *m.* little town
pagare to pay
paio *m.* (*pl.* **paia** *f.*) pair, few
palazzo *m.* palace: **Palazzo Pitti**
  Pitti Palace (*a museum of art in
  Florence*); **Palazzo dei Dɔgi**
  Doges' Palace (*in Venice*)
Palɛrmo *the largest and most important city in Sicily*
pane *m.* bread
panino *m.* bun, roll; **— imbottito**
  sandwich
panorama *m.* view, panorama,
  countryside
Papa *m.* Pope
papiro *m.* papyrus
paragonare (*pres.* **paragono**) to
  compare
parasole *m.* parasol
parco *m.* park
parecchi, –ie several
parɛntesi *f.* parenthesis
***parere** *irr.* to seem; **che te ne
  pare?** what do you think of it?
Parigi *f.* Paris
parlare to speak
parmigiano *m.* Parmesan, *a type
  of cheese*
parɔla *f.* word
parte *f.* part; **far — di** to be a part
  of; **di che —?** from what part?

*partire to depart
partito *m.* match, prospect
passare to spend (*time*), pass; —
la dogana to go through customs
passato, –a past
passato *m.* past
passeggiare (*pres.* passeggio) to
walk, stroll
passeggiata *f.* walk, stroll; fare
una —, to take a stroll
passeggio *m.* stroll; andare a —,
to go for a stroll
passo *m.* step; far due passi to
take a short walk, stroll
pasta *f.* pastry; — asciutta *f.*
macaroni; — in brodo *f.* soup
with noodles
pasto *m.* meal
patatine fritte *f. pl.* French fried
potatoes
paura *f.* fear; aver —, to be afraid;
da far —, frightful
pazienza *f.* patience; pazienza!
be patient! too bad!
peccato! too bad!
pellicola *f.* film
pena *f.* trouble; valer la —, to
be worth while
pendolo *m.* pendulum
penisola *f.* peninsula
pensare (a) to think (of)
pensiero *m.* thought, worry
pensione *f.* pension (*lodging with
meals*)
per to, for, in order to, through;
— di più moreover
pera *f.* pear
perchè why, because; *conj.* so that
perciò therefore
perdere *irr.* to lose; *perdersi to
get lost, be lost
perfetto, –a perfect
perfezione *f.* perfection; andare
a —, to fit perfectly; portare a
—, to perfect
pericolo *m.* danger
permettere *irr.* to permit
però however
persiana *f.* shutter
persona *f.* person; *pl.* people
personaggio *m.* personage
personale personal
personalmente personally

pesca *f.* peach
Petrarca Petrarch (1304–1374) *one
of the most famous Italian poets
and humanists*
petrolio *m.* oil
petto *m.* chest
pezzo *m.* piece, composition
*piacere to please, be pleasing to
piacere *m.* pleasure
piacevole pleasant
piaga *f.* wound
pianista *m. or f.* pianist
piano *m.* story, floor; plan
pianoforte *m.* piano
pianterreno *m.* ground floor, first
floor; al —, on the ground floor,
on the first floor
pianura *f.* plain, valley
piatto *m.* plate
piazza *f.* square; Piazza San
Marco Saint Mark's Square (*in
Venice*)
piccino *m.* little one, little fellow
piccolo, –a small
piede *m.* foot; essere in piedi to
be up; da capo a piedi from
head to foot
Piemonte *m.* Piedmont, *a region in
northwestern Italy*
pietanza *f.* course (*at dinner*)
pinacoteca *f.* art gallery
pino *m.* pine
pioggia *f.* rain
*piovere *irr.* to rain, be raining
piroscafo *m.* ship
Pisa *f. important city in Tuscany,
on the banks of the Arno*
pittore *m.* painter
pittoresco, –a picturesque
pittura *f.* painting
più more; di —, more; il —, the
most; molto di —, much more
piuttosto rather
pizzicagnolo *m.* grocer
placidamente peacefully
poco little; un po' a little
poesia *f.* poetry
poeta *m.* poet
poetico, –a poetic, poetical
poi then, afterward, after all, besides
poichè since
politico, –a political

pollo *m.* chicken; — **arrɔsto** *m.* roast chicken
pomeriggio *m.* afternoon
Pompɛi Pompeii, *a city near Naples, buried by the ashes of Vesuvius in 79A.D.*
ponte *m.* bridge; — **di Rialto** the Rialto bridge
ponticello *m.* neat little bridge
popolare popular
pɔrco *m.* pig
porre *irr.* to put
portagioiɛlli *m.* (*invar.*) jewel box
portare (*pres.* **pɔrto**) to bring, take; wear; — **a perfezione** to perfect
pɔrtico *m.* portico
pɔrto *m.* harbor
posata *f.* place setting (*for a table*)
Posillipo *residential hill in Naples, overlooking the bay*
posizione *f.* position
possedere *irr.* to possess
°**potere** *irr.* to be able, can
pɔvero, –a poor
pranzare to dine
pranzo *m.* dinner
preferire (isco) to prefer
prɛgo you are welcome
prɛndere *irr.* to take; catch; — **freddo** to catch cold; — **un raffreddore** to catch a cold; — **la sua strada** to go one's way
*****preoccuparsi (di)** (*pres.* **mi preɔccupo**) to worry (about)
preparare to prepare
presentare (*pres.* **presɛnto**) to present, introduce
presɛnte *m.* present
prestare (*pres.* **prɛsto**) to lend; — **giuramento** to take an oath
prɛsto early, soon; **far —,** to be quick, hurry
prɛzzo *m.* price
prima *adv.* first; — **che** *conj.* before; — **di** *prep.* before
primavɛra *f.* spring
primo, –a first
principale principal
principalmente principally, mainly
principio *m.* beginning; **al —,** in the beginning
problɛma *m.* problem

prodigio *m.* prodigy
prodotto *m.* product
produrre *irr.* to produce
professione *f.* profession
professore *m.* professor
professoressa *f.* teacher, professor
profondo, –a deep
profumeria *f.* perfume shop
profumo *m.* perfume
promettere *irr.* to promise
pronto, –a ready
pronunzia *f.* pronunciation
proporzionato, –a proportioned
proposizione *f.* sentence
proprietario *m.* proprietor
prɔprio, –a own; **prɔprio** *adv.* exactly, directly, really
prɔsa *f.* prose; **scrittore di prɔse** prose writer
prosciutto *m.* ham; — **cɔtto** boiled ham; — **crudo** smoked (Virginia) ham
prɔssimo, –a next
provare (*pres.* **prɔvo**) to try on
provɛrbio *m.* proverb
provincia *f.* province
provolone *m.* a type of cheese
provvedere *irr.* to provide
pubblico *m.* public
Puccini, Giacomo (1858–1924) *one of the most famous Italian composers of operatic music*
Puglie *f. pl. region of Italy, in the southeast*
pulire (isco) to clean
punto *m.* point, place
punto (*p.p. of* **pungere**) pricked
purchè provided
pure still, as long as; **se —,** *conj.* even if
puro, –a pure

Q

quadro *m.* painting
qualche some; — **cɔsa** *f.* something
quale (qual) *inter. adj. and pron.* which, what, which one; **il —, (la quale, i quali, le quali)** *rel. pron.* who, whom, which, that
qualità *f.* quality
qualsiasi any

qual*u*nque whichever
quando when
quanto how much; how long;
per —, *conj.* no matter how
much
quarantac*i*nquemila forty-five
thousand
quarti*ε*re *m.* quarter, section
quasi almost
quattro four
quello (quel), –a that; *pl.* those;
quel che what, that which
questi *pron.* the latter
questo, –a this; *pl.* these
qu*i* here
quindi therefore

R

racc*ɔ*gliere *irr.* to pick up, gather
racc*ɔ*lta *f.* collection
raccontare (*pres.* racconto) to
tell
radio *f.* radio
Raffa*ε*llo (Raffa*ε*llo Sanzio da
Urbino) Raphael (1483–1520)
one of the most famous painters
raffreddore *m.* cold; pr*ε*ndere un
—, to catch a cold
ragazza *f.* girl
ragazzino *m.* little boy
ragazzo *m.* boy
raggi*u*ngere *irr.* to reach
ragione *f.* reason; aver —, to be
right
rammentare (*pres.* rammento)
to remind; *rammentarsi to
remember
rapidamente rapidly
rappresentazione *f.* performance
raro, –a rare
*rassegnarsi (*pres.* mi rassegno)
to resign oneself
Ravenna *city in Romagna (Emilia),
in north central Italy*
reale royal
regalare to grant, donate
regalo *m.* gift
regina *f.* queen
regione *f.* region
regolare regular
relazione *f.* relation
r*ε*ndere *irr.* to render, make

Respighi, Ottorino (1879–1936)
famous Italian composer
*restare (*pres.* r*ε*sto) to remain,
stay
Riccardo Richard
ricco, –a rich
ricevere (*pres.* ricevo) to receive
riconoscere *irr.* to recognize
ricordare (*pres.* ric*ɔ*rdo) to remember, mention
ric*ɔ*rdo *m.* souvenir; record
*rimanere *irr.* to remain –
Rinascimento *m.* Renaissance
*rinnovarsi (*pres.* mi rinn*ɔ*vo) to
renew oneself
rinomato, –a famous
riparazione *f.* repair
riposare (*pres.* rip*ɔ*so) to rest;
*riposarsi to rest
rip*ɔ*so *m.* rest
ripr*ε*ndere *irr.* to take up again
riscaldare to warm, heat
risp*ε*tto *m.* respect; — a with
respect to
rispondere *irr.* to answer
risultato *m.* result
*ritornare (*pres.* ritorno) to return
ritorno *m.* return; *a*utobus di —,
return bus
riunire (isco) to gather; *riunirsi
to get together
*riuscire (a) *irr.* to succeed (in)
Riva degli Schiavoni *f. promenade
near Saint Mark's Square in Venice*
Rob*ε*rto Robert
Roma *f.* Rome
romano, –a Roman, from Rome;
romano *m. a type of cheese*
rompere *irr.* to break
rond*ɔ* *m.* rondo
R*ɔ*sa Rose
Rossini, Gioacchino (1792–1868)
*famous Italian composer of opera-
tic and symphonic music*
rosso, –a red
ruscelletto *m.* little brook

S

sabato *m.* Saturday
saetta *f.* arrow

sala *f.* room; — **da pranzo** *f.* dining room; — **d'aspetto** *f.* waiting room
salame *m.* salami
***salire** *irr.* to rise, go up; **far —,** to raise
salotto *m.* living room
salsiccia *f.* sausage
salumeria *f.* delicatessen
***salutarsi** to say good-by; greet
salute *f.* health
saluti *m. pl.* regards
salvare to save
San Pietro Saint Peter's (*in Rome*)
Santa Croce *a cathedral in Florence*
Santa Lucia *a picturesque bay in Naples*
***sapere** *irr.* to know, know how to
sarto *m.* tailor
Savoia *f.* Savoy
sbadigliare (*pres.* **sbadiglio**) to yawn
***sbagliarsi** (*pres.* **mi sbaglio**) to be mistaken
La Scala *world-famous opera house in Milan*
scambiare (*pres.* **scambio**) to exchange
scarpa *f.* shoe
scatola *f.* box, can
scavo *m.* excavation
scegliere *irr.* to choose
***scendere** *irr.* to come down
schermo *m.* screen
sci *m.* skiing
scienza *f.* science
scienziato *m.* scientist
scompartimento *m.* compartment
scopo *m.* purpose
scoprire *irr.* (*pres.* **scopro**) to discover
scritti *m. pl.* writings
scritto (*p.p. of* **scrivere**) written
scrittore *m.* writer
scrivere *irr.* to write
scultore *m.* sculptor
scuola *f.* school; — **di ballo** dancing school
scusare to excuse
se if
sebbene although
secco, -a dry

secolo *m.* century; — **decimoquarto** 14th century
secondo, -a second
secondo *prep.* according to
sede *f.* residence; home office
***sedersi** *irr.* to sit down
sedici sixteen
sedile *m.* seat
segno *m.* sign, mark
segretaria *f.* secretary
segreto, -a secret; *m.* secret
seguente following
seguire to follow; — **la moda** to be in style
seguitare (*pres.* **seguito**) to continue
seicento six hundred; *f.* smallest FIAT model
sembrare (*pres.* **sembro**) to seem
semplice simple
semplicità *f.* simplicity
sempre always; **per —,** forever
sentire (*pres.* **sento**) to hear; feel; listen; — **parlare di** to hear about; ***sentirsi** to feel
senza without; — **che** *conj.* without
sera *f.* evening; **di —** *or* **la —,** in the evening
serata *f.* evening; — **di gala** gala evening
serenata *f.* serenade
serio, -a serious; **sul —,** seriously
servire (*pres.* **servo**) to serve, be of use; — **di modello** to serve as a model; **a che serve?** of what use is?
servizio *m.* service; **fare il —,** to make the run
settemila seven thousand
settentrionale northern
settimana *f.* week; **a —,** by the week
severo, -a severe, cruel
sì yes
sì che so that
siciliano, -a Sicilian
sicuro, -a sure
sigaretta *f.* cigarette
signora *f.* madam, lady, Mrs.
signore *m.* gentleman, Sir, Mr.
signorina *f.* young lady, Miss
simbolo *m.* symbol

similar similar
simpatia *f.* sympathy, liking
sincerità *f.* sincerity
sincero, –a sincere, clear
sinfonia *f.* symphony
sinistra *f.* left hand; **a —,** to the left
situato, –a situated
soave soft
società *f.* society
soggiorno *m.* stay
sole *m.* sun
solenne solemn
solito, –a usual
solo, –a alone, single; **solo** *adv.* only
soltanto only
sommo, –a highest, greatest, very great
sonnellino *m.* nap; **fare un —,** to take a nap
sopra above; **al di — di** above
soprattutto especially
sorella *f.* sister
sorpassare to surpass
Sorrento *a beautiful little town on the bay of Naples*
sospettare (*pres.* **sospetto**) to suspect
sospiro *m.* sigh
sotto under
spaghetti al burro *m. pl.* spaghetti with butter
spargere *irr.* to scatter
spazio *m.* space
spazzolino da denti *m.* toothbrush
specialmente especially
spedire (**isco**) to send
spendere *irr.* to spend
speranza *f.* hope
sperare (*pres.* **spero**) to hope
spesso often
spiaggia *f.* beach
spiegare (*pres.* **spiego**) to explain
spilla *f.* pin
spinaci *m. pl.* spinach
spirito *m.* morale; spirit, soul
sponda *f.* shore
sport *m.* (*invar.*) sports
sportello *m.* ticket window
*****sposarsi** (**con**) to get married (to)
sprecare (*pres.* **spreco**) to waste
spremuta *f.* juice; **— d'arancia** orange juice

stamattina this morning
*****stancarsi** to get tired
stanco, –a tired
stanza *f.* room; **— da bagno** bathroom
*****stare** *irr.* to be; **— attento** to pay attention; **— bene** to be well off; **— a far complimenti** to stand on ceremony; **— per** to be about to; **fatto sta** the point is, the fact is
stasera this evening
Stati Uniti *m. pl.* United States
stato (*p.p. of* **essere** *or* **stare**) been
statua *f.* statue
stazione *f.* station, channel; **— ferroviaria** *f.* railroad station
stendere *irr.* to lay, stretch
stesso, –a same; oneself
stile (**stil**) *m.* style
stomaco *m.* stomach
storia *f.* history
storico, –a historical, historic
strada *f.* street, road; **prendere la sua —,** to go one's way
straniero *m.* foreigner
straordinario, –a extraordinary
strumento *m.* instrument
studente *m.* student
studiare (*pres.* **studio**) to study
studio *m.* study
stupendo, –a stupendous
su on; **su, via!** come now!
subito quickly, immediately
succursale *f.* branch office
sud *m.* south
sugo *m.* sauce; **— di pomodoro** tomato sauce
il suo, la sua, i suoi, le sue his, her, its
il Suo, la Sua, *etc.* your; **i Suoi** your family
suonare (*pres.* **suono**) to ring; play an instrument
superiore superior
superiorità *f.* superiority
superlativo *m.* superlative
*****svegliarsi** (*pres.* **mi sveglio**) to wake up
sveglio, –a awake
svelare (*pres.* **svelo**) to reveal
*****svilupparsi** to develop

svizzero, –a Swiss; **svizzero** *m.*
Swiss
svɔlta *f.* turn

T

tabaccaio *m.* tobacco vendor, tobacco store
tabacco *m.* tobacco
tanto, –a so much, so; *pl.* so many;
tanto da vedere so much to see
tardi *adv.* late; **più —,** later
tasca *f.* pocket
taschino *m.* breast pocket
tassì *m.* taxi
tavola *f.* table; **a —,** at the table
teatro *m.* theater
televisione *f.* television
tɛma *m.* subject, theme
temperamento *m.* temperament
tɛmpo *m.* weather; time; **che
— fa?** how is the weather? **fra
pɔco —** soon
tenere *irr.* to keep, hold; **— conto
di** to keep in mind
teɔlogo *m.* theologian
terminare (*pres.* **tɛrmino**) to
end, finish
Tɛrmini: Stazione —, *the main
RR station in Rome*
tɛrra *f.* ground, earth
terrazza *f.* terrace
tɛrzo, –a third
Tevere *m.* Tiber
Tintoretto (Iacopo Robusti)
(1518–1594) *famous Venetian
painter, pupil of Titian*
tipo *m.* type, kind
tirare to pull; blow; **tira vɛnto**
the wind is blowing, it's windy
Tiziano Vecɛllio Titian (1477–
1576) *the greatest painter of the
Venetian school*
tolɛtta *f.* toilette
tomba *f.* tomb
Tommaso Thomas
tonno *m.* tuna fish
Torino Turin, *capital of the region
of Piemonte*
*****tornare** (*pres.* **torno**) to return;
— un'altra vɔlta to come back
Torricɛlli, Evangelista (1608–
1647) *famous Italian physicist
and mathematician*

Toscana *f.* Tuscany, *a province in
central Italy*
Toscanini, Arturo (1867–1957)
*the most celebrated orchestra con-
ductor of our day*
tɔsto che as soon as
totale *m.* total
tovaglia *f.* tablecloth
tovagliɔlo *m.* napkin
tradurre *irr.* to translate
trasporto *m.* transportation
tratto *m.* stretch
tredici thirteen; **alle —,** at one in
the afternoon
trɛno *m.* train
trenta thirty
trentanɔve thirty-nine
trentatrè thirty-three
trombone *m.* trombone
trɔppo, –a too much
trovare (*pres.* **trɔvo**) to find;
*****trovarsi** to be located, find
oneself
tuba *f.* tuba
il tuo, la tua, *etc.* your, yours (*fam.
sing.*)
tuonare *imper.* (*pres.* **tuɔna**) to
thunder
turista *m. or f.* tourist
tutti everyone, all; **— e due** both
tutto everything; **il —,** the whole
thing; **con — ciɔ** *conj.* although
tutto, –a all; **tutto ciɔ** all that

U

ufficio *m.* office; **— informazioni**
m. information desk; **— postale**
m. post office
Uffizi *art gallery in Florence*
ugualmente equally
ultimo, –a last, latest
umanista *m.* humanist
umano, –a human
un, una a, an
unico, –a only
università *f.* university
uno, una *pron.* one
uɔmo (*pl.* **uɔmini**) *m.* man
uɔvo *m.* (*pl.* **uɔva** *f.*) egg
usanza *f.* custom
usare to use
*****uscire** *irr.* to go out

uso *m.* use, style; **all'— antico** old-fashioned

uva *f.* grapes

V

vacanze *f. pl.* vacation

*****valere** *irr.* to be worth; **— la pena** to be worth while

valigia *f.* bag, suitcase

valle *f.* valley

vaporetto *m.* launch

vari, –ie various

Vaticano *m.* Vatican

vecchietto *m.* neat little old man

vecchio, –a old

vedere *irr.* to see; **non — l'ora di** to be very anxious to

veduta *f.* view

veloce fast

vendere (*pres.* **vendo**) to sell

Veneto *m. region of Italy, in the northeast*

Venezia *f.* Venice, *a city in northern Italy, on the Adriatic*

veneziano, –a Venetian

*****venire** *irr.* to come; **— all'incontro** to come *or* go to meet

venti twenty; **ventimila** twenty thousand

vento *m.* wind; **tira —,** the wind is blowing, it's windy

veramente really

Verdi, Giuseppe (1813–1901) *the greatest Italian operatic composer*

vero, –a true, real, veritable; **non è vero?** isn't it so?

verso toward, about

*****vestir(si)** (*pres.* **vesto**) to dress, get dressed

Vesuvio *m.* Vesuvius, *a volcano near Naples*

vetrina *f.* window (*of a store*)

vetro *m.* glass

vi there, in it

via *f.* road, street; *adv.* away, by way of, via

viaggiare (*pres.* **viaggio**) to travel

viaggiatore *m.* traveler

viaggio *m.* trip; **fare un —,** to take a trip; **buon —!** have a nice trip!

vicino (a) near; **da —,** from nearby

vigna *f.* vineyard

villaggio *m.* village

villeggiatura *f.* country holiday; **in —,** on vacation

villino *m.* neat little house

vinaio *m.* wine seller, wine dealer

vincolo *m.* link

violino *m.* violin

visita *f.* visit, social call; **fare —,** to pay a visit

visitare (*pres.* **visito**) to visit

visto (*p.p. of* **vedere**) seen

vita *f.* life; **fare una bella —,** to lead a nice life

vitello *m.* veal; **— arrosto** *m.* roast veal

°**vivere** *irr.* to live

voce *f.* voice; word

voglia *f.* desire; **venire la —,** to get a desire, feel like

°**volere** *irr.* to wish, want; **voler bene a** to like; **vuol dire** it means

volo *m.* flight

volontà *f.* will

volta *f.* time; **una —,** once; **una — l'anno** once a year; **un'altra —,** again; **a sua —,** in turn

vuoto *m.* vacuum

Z

zelo *m.* zeal

zio *m.* uncle

zonzo: a —, wandering, at random

Zurigo Zurich, *a city in Switzerland*

Vocabulary

ENGLISH–ITALIAN

A

a, an un, una, uno, un'
able: be —, potere *irr.*
about di, su, circa; vɛrso; **to be
— to** stare per
accept accettare (*pres.* accɛtto)
accustomed abituato, –a
admire ammirare
after dopo (di) (*prep.*); dopo che
(*conj.*)
afternoon pomeriggio *m.*
ago fa
agriculture agricoltura *f.*
all tutto, –a; **— that** tutto quel
che; **at —,** affatto
almost quasi
along (alòngside) lungo
Alps Alpi *f. pl.*
already già
also anche
although benchè, sebbene
always sɛmpre
ambition ambizione *f.*
American americano, –a; Americano *m.*
and e, ed; **— so** e così
announce annunziare (*pres.* annunzio)
answer rispondere
any qualsiasi
anything (*negative*) niente
Apennines Appennini *m. pl.*
apple mela *f.*
appliance apparecchio *m.*
appreciate apprezzare (*pres.* ap-
prɛzzo)
apricot albicɔcca *f.*
archeological archeolɔgico, –a
architect architɛtto *m.*
arm braccio *m.* (*pl.* braccia *f.*); **— in
—,** a braccetto
around *see* **go**

arrive *arrivare
art arte *f.*
article articolo *m.*
artist artista *m. or f.*
as come, mentre; **as . . . as** tanto
(così) . . . come; **as if** come se; **as
soon as** non appena
ask domandare; **— a question** fare
una domanda
assure oneself *assicurarsi
at a, da; **at all** affatto
aunt zia *f.*
automobile automɔbile *f.*
away via; **far —,** lontano, –a

B

back: to come —, *tornare, *ritornare
backwards: to go —, indietreggiare (*pres.* indietreggio)
bad: too —, peccato
bag valigia *f.*
barber barbiere *m.*
basilica basilica *f.*
bathroom stanza da bagno *f.*
be *essere; **— about to** *stare
per; **— about over** *stare per
finire; **— left** *restare; **— needed
*bisognare; **— worth** *valere;
— worth while *valer la pena
beach spiaggia *f.*
bean *see* **string beans**
bear with *ɛssere indulgente
beautiful bɛllo, –a
because perchè
bed lɛtto *m.*; **go to —,** *andare a
lɛtto
before prima di (*prep.*); prima che
(*conj.*)
begin cominciare (a), *mettersi a
believe credere
bell campanɛllo *m.*; **— tower** campanile *m.*

236

besides per di più
best (il, la) migliore (*adj.*); meglio (*adv.*)
better migliore (*adj.*); meglio (*adv.*)
between fra
big grande
bit poco (po') *m.*
block isolato *m.*
blond biondo, –a
blow (wind) tirare
board pensione *f.*
boiled *see* potato
book libro *m.*
both tutti (tutte) e due
boy ragazzo *m.*
breakfast colazione *f.*; to have —, far colazione
bridge ponte *m.*
bring portare (*pres.* porto)
broiled *see* steak
brook ruscello *m.*
brother fratello *m.*
building edificio *m.*
bus autobus *m.* (*also* autobus)
but ma
buy comprare (*pres.* compro)

C

café caffè *m.*
call chiamare
camera apparecchio *m.*; movie —, apparecchio cinematografico *m.*
can potere (*see* able)
canal canale *m.*
canned in scatola
capital capitale *f.*
car automobile *f.*; macchina *f.*
carry portare (*pres.* porto)
catch prendere *irr.*
cathedral duomo *m.*; cattedrale *f.*
central centrale
century secolo *m.*
characteristic caratteristica *f.*
Charles Carlo
charm incanto *m.*
chest petto *m.*
chicken pollo *m.*; roast —, pollo arrosto *m.*
child bambino *m.*, bambina *f.*, ragazzo *m.*, ragazza *f.*
chilly: it's —, fa fresco
choose scegliere *irr.*

Christmas Natale *m.*
church chiesa *f.*
city città *f.*
civilization civiltà *f.*
class classe *f.*; classroom aula *f.*
clean pulire (isco)
clothes abiti *m. pl.*
coffee caffè *m.*
cold freddo, –a; it's —, fa freddo; raffreddore *m.*
color colore *m.*
come *venire irr.*; — back *ritornare (*pres.* ritorno); — down *scendere irr.*; — out *uscire irr.*
comfortable comodo, –a
compare paragonare (*pres.* paragono)
compartment scompartimento *m.*
composer compositore *m.*
concerto concerto *m.*
converse conversare (*pres.* converso)
cook cucinare
corn granturco *m.*
corner angolo *m.*
cost *costare (*pres.* costo)
country paese *m.*, nazione *f.*
courteous cortese
cousin cugino *m.*; cugina *f.*
cover coprire *irr.*
crest cresta *f.*
cross attraversare (*pres.* attraverso)
cultivate coltivare
cup tazza *f.*; — for drinking tazza da bere *f.*
curve curva *f.*; svolta *f.*
custom usanza *f.*
cutlet: small veal cutlets scaloppine *f. pl.*

D

dad babbo *m.*
daily giornaliero, –a; del giorno
dance ballo *m.*
dark buio *m.*; in the —, al buio
daughter figlia *f.*
day giorno *m.*; giornata *f.*
deal: a great —, molto, –a
dealer: wine —, vinaio *m.*
dear caro, –a
decide decidere (a) *irr.*
depart *partire
descent discesa *f.*

desk: information —, ufficio informazioni *m.*
die *morire *irr.**
different diverso, –a
difficult difficile
dine pranzare
dining room sala da pranzo *f.*
dinner pranzo *m.*
discuss discorrere *irr.*
distinguish distinguere *irr.*
divide dividere *irr.*
do fare *irr.*
dock approdare (*pres.* approdo)
doctor medico *m.*
doubt dubitare (*pres.* dubito)
dozen dozzina *f.*
dress abito *m.;* — **shop** negozio di abiti *m.*
drinking water acqua da bere *f.*
drive giro *m.,* gita *f.*
dry secco, –a
during durante
duty occupazione *f.*

E

each ciascuno, –a
easily facilmente
easy facile
eat mangiare
effective: to be —, fare effetto
eggplant melanzana *f.*
eight otto
electrical elettrico, –a
elegant elegante
empire impero *m.*
enchanting incantevole
end fine *f.*
end finire (isco)
Englishman Inglese *m.*
enjoy godere (*pres.* godo); — **oneself** *divertirsi (*pres.* mi diverto)
enter *entrare (*pres.* entro)
entrance entrata *f.*
enumerate numerare (*pres.* numero)
equally ugualmente
especially specialmente
Europe Europa *f.*
European europeo, –a
even (*negative*) nemmeno
evening sera *f.;* **in the** —, la sera
event fatto del giorno *m.*
every ogni

erbe (grass) — handwritten margin note

everybody ognuno, –a; tutti, –e; — **else** tutti gli altri
everyone ognuno, –a; tutti, –e
everything tutto; — **we needed** tutto il necessario
everywhere dappertutto
excavation scavo *m.*
excellent eccellente
exchange scambiare (*pres.* scambio)
exhibition mostra *f.*
expensive di lusso
express (**train**) direttissimo *m.*
extremely *use superlative*

F

fall autunno *m.*
fall *cadere *irr.**
family famiglia *f.*
famous famoso, –a
far distante, lontano, –a; **not** —, poco lontano; — **away** lontano, –a
fashion moda *f.*
fast presto, –a; *adv.* presto
father padre *m.*
feel sentire (*pres.* sento); **I** — **at home** mi par di essere a casa mia; — **cold** sentire freddo; — **hungry** sentire fame
fellow: little —, piccino *m.*
fertile fertile
few pochi; **a** —, parecchi
fiancée fidanzata *f.*
fifteen quindici
filigree filigrana *f.*
film pellicola *f.*
finally finalmente
find trovare (*pres.* trovo)
fine arts belle arti *f. pl.*
finger dito *m.* (*pl.* dita *f.*)
finish finire (isco)
first primo, –a; *adv.* prima
floor piano *m.;* **first** —, pianterreno *m.;* **second** —, primo piano *m.*
Florence Firenze *f.*
Florentine fiorentino, –a
flower fiore *m.*
foot piede *m.*
for per; — **some time** da parecchio tempo
foreigner straniero *m.*
forget dimenticare (*pres.* dimentico)
fork forchetta *f.*

form formare (*pres.* formo)
fortune fortuna *f.*; **they cost a —,**
consano un occhio
four quattro
French (*language*) francese *m.*
fried *see* **potato**
friend amico *m.*
friendship amicizia *f.*
from da
fruit frutta *f.*; **— vendor** fruttivendolo *m.*

G

garden giardino *m.*
geography geografia *f.*
get prendere *irr.*; **— rich** *farsi ricco
girl signorina *f.*; ragazza *f.*
give dare *irr.*
glad contento, –a
glass vetro *m.*
go *andare *irr.*; **— away** *andar via;
— by (*time*) passare; **— out**
*uscire *irr.*; **— around** girare
good buono, –a
grammar grammatica *f.*
grandfather nonno *m.*
grandiose grandioso, –a
grandmother nonna *f.*
gray grigio, –a
great grande; **the greatest** il maggiore
green verde
greet salutare
greetings saluti *m. pl.*
grocer pizzicagnolo *m.*
group gruppo *m.*
guest invitato *m.*
gulf golfo *m.*
giocatili

H

hand mano *f.*
handbag borsetta *f.*
handkerchief fazzoletto *m.*
happy felice; contento, –a; **— life
of ease** dolce far niente
hat cappello *m.*; **— shop** modista *f.*
have avere *irr.*; **— to** dovere *irr.*
he egli, lui; **— who** chi
head capo *m.*; **from — to foot** da
capo a piedi
health salute *f.*

her *dir. obj.* la; *disj.* lei; *indir. obj.*
le; *poss.* il suo, la sua, *etc.*
here qui; **— is** ecco
high alto, –a
him lo, lui; **to —,** gli
his il suo, la sua, *etc.*
historical storico, –a
history storia *f.*
home casa *f.*; a casa; **at —,** in casa
homework compiti *m. pl.*
hope sperare (*pres.* spero)
hot caldo, –a; **it is —,** fa caldo
hotel albergo *m.*
hour ora *f.*; **the hours** l'orario *m.*
house casa *f.*; **frightful —,** casaccia
f.
housework lavoro di casa *m.*
how come; **— much** quanto, –a;
— many quanti, –e
however comunque
humanist umanista *m.*
hundred cento; **hundreds** centi-
naia *f. pl.*
hungry: to be —, aver fame, aver
appetito; **to feel —,** sentire
appetito
husband marito *m.*

I

I io
ideal ideale
if se
immediately immediatamente
importance importanza *f.*
important importante
impossible impossibile
impression impressione *f.*
in in; a; **— order that** per, di
maniera che, affinchè
inconvenience incomodare (*pres.*
incomodo)
industry industria *f.*
influence influsso *m.*
information informazione *f.*; **—
desk** ufficio informazioni *m.*
inspiration ispirazione *f.*
instead (**of**) invece (di)
intelligence intelligenza *f.*
interest interessare (*pres.* interesso)
interesting interessante
invite invitare
invitation invito *m.*

island isola f.
it dir. obj. lo, la; **of** —, ne
Italian italiano, –a; Italiano m.
Italy Italia f.
its il suo, la sua, etc.

J

jewel gioiello m.
Joseph Giuseppe

K

keep mantenere irr.; **— waiting** fare aspettare; **— on** seguitare (pres. seguito); **— in mind** tener (irr.) conto
kitchen cucina f.
knee ginocchio m. (pl. ginocchia f.)
knife coltello m.
know conoscere irr. (to know a person, be acquainted with); sapere irr. (to know a fact); **— how** sapere
knowledge sapere m.

L

lady donna f.; signora f.; signorina f.
lamb agnello m.
language lingua f.
large grande (gran)
last *durare
last ultimo, –a; passato, –a; **— year** l'anno passato, l'anno scorso
late tardi adv.
latest: the — models gli ultimi modelli
lead condurre irr.; **— a fine life** fare una bella vita; **— by the hand** portare per la mano
learn imparare
leather cuoio m.
leave lasciare; *partire (da)
left sinistra f.; **on the —**, a sinistra
less meno; **the more ... the —**, quanto più ... tanto meno; **— than** meno di, meno che
lesson lezione f.
let lasciare
letter lettera f.
life vita f.
light leggiero, –a; **— wine** vino leggiero m.

like conj. come; verb, see **please**
liking simpatia f.
limit oneself limitarsi (pres. mi limito)
listen ascoltare (pres. ascolto)
liter litro m.
literature letteratura f.
little piccolo, –a; **a —**, un poco di
live abitare (dwell); *vivere (exist) irr.
long lungo, –a
look (at) guardare; **— for** cercare (pres. cerco); **— like** sembrare
luxurious di lusso

M

maid cameriera f.
make fare irr.; rendere; **— oneself at home** *accomodarsi (pres. mi accomodo)
mama mamma f.
man uomo m. (pl. uomini)
manager gerente m.
many molti, –e; **how —**, quanti, –e
map carta geografica f.
mashed see **potato**
matter: no — how comunque
mature maturo, –a
may use potere
me mi, me
meal pasto m.
meat carne f.; **— course** piatto di carne m.
medicine medicina f.
meet incontrare (pres. incontro)
melody melodia f.
meter metro m.
mind mente f.
mine il mio, la mia, etc.
minute minuto m.
model modello m.
money denaro m.
morale spirito m.
more più; **the — ... the —**, quanto più ... tanto più
morning mattina f.; **this —**, stamattina, stamane or stamani
most: the —, il più, la più
mother madre f.
mountain montagna f.
movies cinematografo m., cinema m.
museum museo m.

much molto, –a; **too —**, troppo, –a; **too —**, *adv.* troppo
music musica *f.*
must *use* dovere
mustache baffi *m. pl.*
my il mio, la mia, *etc.*

N

name nome *m.*; **his — is** si chiama
nap sonnellino *m.*; **to take a —**, fare un sonnellino
napkin tovagliolo *m.*
Naples Napoli *f.*
nation nazione *f.*
near vicino, –a (a)
necessary necessario, –a
necktie cravatta *f.*
need *n.* bisogno *m.*; *v.* aver bisogno di; volerci
never mai, non . . . mai
nevertheless nondimeno
new nuovo, –a
news notizie *f. pl.*; **— of the day** fatti del giorno, *m. pl.*
next prossimo, –a; **— to** accanto a
nimble agile
nobody nessuno, –a
noise chiasso *m.*
no nessuno, –a; (non *before verb*); **— one** nessuno, non . . . nessuno
northern settentrionale
not non
note biglietto *m.*
now ora
number numero *m.*

O

object oggetto *m.*
of di
offer offrire *irr.*
office ufficio *m.*
often spesso
old vecchio, –a; **— man** vecchio *m.*
older più grande, maggiore
olive oliva *f.*
on su, a; **— the first floor** al pianterreno
one uno, –a; *reflexive construction;* **the —**, quello, –a
only soltanto
open aprire *irr.*

opera opera *f.*
opposite dirimpetto (a); **right —**, proprio dirimpetto (a)
or o
order: in — to per; **in — that** affinchè
other altro, –a
otherwise altrimenti
ought *use* dovere
our (ours) il nostro, la nostra, *etc.*
ourselves ci (*reflexive pron.*)
oven-baked *see* **potato**
over finito, –a; **to be about —**, stare per finire

P

painter pittore *m.*
painting quadro *m.*
pair paio *m.* (*pl.* paia *f.*)
palace palazzo *m.*
panorama panorama *m.*
parasol parasole *m.*
parents genitori *m. pl.*
part parte *f.*; **to be a —**, far parte
party festa *f.*
pass passare
past passato *m.*
patience pazienza *f.*
peach pesca *f.*
pear pera *f.*
people persone *f. pl.*; gente *f. sing.*
personal personale
piano pianoforte *m.*
picturesque pittoresco, –a
piece pezzo *m.*
pin spilla *f.*; **filigree —**, spilla di filigrana *f.*
pineapple ananasso *m.*
pity: it is a —, peccato
place posto *m.*; luogo *m.*; (*at table*) posata *f.*
plain pianura *f.*
plate piatto *m.*
play giocare (*game*) (*pres.* gioco); suonare (*instrument*) (*pres.* suono)
please *piacere; **please !** per favore !
pleasure piacere *m.*
poet poeta *m.*
Pompeii Pompei *f.*
poor povero, –a
Pope Papa *m.*

porter facchino *m.*
potato patata *f.*; **oven-baked potatoes** patate al forno *f. pl.*;
mashed potatoes purè di patate
m.; **boiled potato** patata lessa *f.*;
French fried potatoes patatine
fritte *f. pl.*
prefer preferire (isco)
prepare preparare
present presente *m.*; — **perfect** passato prossimo *m.*
price prezzo *m.*; **what the — is**
quanto costa
produce produrre *irr.*
product prodotto *m.*
profession professione *f.*
professor professore *m.*
promise promettere *irr.*
prose prosa *f.*; — **writer** scrittore
di prose *m.*
proverb proverbio *m.*
provided (that) purchè
province provincia *f.*
purchase compra *f.*
put mettere *irr.*

Q

quality qualità *f.*
question domanda *f.*; **to ask a —,**
fare una domanda

R

radio radio *f. (invariable)*
rapidly rapidamente
Ravenna *city in Romagna*
reach *arrivare, *giungere
read leggere *irr.*
ready pronto, –a
really veramente
receive ricevere
red rosso, –a
region regione *f.*
remain *rimanere *irr.*
remember *ricordarsi (*pres.* mi
ricordo)
remind rammentare (*pres.* rammento)
repair riparazione *f.*
residence sede *f.*
rest riposare (*pres.* riposo), *riposarsi
rest riposo *m.*

restaurant ristorante *m.*
return *tornare (*pres.* torno)
return trip ritorno *m.*
rich ricco, –a; **to get —,** *farsi
ricco
Richard Riccardo
right destra *f.*; **to the —,** a destra;
— **opposite** proprio dirimpetto;
to be —, aver ragione
ring suonare (*pres.* suono)
river fiume *m.*
roast beef rosbiffe *m.*
Roman romano, –a
Rome Roma *f.*
room stanza *f.*, camera *f.*; spazio *m.*;
waiting —, sala d'aspetto *f.*
rush *andare in fretta

S

same stesso, –a
Saturday sabato *m.*; — **afternoon**
sabato nel pomeriggio
sausage salsiccia *f.*
say dire *irr.*
saying proverbio *m.*
school scuola *f.*
secret segreto, –a
see vedere *irr.*
seem sembrare (*pres.* sembro)
sell vendere
send mandare, spedire (isco)
serve servire (*pres.* servo)
set apparecchio *m.*
set (*a table*) apparecchiare (*pres.*
apparecchio); (*places*) mettere
several parecchi, parecchie; —
times parecchie volte
she essa, lei
ship piroscafo *m.*
shoe scarpa *f.*
shoemaker calzolaio *m.*
shop negozio *m.*; **dress —,** negozio
di abiti *m.*; **hat —,** modista *f.*;
— **window** vetrina *f.*
shopping district mercato *m.*
short corto, –a; **in a — time** in
poco tempo
short-story writer novelliere *m.*
show mostrare (*pres.* mostro)
simple semplice
since siccome
sister sorella *f.*

six sei
sleep dormire (*pres.* dormo)
sleepy: to be —, aver sonno
small piccolo, –a
so così
some qualche; di + *def. art.*
something qualche cosa; — **else** qualche altra cosa
son figlio *m.*
soon fra poco; presto; **as** — **as,** non appena; **as** — **as possible** al più presto possibile
southern meridionale
souvenir ricordo *m.*
speak parlare
speed along filare
spend (*time*) passare; **spend** (*money*) spendere
spinach spinaci *m. pl.*
spoon cucchiaio *m.*
square piazza *f.*
stand: — **on ceremony** far cerimonie
station stazione *f.*; **Termini** —, Stazione Termini
stay *stare *irr.*; *restare (*pres.* resto)
steak: broiled —, manzo ai ferri *m.*, bistecca *f.*
(small) steamer vaporetto *m.*
still ancora
stop *fermarsi (*pres.* mi fermo)
store negozio *m.*
strawberry fragola *f.*
stream ruscello *m.*
street strada *f.*
string beans fagiolini *m. pl.*
stroll passeggiare (*pres.* passeggio)
strong forte; **strong-bodied wine** vino forte *m.*
student studente *m.*
study studio *m.*
study studiare (*pres.* studio)
stupendous stupendo, –a
style moda *f.*; **to be in** —, seguir la moda
subject tema *m.*
such tale, simile; così
summer estate *f.*; — **residence** sede estiva *f.*
Sunday domenica *f.*
surround circondare (*pres.* circondo)
surroundings dintorni *m. pl.*

T

table tavola *f.*; **at the** —, a tavola
tailor sarto *m.*
take prendere *irr.;* portare; — **a walk** fare (*irr.*) una passeggiata; — **a nap** fare un sonnellino; — **a trip** fare un viaggio; — **up** (*space*) prendere; — **up again** riprendere *irr.*
talk parlare, conversare (*pres.* converso)
tall alto, –a
taxi tassì *m.*
teach insegnare (*pres.* insegno)
teacher maestro *m.*; professore *m.*
television televisione *f.*
tell dire *irr.;* raccontare (*pres.* racconto)
temperament temperamento *m.*
ten dieci
terrace terrazza *f.*
than di, che, di quel che
that *rel. pron.* che; *dem. adj.* quel, quello, quella; — (**one**) *dem. pron.* quello, –a; **that** (*near you*) codesto, –a
theater teatro *m.*
their (theirs) *poss. adj. and pron.* il loro, la loro, *etc.*
them li, le; **of** —, ne; **to** —, loro
themselves *use reflexive*
then poi; **and** —, eppoi
there lì; **near** —, lì vicino; — **are** ci sono; — **is** c'è
these questi, –e
they essi, esse, loro
thing cosa *f.*; **such things** cose simili *f. pl.*
think pensare (*pres.* penso), credere *irr.*
this questo, –a; — **one** questo, –a
those *dem. pron.* quelli, quelle; *dem. adj.* quei, quegli, quelle
thousand mille; **thousands** migliaia *f. pl.*
three tre
through per
time tempo *m.*; volta *f.*; ora *f.*; **all the** —, sempre; **what** — **is it?** che ora è? **for a long** —, per molto tempo; **for some** —, da parecchio tempo

tired stanco, –a; **get** —, *stancarsi
to a, ad; in; per
today oggi
together insieme
toilette toletta *f.*
tomorrow domani
tonight stasera
too anche; troppo; — **much** troppo, –a; — **bad** peccato
tourist turista *m.*
toward verso
tower: bell —, campanile *m.*
town paese *m.*; **little** —, paesello *m.*
trade mestiere *m.*
train treno *m.*; **express** —, direttissimo *m.*
travel viaggiare (*pres.* viaggio)
tree albero *m.*
Trevi Fountain Fontana di Trevi *f.*
trip viaggio *m.*; **to take a** —, fare un viaggio
try provare (*pres.* provo)
tuna fish tonno *m.*
turn svolta *f.*
twenty venti
two due; **two-story** a due piani

U

uncle zio *m.*
understand capire (isco)
United States Stati Uniti *m. pl.*
university università *f.*
until fino a
us (to us) ci; *disjunctive* noi
use usare, adoperare; — **up** spendere *irr.*
use uso *m.*; **of what** — **is?** a che serve?
useless inutile
usual solito, –a

V

vacation villeggiatura *f.*, vacanze *f. pl.*; **to go on a** —, *andare in villeggiatura; — **being over** passate le vacanze
valley valle *f.*
veal chop costoletta di vitello *f.*; **small** — **cutlets** scaloppine *f. pl.*
vegetable verdura *f.*
vendor *see* fruit

Venice Venezia *f.*
very molto
view veduta *f.*, panorama *m.*
visit visitare (*pres.* visito)
visit visita *f.*

W

wait aspettare (*pres.* aspetto)
waiter cameriere *m.*
waiting room sala d'aspetto *f.*
wake up *svegliarsi (*pres.* mi sveglio)
walk camminare
walk passeggiata *f.*; **take a** —, fare una passeggiata
want volere *irr.*
warm *v.* riscaldare; *n.* caldo *m.*; **it is** —, fa caldo
waste sprecare (*pres.* spreco)
watch orologio *m.*
watch guardare
water acqua *f.*; **drinking** —, acqua da bere *f.*
way modo *m.*
we noi
wealthy ricco, –a
wear portare (*pres.* porto)
weather tempo *m.*; **how is the** —? che tempo fa? **the** — **is fine** fa bel tempo
week settimana *f.*
well bene; **to be** —, stare bene
what *inter.* che, che cosa; quel che; quale (qual); — **a!** che!
when quando
where dove
wherever dovunque
which *rel. pron.* che; *after a prep.* cui; *inter. adj. or pron.* quale
while mentre
white bianco, –a
who *rel. pron.* che; **he** —, chi; *inter. pron.* chi
whoever chiunque
whom *rel. pron.* che, cui; **with** —, con cui; *inter. pron.* chi
whose *rel. pron.* il cui, la cui, *etc.*
why perchè
wide largo, –a
wife moglie *f.*
wind vento *m.*; **the** — **was blowing** tirava vento
window (*of a store*) vetrina *f.*; **car** —, finestrino *m.*

wine vino *m.*; — **dealer** vin*a*io *m.*
winter inv*e*rno *m.*
wish volere *irr.;* desiderare (*pres.* des*i*dero)
with con
without senza, senza che
woman d*o*nna *f.;* **neat little** —, donnetta *f.*
word par*o*la *f.*
work lavoro *m.*
work lavorare (*pres.* lavoro)
world mondo *m.*
worry *preoccuparsi (*pres.* mi pre*o*ccupo)
worst il peggiore, la peggiore
worth *valere *irr.;* **be** — **while** val*e*r la pena
write scr*i*vere *irr.*
writer scrittore *m.*

Y

yawn *s*badigliare (*pres.* *s*bad*i*glio)
year anno *m.*
yellow giallo, –a
yes sì
young gi*o*vane; **younger** più gi*o*vane, minore
young man gi*o*vane *m.*
your (*fam. sing.*) il tuo, la tua, *etc.*; (*fam. pl.*) il v*o*stro, la v*o*stra, *etc.*; (*pol. sing.*) il Suo, la Sua, *etc.*; (*pol. pl.*) il Loro, la Loro, *etc.*
youth gioventù *f.*

Z

Zurich (*Switzerland*) Zurigo *m.*

INDEX

INDEX

Numbers in lightface refer to pages; numbers in boldface in parentheses refer to sections. Pronunciation aids are not indicated in the index.

a before infinitives, 189 (**121**); with verb **piacere**, 97 (**71**)

absolute superlative, 137 (**90**)

accent: written, 52

address: forms of, 15–17 (**12**)

adjective clauses, 122 (**81**)

adjectives: forms, 9 (**6**)
agreement of, 8–9 (**6**)
capitalization of, xxi
comparison of, 79 (**57**)
comparison of equality, 137–138 (**91**)
demonstrative, 70–72 (**53**)
interrogative, 34 (**26**)
irregular comparison of, 80 (**58**), 135–137 (**89**)
position of, 11 (**9**)
possessive, 33 (**25**)

adverbs: comparison of, 138 (**92**)
formation of, 146 (**97**)
superlative of, 138 (**92**)

advising: verbs of, 121 (**80.2**)

agreement of adjectives, 8–9 (**6**)
of past participles, 53–55 (**38**)

alphabet, xvii

apocopation of words, 24, *footnote*

apostrophe, xxi

articles, 2–3 (**2**): *see* definite *and* indefinite
definite, 4 (**2**), 9 (**8**), 171 (**108**)
indefinite, 4 (**2**), 24–25 (**17**)

augmentatives, 203 (**126**)

auxiliary verbs: *see* **avere, essere,** reflexive verbs

avere: agreement of verbs conjugated with, 55 (**38**)
present perfect of verbs conjugated with, 40 (**28**)

belief: subjunctive with expressions of, 122 (**80.4**)

bello: forms of, 55 (**41**), 15, *footnote* 1

buono, comparison of, 80 (**58**)

capitalization, xxi, 15, *footnote* 2

-care: verbs in **-care,** 64 (**49**)

ch-sound, 29–30, 45

che, interrogative, 33–34 (**26**)
relative, 146 (**98**)

chi, interrogative, 33 (**26**)
relative, 146 (**98**)

ci, pronoun, *see* object pronouns
particle, 106 (**74**)

-ciare: verbs in **-ciare,** 64 (**49**)

ciò che, 147 (**99**)

codesto, *see* **cotesto**

colei che, 147 (**99**)

coloro che, 147 (**99**)

colui che, 147 (**99**)

combined letters, xviii–xix

commanding: subjunctive with verbs of, 121 (**80.2**)

commands: second person singular and plural, 61 (**44**)
first person plural, 61 (**45**)
polite, 63 (**46**), 127–128 (**83**)

comparatives: irregular, 80 (**58**)

comparison of adjectives, 79 (**57**), 135–137 (**89**)
irregular, 80 (**58**)
of adverbs, 138 (**92**)
of equality, 137–138 (**91**)

compound tenses: *see* tenses, subjunctive
uses of the compound tenses of the indicative, 155 (**102**)

concession: subjunctive with adverbial clauses of, 145 (**95.3**)

condition: subjunctive with adverbial clauses of, 145–146 (**95.4**)

conditional, formation of, 93–94 (**68**)
uses of, 94 (**69**)

conditional perfect, 154 (**100**)

conjugations, 17 (**13**), 22–24 (**15**)

conjunctive personal pronouns: *see also* direct *and* indirect
position of, 112 (**76**)

table of, 111 (**75**)
with dependent infinitive, 112
(**76.5,6**)
with **ecco**, 112 (**76.4**)
with monosyllabic verbs, 112
(**76.3**)
conoscere and **sapere**, 155–156 (**103**)
consonants, xviii
long consonants or double consonants, xix, 37
contractions of articles and prepositions, 11 (**10**)
table of, 88 (**65**)
contrary-to-fact sentences, 194–195
(**122**)
cosa, interrogative, 33 (**26**)
che cosa? 33 (**26**)
cotesto, 104–105 (**73**)
cui, relative pronoun, 64 (**50**), 147
(**99.2,3**)
il cui, relative pronoun, 146
(**98**)

da: special meaning of, 88 (**67**)
days of the week, 26 (**21**)
definite articles: forms, 4 (**2**), 9 (**8**)
uses of, 25 (**19**)
summary of, 9 (**8**)
with name of a language, 25
(**19**)
before nouns expressing a general
characteristic, 25 (**19**)
omission with possessive adjectives,
33 (**25**)
demonstrative adjectives, 70–72 (**53**)
pronouns, 104–106 (**73**)
desire: subjunctive with verbs expressing, 121 (**80.1**)
diminutives, 203 (**127**)
diphthongs and triphthongs, xx
direct object pronouns, 41 (**31**), 49
(**36**), 111 (**75**)
position of, 41 (**31**), 49 (**36**), 88
(**66**), 112 (**76**)
disjunctive personal pronouns, 94–95
(**70**), 111 (**75**)
uses of, 95 (**71**)
double consonants: *see* consonants
double object pronouns: *see* object
pronouns
doubt: subjunctive with expressions
of, 122 (**80.3**)
drinks and foods, 185–186

e, open, close, 21
e (ed), 7, *footnote*
ecco: pronouns with, 112 (**76**)
emotion: subjunctive with verbs
expressing, 122 (**80.5**)
infinitive with expressions of,
129 (**86**)
equality: comparison of, 137–138 (**91**)
essere: agreement of verbs conjugated with, 40–41 (**29**), 53–55
(**38**); verbs conjugated with,
40–41 (**29**)

fare with dependent infinitive, 113
(**77**), 171 (**109**)
fear: subjunctive with expressions
of, 122 (**80.3**)
foods and drinks, 185–186
future tense: forms, 48 (**35**)
future perfect, forms, 154 (**100**)

g-sound, 37, 45
-gare: verbs in **-gare,** 64 (**49**)
gender, 2 (**1**)
gerund, uses of, 163 (**106**)
gli-sound, 7
gn-sound, 7
grande: comparison of, 80 (**58**) *and
footnote*

hours: *see* time

imperative, 61 (**44**), 63 (**47**)
position of object pronouns with,
63–64 (**48**), 112 (**76**)
imperfect indicative: forms, 85–87
imperfect subjunctive, 144–145 (**94**)
in after a superlative, 80 (**59**)
indefinite articles, 4 (**2**)
plural of, 24–25 (**17**)
uses of, 25 (**19**)
omission with predicate nominative, 25 (**19**)
independent clauses: subjunctive in,
146 (**96**)
indirect object pronouns, 55 (**39**),
111 (**75**)
position of, 55 (**39**), 88 (**66**)
with **piacere**, 97 (**72**)
infinitive, as a substantive, 188 (**117**)
complementary, 188–189 (**121**)
compound tenses of verbs followed
by infinitive, 186–188 (**116**)

infinitive (*cont.*)
  preceded by **a**, 189 **(121)**
  preceded by **di**, 189 **(121)**
  with adjectives, 188 **(119)**
  with expressions of emotion, 129
    (86)
  with **fare**, 113 **(77)**
  with nouns, 188 **(120)**
  with pronouns when depending
    on another verb, 112 **(76)**
  with prepositions, 188 **(118)**
interrogative form, 4 **(3)**
interrogatives, 33–34 **(26)**
intonation, 84
irregular comparison of adjectives,
  80 **(58)**
  comparison of adverbs, 138 **(92)**
  past definite, 160–161 **(104)**
  past participles, 41 **(30)**

j-sound, 30, 45

k-sound, 37, 45

Lei-form, 15–17 **(12)**, 15, *footnote 2*
letters: missing, 45
  combined, xviii–xix
like: see **piacere**
Loro-form, 17 **(12)**; 15, *footnote 2*

metric system, 171–172 **(110)**
months, 42 **(33)**

ne, 42 **(32)**, 106 **(74)**
negation: subjunctive with expressions of, 146 **(95.5)**
negative form, 4 **(4)**
noun clauses: subjunctive in, 121–
  122 **(80)**
nouns: gender of, 2 **(1)**
  plural of, 8 **(5)**
  summary of plural of, 180 **(115)**
numerals, cardinal, 32 **(24)**, 72–73
  (54)
  ordinal, 80 **(61)**

o, open, close, 21
object pronouns: *see also* direct,
  indirect, disjunctive
  direct object pronouns, 41 **(31)**,
    48–49 **(36)**
  disjunctive personal pronouns, 94–
    95 **(70)**

uses of disjunctive pronouns, 95
  (71)
double object pronouns, 88 **(66)**,
  170–171 **(107)**
indirect object pronouns, 55 **(39)**
object pronouns with participles,
  195 **(124)**
position of object pronouns, 55
  (39), 63–64 **(48)**, 112 **(76)**
position of object pronouns with
  imperative, 63–64 **(48)**
position of object pronouns with
  infinitives, 55 **(40)**
position of object pronouns with
  polite commands, 127–128 **(83)**
omission of the definite article, 33
  (25)
  of the indefinite article, 25 **(19)**
opinion: subjunctive with expressions of, 122 **(80.4)**
optative subjunctive, 146 **(96)**
ordinal numerals, 80 **(61)**
orthographical changes, 64 **(49)**

participle: past, 40 **(27)**
  agreement of past participles, 53–
    55 **(38)**, 195 **(123)**
  irregular past participles, 41 **(30)**,
    56 **(43)**
  object pronouns with participles,
    195 **(124)**
particles: *see* **ci, vi, ne**
partitive construction, 25 **(18)**
passato prossimo = present perfect
passato remoto = past definite
past definite, 77–79 **(55)**
permitting: subjunctive with verbs
  of, 121 **(80.2)**
personal pronouns: *see* conjunctive,
  direct, disjunctive, indirect, reflexive, subject
piacere meaning *to like*, 95–97 **(72)**
pluperfect subjunctive, 178–179 **(112)**
polite commands, 63 **(46)**, 127–128
  (83)
possessive adjectives, 33 **(25)**
  pronouns, 113 **(78)**
  definite articles with possessives,
    113 **(78)**, 171 **(108)**
  definite article omitted with certain
    words, 33 **(25)**
present indicative, 17 **(13)**, 24 **(15)**
  subjunctive, 120–121 **(79)**

present perfect: indicative, 40 (28), 154 (100), 40–41 (29)
subjunctive, 128 (85)
pronouns: table of pronouns, 111 (75)
see also conjunctive, disjunctive, object, personal, reflexive, subject
punctuation, xxii
purpose, 26 (20)
subjunctive with clauses expressing, 145 (95.1)

quale, 34 (26); il quale, 147 (99.4)
quello, 71–72 (53), 104–105 (73)
di quel che, 138 (93.4)
questo, 71–72 (53), 104–105 (73)

r-sound, 7
reflexive: pronouns, 111 (75)
auxiliary with reflexive verbs, 155 (101)
reflexive for first plural, 129 (87)
reflexive for the passive, 71 (52)
verbs, 69–70 (51)
relative: clauses, 122 (81)
pronouns, 64 (50)
subjunctive after relative pronouns, 122 (81)
table of relative pronouns, 146 (98)
use of the relative pronouns, 147 (99)
requesting: subjunctive with verbs of, 121 (80.2)

s-sound, 21
sapere and conoscere, 155–156 (103)
seasons, 42 (33)
sequence of tenses, 177–178 (111)
sh-sound, 60
should-would and contrary-to-fact sentences, 194–195 (122)
sk-sound, 60
sounds: writing from sounds, 76
special masculine words, 9 (7)
special meaning of da, 88 (67)
stare with gerund, 163 (106)
stress, xix–xx
subject pronouns, 15 (11), 111 (75)
subjunctive: present, 120–121 (79)
present of irregular verbs, 122–123 (82), 129 (88)
present perfect, 128 (85)

imperfect, 144–145 (94)
compound tenses, 178–179 (112)
pluperfect, 178–179 (112)
in adjective clauses, 122 (81)
in adverbial clauses, 145–146 (95)
with impersonal expressions, 128 (84)
with indefinite words, 179–180 (114)
in indirect questions, 180 (113)
in noun clauses, 121–122 (80)
in polite commands, 127–128 (83)
optative subjunctive, 146 (96)
suffixes with nouns, 201–203 (125–127)
with adjectives, 203 (128)
superlative: absolute, 137 (90)
relative clauses depending on, 122 (81.3)
supposition: subjunctive with expressions of, 122 (80.4)
surprise: subjunctive with expressions of, 122 (80.5)
syllabication, xx–xxi

t-sound, 14
tenses of the indicative: present, 17 (13), 22–24 (15)
present perfect, 40 (28), 154 (100)
present perfect of verbs conjugated with essere, 40–41 (29)
future, 48 (35)
future perfect, 154 (100)
imperfect, 85–87 (62)
verbs irregular in the imperfect, 87 (63)
first pluperfect, 154 (100)
past definite, 78–79 (55)
past definite of irregular verbs, 160–161 (104)
second pluperfect, 154 (100)
imperfect and past definite, 87 (64)
distinction between present perfect, past definite, and imperfect, 162 (105)
compound tenses of the indicative, 152–155 (100)
uses of the compound tenses of the indicative, 155 (102)
than in comparisons, 80 (60), 138 (93)
time: expressions of, 32 (23)
subjunctive with adverbial clauses of time, 145 (95.2)

triphthongs, xx
tu-form, 15–17 **(12)**

urging; subjunctive with verbs of, 121 **(80.2)**

verbs conjugated with **essere,** 56 **(42)**
vi, 106 **(74)**
voi-form, 15–17 **(12)**
vowels, xvii–xviii, 1

w-sound, 14
weather: expressions about, 49 **(37)**
week: days of, 26 **(21)**
whose, relative pronoun, 146 **(99)**
wish: subjunctive with verbs expressing, 121 **(80.1)**
writing from sounds, 76

y-sound, 14

z-sound, 29